A Wind to Shake the World

Books by Everett S. Allen

ARCTIC ODYSSEY
The Biography of Rear Admiral Donald B. MacMillan

FAMOUS AMERICAN HUMOROUS POETS
(*For young people*)

THIS QUIET PLACE
A Cape Cod Chronicle

CHILDREN OF THE LIGHT
The Rise and Fall of New Bedford Whaling and the Death of the
Arctic Fleet

A WIND TO SHAKE THE WORLD
The Story of the 1938 Hurricane

A WIND TO SHAKE THE WORLD

The Story of the 1938 Hurricane

EVERETT S. ALLEN

Little, Brown and Company — Boston – Toronto

Fourth Printing
т09/76

The author is grateful to the following for permission to reprint from previously copyrighted materials:

Russell & Volkening, Inc., for "A House by the Sea" by Benedict Thielen, pub- lished in *Yale Review*, Spring, 1939. Copyright 1939, © 1967 by Helen Thielen.

Marcelle Hammond Ham, for the Watch Hill, Rhode Island, hurricane accounts taken from *Seaside Topics*. Copyright 1938 by Charles F. Hammond, renewed © 1966 by Marcelle Hammond Ham.

Marguerite F. Fetcher, for excerpts from the poem "The Hotel" from *You and I* by Harriet Munroe. Copyright 1914 by The Macmillan Company.

LIBRARY OF CONGRESS CATALOGING IN PUBLICATION DATA

Allen, Everett S
    A wind to shake the world.

    Includes index.
    1. New England — Hurricane, 1938. 2. New York (State)
— Hurricane, 1938. I. Title.
QC959.U6A44   974'.04   76–18693
ISBN 0–316–03426–6

Designed by Susan Windheim

Published simultaneously in Canada
by Little, Brown & Company (Canada) Limited

PRINTED IN THE UNITED STATES OF AMERICA

To Anna
who made my father happy

Preface

PERHAPS WHAT I HAVE TO SAY here would go better at the end; yet as I write these words, I feel I have the right to claim a certain perspective on this book. For many months now, recalling my own experiences and those of others on September 21, 1938, I have relived the hurricane in detail. Although I believe it is the major untold American story of that period, I am glad my task is behind me.

For two years, I have forced myself — and countless others — to see again the sick color of sky and sea on that day, to hear the scream of the wind, which was everywhere; to confront anew the shocking, instant obliteration of what had always been assumed permanent, mile upon mile of man's work reduced to rubble. And I have forced myself and others to see man himself, face down and weaving like weed in the roiling shallows or open-mouthed and still, half-buried in the damp sand. I have made people weep by asking them to remember what for many of them remains their most terrible day.

The remembering was not all bad. The hurricane was a crisis for thousands. It had to be confronted, individually or collectively. Men, women, and children met the challenge variously, but mostly with strength of spirit and physical endurance that are astonishing even in retrospect. If I have achieved here no more than the broad outlines of man's magnificence and determination and, on occasion, his ignoble defeat, the heroic proportions of his struggle to survive are obvious. Inevitably, some lived, despite all the odds against it, and certainly the reverse was true. I shall not forget one man whom I interviewed, who cried out, even after all these years, "That was when I stopped believing in God!"

I could not have written this book a decade, even half a decade from now. Several survivors I talked to were in their late seventies when I met them; some were in their eighties, and at least two I interviewed are now dead.

I seek to evade no responsibility in pointing out that the margin for error in this chronicle is necessarily large. Even the most superficial investigation of hurricane accounts reveals lapses and contradictions born of the mind distraught, pressure of deadline, lack of reliable communication, and absence of solid information. The problem is compounded by the human tendency to tell a spectacular story in a spectacular way. In some cases, this has produced versions of events that actually happened very differently; in others, it has resulted in both published accounts and neighborhood legends of things that really did not happen at all. I have endeavored to thread my way through the labyrinth, holding to what I hope is truth or at least practical possibility.

Having finished my work, I feel somewhat as I did when the hurricane itself was over. I remember on that day how spent one emerged, how quiet people were, as nature was finally quiet, and how incredible it was, not only that the storm was over, but that it could have occurred at all. And so the writing of this book, having occupied and preoccupied my waking moments for a long time, is now all over, too, leaving an equally strange quiet in its wake.

E. S. A.

Poverty Point
Fairhaven, Massachusetts

Contents

Illustrations

[*xi*]

Book I

The Summer of 1938

Chapter 1

Martha's Vineyard, Massachusetts

IT WAS A TIME OF SUSPENSION AND TRANSITION, a time of reluctant emergence from dreamless sleep, not only for the world and nation, but for me.

One still had the deceptive sense that things were as they had always been — the remoteness of government, the notion that education guarantees success, albeit at a loss of virility; the solid striking of the big Methodist Church clock across the street from our house, the leisurely gait of Al Luce's dray horse coming up from the steamboat dock with cartons of romance-saving Lifebuoy soap, and the fact that you could count the registered Democrats in town on the fingers of one hand. (And, as everyone knew, at least three of them were not right in the head.)

Yet like smoke upon the wind in the forest-fire season, there was the smell of raw and ill-defined change.

"Marx predicted it all!" cried the green-eyed girl with whom I had gone to college until June. It was easy to believe that he had. As of July 1, 1938, Franklin Delano Roosevelt, President of the United States of America, began what he called "the real drive on depression." There were 10.5 million unemployed; the President proposed to spend $8.5 billion, or $66 for every person in the nation, to revitalize the economy. The navy was spending faster than at any time since World War I, engaged in the construction of 39 vessels, including four $70-million battleships.

I do not know who delivered my college commencement address that June or what he said, wisely or otherwisely. I chewed a blade of grass, fiercely and absentmindedly, during the ceremony in the New England chapel and heard nothing but my name when they called it, for I sat there in the shock of relief, soaked in sweat to the waist beneath my black gown. I was in debt for my education; my father was in debt for my education; I had worn a donated pair of ski boots all one winter because I could not afford shoes; I had slept in a windowless linen closet during my junior year; I had ulcers and I had had two nervous breakdowns; I had never attended a formal dance in four years; I had had as many as five jobs at one time, including stoking a furnace, digging a cellar under an existing building in a Vermont winter, and shoveling manure. I attended my course in the European novel five times in two semesters because it conflicted with my job of waiting on table and if I had given up the job, I would have had to leave school. I received an "A" in the course, in part, because the professor also had had to work his way through college. (After each class, he loaned me his lecture notes to copy.)

Now, it was done. My family had been in this country since early in the seventeenth century. I was the first member to complete four years of college.

For a little while after graduation, I tried to find a job on a newspaper. A Boston editor removed his glasses, looked at me, and sighed. "You were managing editor of your college weekly. You were the editor of the school literary publication. You won a couple of local prizes for short stories and poetry. You majored in English. Now you want to write and you think a newspaper is the place to start.

"All of these things apply to my kid brother. He got out of college last year. I got him a job here because I am an executive of this newspaper and have certain influence here. Let me introduce you to him."

We took a grubby elevator and went down into the bowels of the building. I shook hands with his brother. He had an ink smudge on his cheek. He was wrapping newspapers in the mailing room.

So I went back to Martha's Vineyard because, as Robert Frost and others have observed, home is where you go when the world won't have you. The people of my town gave me a job, for which I have always been grateful. They provided me with a substantial, ten-foot skiff and a pair of ash oars, and for $18 a week (a lot of money when you could buy fresh cod at retail for six cents a pound), I was the harbor patrol. My job was to greet visiting yachtsmen, to acquaint them with the local rise and fall of tide, assist them in making fast to the town moorings, tell them where they could buy booze, ice, food (and, for that matter, contraceptives) and, if they invited me aboard, to regale them with local lies and legends. Actually, that last part was not in the contract but I thought I ought to flex my literary muscles occasionally to avoid atrophy. Besides, a good many of the sailing women were pretty and appreciative.

Those were the days, believe me. I was one with the world in not knowing where I was going or whether I could avoid failure in trying to hold together an obviously disintegrating moment. I was twenty-one and that in itself was frequent cause for both tears and laughter. I did not necessarily want to go where I had to go, wherever that proved to be. Yet, obviously, however dear today was in its best aspects, it could not last.

In the morning, the rags of night fog were gone by the time I came to the beach. The braying horns had ceased their warning. Still, it was early enough for the clean silence, salt and wet, sparingly etched with one gull's sad and ageless cry. The harbor's fringe advanced and retreated across the sand, the pebbles rolled and chittered.

[5]

At the bend of the beach, "Poker" Norton was swaying up the high-peaked mainsail of his stately catboat *Victor;* the varnished halyard blocks went "chuckle, chuckle" and he was swiftly away in his white boat. I watched man and boat as through a sheet of glass. He raised his arm to me; at sea, this is how you say, "Are you all right?" but he did not call out because he was a silent man and even if he were not, what manner of fellow would make unnecessary noise at such a moment?

I sat in the big skiff, floating off the end of the breakwater, watching three jellyfish — first like toadstools and then like parasols — propel themselves transparently through the light green water. I was brown from the sun, sitting there in my red swimming trunks and drifting upon the surface of a sea so hypnotically bright that I could not stare at it very long.

But *being* in water was, of course, better than simply watching and touching it. Sunday, my day off, I went to the vast emptiness of the South Beach with a few bottles of beer and got boiled in the rollers. Then I cooked three or four short lobsters in a bucket of seawater over a driftwood fire and squatted comfortably in the sand cracking them and pondering how different man's life might be if the sun were green.

Monday through Saturday, as the working day ebbed, the yachtsmen came into harbor for the night. Like their boats, they were of many kinds and incomes. The symbol of the richest was the big steam yacht, concerning which Marx undoubtedly would have made a prediction if he had thought of it. From gilded billethead to snapping ensign at the mahogany taffrail, it was an oasis of gentility in a gradually less gentle world, a bastion of brass and teak. Its owner wore a dark blue jacket and white flannels, its master declined the public mooring, its women were evenly tanned and did not perspire, and its shiny little launch, deftly guided by a uniformed seaman, purred to the dock in search of White Rock water and Roquefort. Those aboard steam yachts usually said to me, "Why don't you have a motor in your boat?" and I couldn't think

[6]

of any way to get into that without explaining the whole tax structure of the town of Tisbury, so I replied, "I'm training for crew in
the fall," and they said, "Oh yes, of course."

The owner's party on the big yachts reflected the national pen-
chant for listening to the radio; it was a ritual performed with
reverence, and the choices were a reflection of caste. Favorite
broadcasters were like members of the family.

Sometimes, I would be invited aboard a steam yacht and I would
sit there in a wicker chair on the afterdeck under the white canvas
eating anchovy paste on a cracker and drinking a gin and tonic. If it
was time for a news broadcast, I would sit through it with them
(Vincent Astor regularly halted dinner conversation to listen to
Amos 'n' Andy), but I did not really listen, even though we did
not have a radio at home, because I was thinking how expensive
everything was that I was looking at. Of it all, I tried to figure what
I could afford. Six teaspoons? A coil of rope? I could not imagine;
it was beyond me.

When I sat through a radio news broadcast aboard a yacht,
somewhat conscious of the hole in the toe of my left sneaker, I
used to play a game inside my head. In my senior year at college, a
professor who was a favorite of mine had acquainted me with
Harriet Monroe's poem about the hotel. It appealed to me so much
that I memorized it and when I was listening to the news broad-
casts, I recited pieces of the poem to myself in what I suppose was
some kind of litany of silent protest against what I thought was
wrong with the world. Whatever it was, it was something deeply
and importantly related to being twenty-one and emotionally and
professionally adrift.

It went something like this:

*Good evening, ladies and gentlemen, this is your lares and pe-
nates, Gabriel-Lowell Heatter-Thomas —*

*A plan for ending the Chinese-Japanese war by carving China
into at least five autonomous parts is being drafted by Chinese
members of the Peiping Provisional Government and their Japanese*

[7]

advisers. . . . Helen Wills Moody, whose feud with Helen Jacobs could be no more intense had one been born a Hatfield and the other a McCoy, trounced Miss Jacobs 6–4, 6–0, at Wimbledon to win the singles crown for the eighth time today. . . . Alf M. Landon, former governor of Kansas and 1936 GOP presidential candidate, replied to the President's recent fireside chat and called the depression a "political depression." He criticized Roosevelt for the New Deal policy of deficit spending and added, "Let Mr. Roosevelt forswear all further attempts to tamper with the Supreme Court and to get power into his own hands. Let him put a stop to the use of WPA money to buy votes."

(Harriet Monroe had written: "The stout and gorgeous dowagers in lacy white and lilac, bedizened with many jewels, with smart little scarlet or azure hats on their gray-streaked hair./ The business men in trim and spotless suits, who walk in and out with eager steps, or sit at the desks and tables, or watch the shining women.")

Howard Hughes and his four companions landed in New York with a smashing new round-the-world plane record of less than four days. The airmen rode triumphantly up lower Broadway from the Battery to City Hall in the most tumultuous heroes' parade New York has held in a decade. Downtown New York screamed its praise for the multimillionaire Texas sportsman and his mates and showered them with ticker tape torn up and emptied from the windows of the world's greatest skyscrapers. . . . Chelsea Sherlock, 42, former editor or managing editor of St. Nicholas *magazine, the* Ladies Home Journal, Better Homes and Gardens, *reportedly depressed over finances, killed his wife with a shotgun and then blasted away his own life. . . .*

("The telegraph tickers sounding their perpetual chit-chit-chit from the uttermost ends of the earth," Harriet Monroe had written. "The waiters, in black swallow-tails and white aprons, passing here and there with trays of bottles and glasses./ The quiet and sumptuous bar-room, with purplish men softly drinking in little alcoves, while the barkeeper, mixing bright liquors, is rapidly plying his bottles.")

In London's Bow Street court, Countess Barbara Hutton Haug-witz-Reventlow's battery of noted legal talent accused her titled Danish husband of demanding $5 million and their two-year-old son, Lance, in return for a divorce. In 2½ hours of sensational testimony, he was further accused of threatening to shoot an unnamed Mayfair society man "like a dog." The golden-haired, black-clad Woolworth heiress kept her sad, childlike eyes on the back of her husband's head as her attorneys declared that he had threatened to "put her on the spot" and give her "three years of hell and headlines." . . . Walter Lippmann wrote today, "Barring incidents which cannot be foreseen, incidents which might take matters out of Hitler's hands, there would seem then to be no great probability of war in the near future. . . ."

("The great bedecked and gilded cafe," Harriet Monroe wrote, "with its glitter of a thousand mirrors, with its little white tables bearing gluttonous dishes whereto bright forks, held by pampered hands, flicker daintily back and forth.")

Mrs. Nicholas Brown's gardens at Harbour Court were open for the benefit of the Newport Civic League. Mrs. Brown, with her nieces, the Hon. Nadine Stonor and Miss Natalie Bayard Meril, sailed from New York today on the Queen Mary to attend the marriage of the Hon. Sherman Stonor, son of Lord and Lady Camoys, to Miss Mary Jean Stourton. Mrs. Brown plans to remain abroad two months. . . . Two dead, one shot was the record today of violence in London, Kentucky, during the Harlan labor conspiracy trial now in its eighth week. Frank White, 36, a defendant in the anti-union indictment involving 39 persons and 17 corporations, was shot through the head as he sat on the front porch of a tourist camp. . . . A record advance entry is announced by the tournament committee of the seventh annual Southern New England contract bridge championships, which are to be held at the Mohican Hotel, New London. . . .

[9]

("The white-tiled immaculate kitchen," Harriet Monroe wrote, "with many little round blue fires, where white-clad cooks are making spiced and flavored dishes. The cool cellars filled with meats and fruits, or layered with sealed and bottled wines mellowing softly in the darkness.")

In Chicago, John H. Seadlund, convicted of the kidnaping and slaying of Charles S. Ross, 72, retired greeting card manufacturer, died in the electric chair, with 22 witnesses. . . . In the third year of Spain's civil war, Socialist resistance along the Teruel-Mediterranean highway collapsed. Fascist warplanes were flying over the routed troops, retreating along the road toward Sagunto, fifteen miles north of Valencia, bombing and machine-gunning them. . . . Dowager Queen Marie of Romania, who died of cirrhosis of the liver, requested that dark lilac be the color of mourning for her and that her heart be buried at her favorite resort on the Black Sea. . . . Boston's rejuvenated Red Sox were in second place after bombarding Cleveland's pitching for over five hours yesterday to win both ends of a doubleheader, 13–3, 14–12, with their greatest surge of batting power this season. Foxx's 35th homer, with the bases full in the ninth inning of the second game, climaxed the Sox drive against the fading Indians. . . .

("The people inside of the clothes," Harriet Monroe wrote, "the bodies white and young, bodies fat and bulging, bodies wrinkled and wan, all alike veiled by fine fabrics, sheltered by walls and roofs, shut in from the sun and stars. The souls inside of the bodies — the naked souls; souls weazen and weak, or proud and brave; all imprisoned in flesh, wrapped in woven stuffs, enclosed in thick and painted masonry, shut away with many shadows from the shining truth.")

Representative Martin Dies, D-Texas, chairman of the House committee investigating un-American activities, demanded today that Secretary of Labor Frances Perkins act immediately to deport Harry Bridges, Pacific Coast director of the Committee for Industrial Organization. He said Department of Labor files in the Bridges

[10]

case disclosed that one witness testified he had heard Bridges say,
"Jo hell with the President of the United States." . . . Neville
Chamberlain and Adolf Hitler bargained face to face at Berchtes-
gaden, Germany, in the Bavarian Alps today while a worried world
waited to hear whether the result would mean peace or war in
Europe. . . .

("God inside of the souls," Harriet Monroe wrote, "God veiled
and wrapped and imprisoned and shadowed in fold on fold of flesh
and fabrics and mockeries; but ever alive, struggling and rising
again, seeking the light, freeing the world.")

Then, while I was wondering what man would have invented if
he hadn't invented religion, the people on the big steam yacht
would give me another gin and tonic and ask me what I thought
about "the mess the world is in today," mostly because they wanted
to know whether the young had any sense, I suppose.

But I was not much help to them in that way.

The girl with green eyes who had cried "Marx predicted it all!",
who carried a clumsily lettered banner saying "Unite!" in a rain-
soaked May Day parade of small proportions and less enthusiasm,
had been arrested somewhere, for something. Somebody named
Roger had sent me a postcard about it, but there wasn't much
information on it and he didn't give me his address because he said
he was moving.

I had co-authored in college a published interview with an American newspaperman recently returned from Spain, a fellow who had
managed to talk to Franco. On the basis of what this newspaperman (who was also my world politics teacher) said, my colleague
and I concluded in the article that Franco intended to create a
broad middle class, American-style. At least, I think that is what
we concluded. In any event, whatever we wrote provoked the
wrath of a local editorial writer, who wanted to know what in the
hell that was subversive we were being taught in college. I had to
go see the dean and I thought perhaps he would throw me out of

school, in which case, I would kill myself. But he didn't and I didn't.

I suppose you could conclude from this that I either did not know the difference between fascism and communism or could not choose between them, or that I did not know much about either of them. I also received the lowest mark in a mid-semester examination in economics ever given in the 136 years of my college's existence. I got an 18. What I wrote was so funny (the professor said) that he asked my permission to read the exam paper to all of his classes. I told him to go ahead, feeling that somebody might as well get something out of it.

I never did understand economics and felt bad about it because, being twenty-one, I labored under the misconception that everyone else did. But just before I got out of school, I wrote a bitter piece about "the men with the concrete faces and the concrete hearts behind the glass-topped desks" because I had already concluded there was no job waiting for me anywhere, and I was thinking about joining the Civilian Conservation Corps, which we called FDR's Brownshirts, that being a sophomoric reference to Hitler's storm troopers of the same name. I knew a couple of fellows who had gone into the CCC, and one of them said, "Well, somebody cooks your meals, there's plenty of hot water, and it's a relief to talk to people who *didn't* go to college."

Sometimes, even sitting in the sun, I became depressed when I thought about all these things and the whole damned business dropped over me like a wet horse blanket flung from a second-story window. But it's hard to stay depressed in the sun, floating in a boat. Especially at twenty-one.

The smaller craft I boarded were more crowded, less expensive and more fun. Mostly, their people were younger and looked as if they made love often. One day, I rowed out to a big old Friendship sloop that was hunkering up the harbor in light air as if she had a week to do it in. She was hogged and weatherworn and her mud-

[12]

colored sails hung in bags. I asked the man and woman aboard if they would like a public mooring and they were delighted because the sloop had an anchor that weighed seventy-five pounds and nothing to haul it up with but back muscles, his and hers.

They were both sunburned; they had borrowed the sloop two days before. "We're learning about it; it's learning about us," they said amiably.

I rowed to the mooring, picked up the line from the buoy and held it, waiting for the sunburned man to sail up to me. It was not until too late that I realized he was no sailor, that he had, in fact, started his ancient, clutchless engine and that, under power and sail, he was bearing down on me from to windward in a heavy vessel about as hard to stop as a truckload of brick on a mountain grade. Six feet away, with foam at the cutwater, boom winged out, that Friendship looked enormous.

I ducked his bowsprit and jumped overboard just as the sloop crunched into my skiff and rolled it under. I tried to get away from the vessel but couldn't because he changed course in sudden panic; her rough side rasped my arms and hands as she slid by. I yelled at the two aboard to shut off the engine — I thought likely some part of me might go under her stern and get ground up in the propeller — but they were running about the cockpit yelling, and the engine kept chunking away. I banged my head on something and thought angrily that I did not wish to be crippled or killed because of somebody else's stupidity.

I felt the surging water from the sloop's propeller around my feet and ankles and yanked my knees up against my chest to get clear if I could. Suddenly, the sloop was past me, and it was over. Frankie Vincent, short and leathery, perpetually paddling about the harbor with his oars worn thin at the rowlocks, looked down at me from his skiff and said, " 'y God, I thought sure they got you that time." He helped me bail the water out of my boat and get back into her. Later, when the man and his wife got the Friendship sloop calmed down, I boarded them. They were nice people. She kissed me and said, "We could have killed you!" and, tasting her lipstick, I said, "Well, it really wasn't anything."

Afterward, when I thought about it, I shook for a while, but it's like being depressed; at twenty-one, in the sun, things pass, or at least you can file them.

And those nights that summer were such nights.

They began in and about Circuit Avenue, which embraced, in a matter of a few blocks, the essence of the fading national illusion, complete with $1.50 full-course dinner and colored paper lanterns. At the Strand, management was showing Barbara Stanwyck ("the Stella Dallas star at her greatest") with Herbert Marshall in *Always Goodbye*. In those days, people often wept over sad movies and emerged, wiping their red eyes and blowing their noses, generally feeling much better.

At the Tivoli, they played dance music made famous by Bing Crosby's "Music Hall," the Ink Spots, Rudy Vallee, Shep Fields, and Guy Lombardo. ("Every star above/ Knows the one I love/ Sweet Sue . . .")

As a relatively incompetent saxophonist who had toured the Grange Halls of northern New England with a Saturday-night orchestra of no consequence and a vocalist named Deborah, who never could remember lyrics (she invented "la de ah de ah") but who was all heart, I listened to such music with my mind. Which is to say that every piece reminded me of something or somebody and the whole montage of wilted corsages, pancakes on a mountain morning, rainstained wallpaper and farewell in the hissing steam at the depot flooded through me bittersweet and scarcely bearable.

This, then, was the "swing" era, the brief interlude of the Big Apple (which osteopaths, in convention, heard denounced as likely to give girls thick ankles), of the rug cutter, alligator, and hepcat. "Kill me," said the fine dinner, which is to say, "Show me a good time," said the good-looking girl.

It was long ago in so many ways. If you had $694, you could buy a new three-passenger Hudson coupe; if you had $2.50, you could get a room with bath and radio at New York's Hotel Taft; if you had $1.98, you could buy a lady's soft, all-wool (one-piece) swim-suit; if you had . . .

And the Flying Horses, with music like no other — an exciting, thin, metallic strumming; a sometimes martial, sometimes hoyden-ish invitation to the wooden steeds, rising and falling, whirling and gold, red, green and blue, and to the brown-legged, shiny-haired girls swinging out from the bright brass vertical bars to catch the ring. If you had . . .

Circuit Avenue itself, blobs of pale light puddling the black tar, was warm with life. In the bars, there was laughter; behind screen doors, the glass chimes tinkled in the evening breeze, and in the shadows of the long verandahs, the red eyes of Havana cigars punc-tuated the murmurings of conversationalists unseen.

Such sights and smells! Within glass, a fountain of yellow but-tered popcorn, erupting and tumbling; regiments of browning frankfurters, awaiting their epaulets of onions; fat pickles, warted and awash in brine; gallons of orange drink; red pennants or slen-der bamboo canes and little carved figures from Japan.

Upon the wind, the boom of bowling balls and phrases caught and lost of a Sousa march; the town band playing in the park, silver trombone flashing under the overhead lights, and deep in the darkness upon the grass, couples hearing only their own music.

When the lights went out on the avenue at a fairly early hour, the lady in the print dress who had sucked a Ward Eight through a straw before dinner of broiled swordfish with lemon walked back to the hotel with her husband, he fanning the still air with his straw hat. The drifting away of the people, the gathering dark, until only the streetlamps remained, the dying away of the last note of music, these were so gradual, so subtle, that one was always surprised to discover that it was all over for another day.

With Circuit Avenue dark, I climbed into a borrowed Model A, the driver's door of which would not open, and headed out of town.

It was a splendid automobile; it had no top and therefore encouraged the notion that if rain did, in fact, come, it would arrive conveniently, that is, when the automobile was not in use. The car had been owned by a fisherman, who drove it twenty miles a day to the dock where his boat was, drained the crankcase, put the oil into his boat engine, used his boat all day, drained the oil from the boat engine, and put it back in his car for the return trip home.

Once, the radiator ran dry and the car engine got so hot that it kept running after I had turned off the ignition. I said to the fellow at the gas station, "That's eerie, isn't it?" He stuck his head under the car's hood and said, "You wanna blow the goddam thing up, that's your business."

Driving along, I was thinking how close the stars were; they burned and shimmered. ("Every star above/ Knows the one . . .") I stopped singing, realizing there were two girls thumbing at the roadside. I pulled over and they got in; where they wanted to go was twelve miles out of my way, but at twenty-one, that is no matter. I was as expansive as the night itself.

They were neither handsome nor otherwise; they were slightly older than I, but not much; most important, they were in keeping — they went with the night and the way I felt about it.

It was no more than a little after midnight. The lush growth at the roadside spilled upon itself, acres and miles of it, as if there were no end to nature's munificence, nor to time, nor to youth. We sang together, "Every star above . . . ," and the sound pattered against the arched leaves overhead; we pitied those in the unlighted farmhouses — dark blots against the moonlit fields — who had nothing better to do than sleep, and the little engine thundered under the floodboards. We were bound for Menemsha.

I cannot remember what the tall girl's name was. I think it was Evelyn, but no matter. She had pierced ears and we sat on a screened porch discussing *Mourning Becomes Electra.* She said she thought it possessed great universality and I said I thought she was most perceptive. At some point, she offered me what she called "a cigarette with a difference" and she smiled. I knew it was marijuana because some of the band players I had worked with smoked reefers. I never had because I couldn't afford to. I smoked the cigarette she gave me, and I told her again that I thought she was most perceptive.

When I drove home alone it seemed to me that the road was like a river and that each mile was identical to the last one — the same curves, the same trees, the same houses. When I got home, I was climbing in the kitchen window, crawling over the sink, and my father stomped into the room in his pajamas, pulling on the light. He said, "What in hell are you coming in the window for? Don't you have a key?" I looked and there the key was, in my jacket pocket. I said, "Yes, I have a key." Then I thought a minute and I told him about the cigarette that the girl had given to me. "Sounds to me like some kind of dope," he said; "that's what it sounds like to me." And he went back to bed.

In bed, I thought, lying there in the dark with moonlight streaming across the kitchen chimney outside my window, how uncluttered everything was if you just looked at the larger aspect — the sky, the sea, love, and the miracle of the seasons. Then I fell asleep.

There was one other thing about that summer. If the world, the nation, and I were fouled up — in suspension and transition, if you will — so was the weather. The minimum temperature on June 1 was 44 degrees, surpassed only once and equaled only once in the decade preceding. Half of the days of June were cloudy and total rainfall for the month was 9.47 inches.

As of July 22, Boston had chalked up 6.12 inches of rain for the month, the heaviest July rainfall in seventeen years. (On the twenty-first, it had a 2.31-inch downpour.) By July 23, rain was falling for the sixth consecutive day in Massachusetts and damage was estimated at $500,000 to $1,000,000, with showers predicted for the next two days. Rivers and lakes were overflowing their banks; highways were pitted with holes; railroad beds were washed out, and crops ruined.

On July 25, total rainfall for most of the state was 9.28 inches — everywhere but Nantucket, which had had a fine spell of sunshine. Nor was the unusual weather regional. On August 29, a hurricane struck Monterey, Mexico, dumping 9 inches of rain in thirty-six hours, and leaving nine dead and four hundred families homeless. A severe thunderstorm swept the Merrimack River valley in Massachusetts, uprooting trees and knocking out electrical service. A landslide precipitated by storms and flood waters took eight lives in Quebec Province and a sixty-mile wind whipped the heavy rainfall, which in at least one location measured 3.75 inches.

"I don't know what's come over the weather," said Frankie Vincent, paddling across the harbor, "but I shouldn't be surprised if we had one real good line storm this year, the way things are going."

"What about Nantucket?" I asked. "Nantucket hasn't had a weather problem."

"I ain't about to try to account for Nantucket," Frankie said.

A few days later, I received a letter from the editor of *The Standard-Times* in New Bedford, Massachusetts, saying, "I would be pleased to see you for an interview in my office. . . ."

I put away my oars and the summer of my majority.

Chapter 2

New Bedford, Massachusetts

IF YOU HAVE LIVED ON AN ISLAND and are not going to live there any more, there is probably no good time of day to leave it.

I left Vineyard Haven at 6 A.M. on September 19, 1938. It was warm. The sky was overcast and weepy. I did not know that I was not coming back but, on the other hand, there was a sense of things winding down. My harbor patrol job was over; most of the yachtsmen were heading for home.

Of course, New England weather in the early fall perennially deludes even the natives, who know better than to believe it. It is still warm enough for swimming; if it is fair, the sky is so clear as to encourage the notion that summer is forever. Even when it is cloudy, there is a benign quality about the overhead in this season, a persistent promise that it will burn off before noon. Although on this morning in question the atmosphere did seem oppressive, I put it down to my mood.

There were not many passengers on the steamer *Martha's Vineyard* and I did not know any of them. I went aft and out on deck, watching the village grow smaller with the distance. I knew every house, every store; I even knew who was up and who wasn't up at that hour. The big screw throbbed beneath me and the boiling wake made almost identifiable profiles that floated into oblivion before I could decide who they were.

"Good luck, boy," my father had said while I downed my coffee before walking down to the boat. So many things that had been, had never been, never would have been welled up in me, for this was the moment of striking out alone — if not in New Bedford, then somewhere else. At such a moment, there is no point in looking back. There is no way of coming back, except in failure. All the little houses in the village were now far astern. They melted into the trees. I could no longer distinguish one from another.

I was hired by *The Standard-Times* of New Bedford to cover the waterfront. Principally, I got the job because, after I had filled in the usual application form, I scribbled in at the bottom that I was familiar with boats and the ways of salt water. I had not put that on any other application because I had not learned it at college. My father had insisted on teaching me what boats and ships were about, often against my will. I had memorized all the sails on a full-rigged ship (totally without enthusiasm) by the time I was ten. I took no particular pride in the knowledge, equating it with other homely capabilities, such as being able to skin a tautog.

But *The Standard-Times*, although I did not know it then, had just lost its waterfront reporter and the breed was already vanishing; there weren't many about. On September 19, I picked up my Social Security card. The pay was $20 for a six-day week, $19.80 take-home, the only deduction being Social Security. On September 20, the editor said, "Take today to walk around the city and read some back issues of our newspaper. Tomorrow, you can start writing something about the waterfront."

I was not a stranger to the place nor it to me. But we had not been thus wed before and I regarded it with different eyes, seeing things I had not seen before. With the complex of towns surrounding it, the place represented a fairly typical New England portrait of Catholic and Yankee, wealthy and otherwise, seasonal visitor and

[20]

native, industry and small business, tenement and suburb, all with a characteristic amphibious orientation.

There were the textile factories ("And was Jerusalem builded here/Among these dark Satanic mills?"), great brick piles, with their chimneys and saw-toothed sheds thrust against the sky. Leon Huggins, a pleasant Dickensian gentleman in whose journalistic trust I was placed in those first few hours, quoted somebody as calling the mills "the college of the poor, the opportunity of the ambitious, and the security of the rich." Within those acres of walls, thousands, young and old, had made the city's name synonymous with cotton cloth, and shuttle and bobbin continued to work their repetitious magic, but not so much as they once had.

Less than ninety days before, employees of the Dartmouth Mills, Inc., had met in Polish Hall on Rodney French Boulevard to listen to a plan for reorganization and resumption of operations at the plant "with active participation of all workers in refinancing the company." Creditors had indicated willingness to accept common stock in liquidation of their claims and the proposal involved purchase by workers of 15,000 shares of nonvoting preferred stock with a par value of $10 per share.

Both the city and the industry were having lean going. New Bedford's tax rate for 1938 stood at $45.60; only one other community in the state equaled it, and the high rate was blamed on "increased welfare costs and continued industrial depression." By August, a minimum wage of 30 cents an hour — 5 cents above the statutory standard — appeared likely for the textile industry.

The waterfront was older than anything else, far older than Melville, although most of the books concerning its earlier years were filled with figures, rather than words. Its slates and cobbles sloping to the river, smooth with the traffic of generations; its deep stone steps at the boat landing, the austere structures at the dock head where meticulous clerks spent their lives recording in idioms of blubber and bone the fortunes lost and won, a sundial on the

[21]

side of a building pale with age, a heaving-down spile, lonely as an old elephant who has outlived his herd — all these were yesterday's signals — in the past tense, certainly, yet still just beneath the surface of the city. They were being overlaid impatiently by a new generation of filleters, lumpers, longshoremen, diesel doctors, purveyors of scallop dredges, shoers of trawl doors, welders and winch builders, and all of their latter-day paraphernalia. Yet the brawling business of one seagoing era melded with another. There was not that much difference.

The handliner's matronly, engineless catboat, the bluff-bowed bark were gone, but at the same caplogs now lay the haddock hunter, the dark green otter trawler (*Evelina Goulart, Nashawena, Growler*) with the salt-rusted deck clutter, towing cable and pen boards, and a net, armed with water-blanched cowhide, hung aloft to dry. Here now was the deep-legged scalloper, a battery of lights along the rail for night shucking, engine stack panting blackly above the wheelhouse, eager to be gone. And some little way to the south, the "navy yard" of the Portuguese, the day-trippers who pursued the iridescent scup and the dripping, flipping lobster.

These booted ones and their boats; the bull-voiced freighters that swung their big booms over the pier apron and dropped baled cotton from the South; the three- and four-masters with miles of spruce from the West Coast, shepherded to the dock by a snorting tug; these were what came when whaling went, and they were of the same strong and reticent mold.

I walked along the dock and there was Bob Howland, aboard the *Uno*. I had known him most of my life. "What're you doing up here?" he asked, and I told him. I said, "If you hear any news, tell me first, hey?"

"Boy, I hope you ain't getting paid by the inch," Bob said. "Last thing happened around here was my cat fell overboard and I got him back in a bucket. And that was three years ago."

Some people fished for the fun of it or because they weren't working or both. There were men and boys jamming the Coggeshall

[22]

Street bridge across the Acushnet River, their bamboo poles cocked at all angles. Beneath them in the dark water, the bluefish surged like little torpedoes; they struck savagely at the lead jigs scraped bright with a fish knife. Then the poles arched and up came the flapping fish, silver bellies shining. A sign on a nearby market read: "Native swordfish, 43 cents a pound. Fresh mackerel, four pounds for a quarter."

It was a city of trees, no matter what the neighborhood. In the older sections, these were principally elms planted long before the wealthy moved westward from the waterfront that made their money, before the fanlight over the double Christian door fell into decay, with its broken pane plugged with rags; before the peak of the eighteenth-century roof sagged with neglect and the front parlor of the mansion became a variety store with a red and yellow tin sign tacked under the window, "Chew Barlow's Cut Plug." So in many places, both the rich and poor had elms.

North and south of the city's center — with its trolley cars on their shiny tracks, its ice cream parlors with tessellated floors and slowly swishing overhead fans, its noiseless stone banks, its unhurried men in white coats with straw wristlets cutting tub butter and gutting the bright-eyed codfish on slate slabs — north and south of all this sprawled the three- and four-decker tenements.

They were enormous lumber monuments to a day when both men and wood were cheaper. I was looking at one and a fellow in paint-stained white overalls came by, pushing three or four short ladders on a pair of wheels. He asked me for a match and I gave him one. He shoved his hat back on his head, hauled a green can of Half and Half out of his pocket, shook some into his pipe, and pushed it down with a thumbnail that looked as if it were made of elk horn.

"Them," he said, jerking his chin in the direction of the row of tenements, "is bad news. Get up there to paint, fix gutter, y'r life ain't worth nawthin'. Hook onto somethin', it lets go, y'r all through. Father's stagin' come down seven years November, broke

[23]

his back, and he ain't earned a dollar since. Bad news," he said, and pushed off, wheel squeaking and blue smoke wisping over his bent shoulder.

As in Melville's time, the community possessed an international flavor that was charming, desirable, or a damned nuisance depending on whom you asked. There was no real trouble among ethnic groups — that is, between the Anglo-Saxons and "others" — but they had virtually nothing to do with each other except for their working-day relationships. Yet the cosmopolitan flavor was there. I read the street signs with fascination: Pilgrim, Lafayette, Jacintho, Aquidneck, which is Indian, and Kosciuszko Square. When Britain's Queen Victoria celebrated her diamond jubilee, the city's mills closed for the day in deference to the thousands of workers from Lancashire who had settled there.

The North End was "little France." And the city was recognized in Lisbon as the "capital" of the Portuguese communities in the United States. The altars of eighty churches offered spiritual comfort to English, Portuguese, French, Polish, Greek, Canadian, Russian, Irish, Italian, Scandinavian, Lebanese, German, Lithuanian, and Syrian. Their clubs, festivals, parades, slang, their breads, sausages, and soups (carne de espeto, kielbasa, moussaka, and blood pudding) were the warp and woof of this place.

There was still a coffeehouse where you could sit on a straw mat on the floor, pay a nickel, fish a silver mouthpiece out of boiling water with a pair of tongs, and smoke a hookah. Outside the shop, the owner displayed for sale candle lanterns of pierced tin and round brass trays, with the short-horned deer of another country and another culture etched around the edge. The old men smoked in that shop in the mornings, if they had the money, and talked about what it was like wherever they came from in the days when they were unwrinkled and women looked at them.

Tomorrow was uncertain for the city, yet yesterday and today commingled everywhere, and often in unlikely patterns. To the west and uphill from the river, the homes that whaling and textiles

[24]

built survived variously. Still solid and pretentious without, high-ceilinged and formidable within, some retaining the vestigial remains of illuminating gas fixtures and all of them hard to heat, there now were many mansions in which the butler's pantry had outlasted the butler. I remember walking through a living room — still with the aura of oolong and purple velvet about it, yet there was precious little left in it — and observing a great rectangle of wallpaper that was lighter by far than the rest.

There had hung for years the huge portrait in oil of the thin-lipped, mutton-chopped Quaker who had started the whole business. He had stared down unfathomably upon his issue and their issue until the day came when they sold the painting to a Boston art dealer, of necessity, and the mansion was whacked up into apartments. Like the elms, but not so successfully, the houses hung on beyond their time; attempts to adapt them to change were none too successful because those who built them had never envisioned the need for great change in anything.

With the exception of a street or two on which the rich lived and had lived for long enough to give that area a reputation for social prominence, the West End was a snug, well-kept place of one- and two-family homes tenanted by the careful middle class. Their religions, backgrounds, and nationalities varied, but they were tacitly and solidly agreed upon the principles of avoiding second mortgages, keeping the catalpas well pruned, and putting the screens on early. They were an ingenious, thrifty lot; some cobbled their own shoes down cellar, many salvaged wooden boxes from the corner grocery for kindling; they did not forget to empty their icebox pans. Their children had library cards. They kept their dogs tied up. They thought of themselves as the ones who made things go, wherever they worked or went to church. They were right in so thinking.

The percentage of college graduates in Greater New Bedford was not large; the wage level was low; the number of unemployed was high, and because diversification of industry was hardly more

[25]

than being thought of, the slump in textiles was painful. There was, however, some kind of spirit about the place. Its critics called it resignation, its proponents praised it as stubbornness, but, for whatever reason, the community never considered giving up, although its population did drop somewhat. As in all places, threat of war and reality of recession notwithstanding, a great deal of life went on as usual, sometimes with less butter, sometimes with about as much butter as usual. There was more news than Bob Howland was aware of.

In midsummer, Captain Fred W. Phillips of Fairhaven, for the past nineteen years captain of Andrew G. Pierce's schooner yacht *Palestine*, had assumed command of a 90-foot power boat recently purchased by A. B. Houghton of Washington, D.C., and Salters Point. Furnans Yacht Agency had planned half the body and drawn the underbody lines for a 62-foot motor sailer for Dr. Austen Riggs. The New Bedford dragger *Winifred Martin*, shoaled by an inside rip, grounded off the Cape, but the Coast Guard got her afloat at high water, with all hands safe.

August was busy. Miss Mimi Little, daughter of the Harry B. Littles of Concord and Wianno and a frequent visitor in South Dartmouth, sailed for Europe with her parents. They planned a motor trip through the Austrian Alps, following the route Mr. and Mrs. Little took on their honeymoon, and a visit to Henry Laughlin of Concord, who had a castle in Ireland. A fleet of 119 boats turned out for opening day of the New Bedford Yacht Club's seventeenth annual Race Week regatta. Clarence Worden's *Tar Baby* took the Cruising Class B honors on corrected time, winning by 52 seconds over the scratch boat. In nearby Marion, Tabor Academy's eight-oared crew defeated Radley College, visiting English oarsmen, by one-third of a boat length in Sippican Harbor over a sloppy mile course kicked up by a following northeast wind.

Admissions to the whaleship *Charles W. Morgan*, enshrined at Colonel Edward H. R. Green's estate at Round Hill, South Dartmouth, were about half for the summer season because of the rainy weather. New Bedford's Thanksgiving Assembly was scheduled for November 25 and eleven debutantes were scheduled to make their bows.

Thus, the area, with its rich and poor, its "summer people," its waterfront, its old elms, its heritage rooted in the Yankee tradition and with the new, rich strains of the immigrant already coloring the society in increasing depth, with its smoky city industry and its suburban harbors filled with yachts, was much like many another New England coastal complex on September 20, 1938.

Most of the young had returned to school. Adults whose winter homes were not too far away were encouraged by high temperatures to stay a few more days at their beach houses, hoping for one touch more of fine weather, another weekend of swimming and sailing. Many of those who had departed the beaches had left behind their domestics, who were packing family belongings and preparing the summer houses for closing.

That is how it was on September 20. "Tomorrow," the editor said, "you can start writing something about the waterfront." I went to Jules', a hole in the wall, had a meat pie, a glass of milk, and an apple tart, all for a quarter, and went to my room and to bed. The last thing I recall was wondering what I would write about the next day.

Book II

New Jersey, New York City, and Long Island

Chapter 3

WHAT YOU HAVE TO REMEMBER FIRST is that nobody expected anything to happen. It was not as it is now, when almost nothing, however awful, would be surprising. In those days, there was a remoteness about most things that was reassuring because it was predictable. If there was a disaster, it always occurred in one of those vague locations where they didn't wash and built their houses out of straw. There was no reason to assume that this Wednesday would be appreciably different from any other September 21; the people who had watched the weather in this place all their lives knew what they knew about it.

It is appalling, in retrospect, to reflect upon how little we expected what happened, to discover how little we knew about what was going on elsewhere on the day of the storm and to realize how long it was before we did know. That was because New Bedford was not the first to get the hurricane. It came from the south. Consider then, those who were to the south of us.

A *New York Times* editorial on September 21 entitled "Hurricane" concluded, "Every year an average of three such whirlwinds sweep the tropical North Atlantic between June and November. In 1933, there was an all-time record of twenty. If New York and the rest of the world have been so well informed about the cyclone, it is because of an admirably organized meteorological service. From every ship in the Caribbean Sea, reports are radioed to Washington, Havana, San Juan, and other stations.

"Hour by hour, a cyclone is watched, peril that it is, until at last it whirls out into the Atlantic to make passengers on liners wonder why the wind whistles past glass-enclosed decks and why a 50,000-ton hull begins to roll and pitch. In ships and scientific stations are men sending wireless warnings to all the world, caring nothing about nationality or economic prizes. There is a lesson in all those stations and ships of many nations warning the Western world that a cyclone is on the loose. Science is doing its best to teach the world the worth of cooperation."

In the larger sense, New York City and, for that matter, much of the state — excluding Long Island — and neighboring New Jersey were not immediately aware of the vastness˙ of what occurred on the twenty-first because the hurricane's full fury was for other places. Yet the explosion of weather left its mark here.

The peak of the storm passed over New Jersey in the late afternoon. It was the worst in fifty years and met the home-going commuter just in time to disrupt his return from New York to examine the damage.

At Manasquan, the sea tore the entire fourteen blocks of the boardwalk off its foundations and distributed it two blocks inland. On the way, the breaking sections crashed into casinos and pavilions fronting the ocean and into cottages on the side streets. Porches were torn away and doors and windows were smashed open to the wind, and the slashing rain and sea left behind a three-foot deposit of sand, burying Ocean Avenue its full length. Nature's brief onslaught cost a quarter of a million dollars at Manasquan. There were no lives lost, but James Golden was swept more than a block inland in the swirl of water and splintered timber before he was hauled to safety.

The bridge across Absecon Inlet, separating Atlantic City and the island of Brigantine, a one-million-dollar structure, had already been weakened by high winds and heavy seas; it collapsed with the high tide that followed, marooning more than two thousand people at Brigantine.

From Cape May to Sussex, the storm delivered a final blow to the 33,000-acre tomato crop and caused widespread damage to the forty percent of the state's 3.5 million bushels of apples still on the trees. The combined pressure of wind and rain on the laden boughs broke them down and uprooted thousands of trees in ground that had been softened by the steady downpour of the previous four days. In North Haledon, Fred Yahn's flock of four thousand young pheasants were so jammed together by the wind and panic in the run that a thousand of them were smothered before he could pry the birds apart and get the survivors under cover. The birds were worth two dollars apiece.

New York City did not officially have a hurricane, since average intensity of the gale was 65 miles an hour and a hurricane must be at least 75. Yet because of the wind, high tides, and a four-and-a-half-inch rainfall, the routine of city life was virtually at a standstill from 3 to 6 o'clock in the afternoon.

The storm uprooted thousands of trees, flooded cellars, caved in houses and garages, inundated streets and highways, and grounded innumerable small craft along the waterfront. Police emergency squads worked to cut away dangling signs and blocked off parts of buildings that were undermined or weakened, and the ambulance services of the city's hospitals, sirens wailing, crawled cautiously through the storm-swept streets to treat scores of the injured. Thousands of office workers, seeking to return to their homes, were marooned in business buildings because transit schedules had been disrupted by washouts. At 8:45 P.M., a power failure on the lines of the Consolidated Edison Company left parts of Manhattan and all of the Bronx in darkness.

All the lines of the Independent Subway System except those

[33]

running to Queens were affected. Hospitals without emergency apparatus turned to candles, as did thousands of residents. The power failure stemmed from a breakdown of the Hell Gate Plant at 133rd Street and the East River, one of the largest in the world and the chief source of supply for most of the electrical energy consumed in Manhattan and the Bronx. The breakdown was caused by overflowing of the East River, which flooded three blocks inland to Willow Avenue, where it was four feet high at nine in the evening. By then, access to the power plant was possible only by boat.

The flooding made it impossible to operate the boilers, and the generators had to stop for lack of steam. Since the Hell Gate station was built well above ordinary high-water marks, it was immediately obvious that the tide which flooded the plant had broken all records.

Loew's 83rd Street theater and the RKO 81st Street theater, both on Broadway, were left in darkness and with projection mechanism out of commission. A few members of the capacity audiences stomped out about 9:30 to get their money back, but most remained good-naturedly for another ten minutes, at which time the power returned.

Along the waterfront, both in the afternoon and evening, there was, of course, a more acute awareness of what was going on. The French liner *Ile de France*, due to arrive at quarantine at 1:45 in the afternoon, was awaited by the Coast Guard cutter *Navesink*, with about seventy-five customs inspectors, immigration agents, visitors, and newspaper representatives aboard. In driving rain that reduced visibility to less than one hundred yards, the cutter searched in vain for the ship and finally returned to dock at the foot of Whitehall Street.

Shortly thereafter, the liner appeared at the entrance to the Hudson River, the force of the wind then so strong that, as she proceeded to the French Line pier, the big ship listed sharply to starboard. At the pier, where five or six tugs normally were used for docking, a dozen were on hand, and even with these at bow and stern, warping the ship in against the wind, Captain Jules Chabot had to drop his port anchor to aid in swinging the vessel around.

Warned by the Coast Guard that the *Queen Mary*, scheduled to sail from New York at 4:30 P.M. with 868 passengers, might encounter the center of the hurricane, officials of the Cunard White Star line postponed her departure until 5 the next morning.

Near-panic occurred on the Staten Island ferryboat *Knicker-bocker* at 6 P.M. when the storm-lashed waters of the bay rolled the vessel down in her slip at the Battery and left her hanging at a 45-degree angle, her port guard rail caught under an iron bumper attached to the piling. The cries of two hundred passengers on board mingled with those of hundreds of homeward-bound commuters waiting to take the ferry to Fort George on Staten Island as they saw the craft assume and retain her alarming slant. It required two tugs and nearly a half-hour to work the *Knickerbocker* loose so that her passengers could be landed safely.

Because today there are no police records pertaining to the matter, the name of the man initially described in metropolitan newspapers as New York City's "only storm death" remains unknown. He was a hitchhiker, who was picked up by an unidentified Queens motorist. The car in which they were riding stalled in high water at 20th Avenue and 133rd Street, Whitestone Landing, in Queens. As water filled the interior, both men climbed to the top of the car. After several hours, the drenched hitchhiker said he thought he could swim to higher land, about a block away. He plunged into the current that swirled about the car, and was quickly lost to sight in the twilight. Much later, Coast Guards rescued the motorist from the top of his car and found the body of the hitchhiker washed up on the higher land he had tried to reach.

The flood waters of the East River and Long Island Sound at Throgs Neck, near Fort Schuyler Road, were nine feet deep at 7:30 that night. There were foot-high choppy waves over what normally was dry land; the tide was rising, the wind was from the

[35]

west, and blowing at least 40 miles an hour, and the water was full of drifting debris.

For nearly an hour, J. Gilbert Finning, forty, a bowling alley manager and (although he had had his left arm amputated below the elbow) a fair swimmer, and William P. McGrath, thirty, unemployed, and some other samaritans had waded among the small frame bungalows in the area, assisting residents on Fort Schuyler Road to high ground.

Finning, McGrath, and four boys ranging from fourteen to sixteen waded through water three to four feet deep to get a woman out of a flooded house; one of the boys was Finning's sixteen-year-old son. They found a rowboat which was filled with water lodged against a hedge, between a bungalow and the road; after bailing out the skiff, they pushed it to the house and the woman got into the boat, holding her six-year-old son in her arms. The men and boys then waded and pushed their boat toward dry ground.

Then Finning lost his hold and his footing. McGrath called to him; Finning said that he was all right, but McGrath — not a robust man — decided to go to his aid. McGrath worked his way around the stern of the boat, made a shallow dive and started to swim toward Finning. In the gathering darkness, both were immediately out of sight and four hours later, when the tide had fallen, their bodies were recovered not far away. McGrath was posthumously awarded the Carnegie Hero Fund Commission's Bronze Medal for his attempt to save Finning's life.

Offshore, one liner met the hurricane and one did not. The Red Star's *Königstein* nosed into it forty miles off Block Island and was consequently nine hours late in reaching Hoboken. Her skipper, Captain Alfred Leidig, said the ship's barometer had fallen to 28.40 and the wind had risen to 100 miles an hour during the worst of the storm. None of her 294 passengers suffered injury. The *Conte di Savoia* of the Italian Line, bound for New York from the Mediterranean, was fortunate in having aboard a passenger who predicted the hurricane two days in advance — that is, on the nineteenth. The passenger was the Reverend Ernest Gherzi, sometimes referred to as the "Father of Typhoons," an Italian Jesuit who had been a meteorologist for twenty-three years at an observatory near Shanghai. On the Monday morning preceding the hurricane, Father Gherzi went to the ship's bridge and remarked, "One of my children will be around in about three days."

In relating the story, he added that the passengers had jovially suggested he be thrown overboard because of the forecast. From then on until Wednesday, he spent long periods on the bridge, examining weather charts and predicting the hurricane's course.

"The path of the hurricane and our path seemed to be converging," Father Gherzi said, "but after studying the warning from the Naval Observatory in Washington, as well as the signs at sea, I was able to assure Captain Alberto Ottino, commander of the liner, that the hurricane, reportedly passing rapidly northward, would go by before we reached it, so we did not have to change our course or reduce speed when we ran into the outer edge of the disturbance and encountered squalls on the night of the twenty-first. The squalls were not dangerous."

Captain Ottino praised Father Gherzi's forecast for its accuracy and said the worst the ship struck was a forty-mile wind for a brief period Wednesday night.

Some beavers also received due credit, although how they knew what was expected of them, or how far in advance they knew it, is less clear than what they accomplished. At Stony Point, sixty colonies, numbering more than five hundred beavers — the progeny of three pairs trapped in the Adirondacks and placed in Palisades Interstate Park eighteen years before — manned their dams in the park's 42,000 acres when the storm broke. There were sixty dams in the beavers' defense line, the principal restraining force against rain-swollen rivers, streams, and ponds.

The size of the problem confronting the animals was impressive. Long Mountain beaver pond, for example, was created by a dam in what normally was a three-foot-wide stream; the pond ordinarily covered about five acres in the center of the park. On Wednesday night, with a roiling stream widened to almost twenty feet and the pond doubled in size, the beaver dam, made of mud, sticks, stones, and sod, withstood the pressure and fed eighteen inches of fast-moving water over its top. That particular dam, five years old at the time of the hurricane, was one hundred and fifty yards long, with a fourteen-foot base and a height of six feet at the midpoint.

In the west central section of the park, Cedar Hill Pond, made by a dam at Stony Brook, doubled its normal four acres when the stream widened from five to twenty feet. Over this dam, which was only forty feet wide, water rose two feet.

Another dam of critical importance was wedged between boulders thirty feet apart; as with all the others, it was completely submerged at the storm's peak, yet never showed a sign of yielding to the strains of the water upon it. John J. Tamsen, superintendent of Bear Mountain Park, and William H. Carr, director of the Trailside Museum, maintained by the American Museum of Natural History, credited the beavers — who cut down trees all through the night of the hurricane to reinforce their wood-and-mud bulwarks — with having saved three arterial highways from serious flooding, preventing the certain destruction of at least one bridge, and retarding the erosion of hundreds of acres of soil.

Carr said had it not been for the beaver dams "backing up perfectly terrific bodies of water, in some cases, more than two hundred yards across," Long Mountain Road, U.S. Highway 6, and the Johnstown Road would have been transformed into rivers for distances of up to a quarter of a mile and the same would have held true of U.S. Highway 9-W, the main road along the west shore of the Hudson, and Route 17, linking Tuxedo Park and Harriman, to the north.

Even with the beavers' help, what the roads in the area were like that night — wild, black, suddenly foreign, and even hostile — can be really known only by those who drove them. Frederic Foster de

Rham, fifty-four, was vice president and trust officer of the Fulton Trust Company of New York and a prominent member of the Tuxedo Park colony for many years. The afternoon train on which he was returning from New York City was marooned by the storm at Warwick and he made the remainder of the journey in his own car. The trip, which ordinarily would have taken fifteen minutes, required two hours, on an almost impassable road.

Mr. de Rham arrived at his house shortly before 8 o'clock that night, suffering from exhaustion and exposure. He went into the bathroom to prepare for dinner and collapsed a moment later, dying almost instantly.

To appreciate how such a thing could happen, consider what it was like on that Wednesday if you were driving the length of Long Island, say from Times Square, starting at 3 in the afternoon, to the ocean's edge at Southold.

The most sobering — and eventually frightening and defeating — aspect of the journey derived from its cumulative effect, which most who went through the hurricane did not have because they remained in one place. Making one's perilous way through town and village, the principal impression was one of gradually building devastation, beginning with comprehensible proportions that finally were swollen beyond the mind's grasp.

There was hardly more than a nasty blow in New York City in midafternoon. Traffic was proceeding normally through the streets, across the bridge and over the boulevards of Queens, and it was not until one reached the World's Fair site that anything approaching flood conditions was in evidence. Here, automobiles were parked in puddles that reached to the hubcaps.

At Westbury, the Northern State Parkway was more wet and slippery than usual and here and there, a tree was uprooted. The wind was accelerating with disturbing persistence and there was now an unnatural whine about it, such as no ordinary Long Island wind ever made. Traffic was slowing and Grand Central Parkway was beginning to fill with water. The time was about 4:30. It was apparent that a bad storm was getting under way.

A little farther on, the picture got worse. Jericho Turnpike revealed the first real evidence of devastation. Here, the passing motorist looked anxiously at bending trees and fallen branches which began to strew the highway. The wind kept picking up. Drivers felt their cars begin to jump a little under the more forceful gusts, and even tightly closed automobile windows dripped moisture as the gust-driven rain began to pelt from a variety of directions.

One now passed old villages caught in the full rip of the gale. Shutters and awnings were dangling; trees were beginning to fall over the streets. All manner of sodden debris, curiously unidentifiable and shapeless, was being thrown about. Drivers moved ahead at ten miles an hour, peering through the meager hole left by the swishing wiper blade. Darkness was settling over the countryside.

By this time, the wind was roaring; car headlights pierced the torrents of rain no more than fifty feet. Over and over, a tree would appear unbelievably across the road — sometimes flat, in a massive heap, sometimes at a threatening angle — and three or four cars would halt, their lights puny in the turmoil. The drivers, half-soaked, forced car doors open against the wind, braced and struggled to get to the downed tree, yelled some word of advice and then, clothing whipping, battled back to their vehicles and, with luck, drove gingerly around the obstruction. Now and then, a car slipped into a water-filled ditch and there it stayed.

At Laurel, huge trees were not only down across the highway, but thrown against houses and even shoved through walls of buildings. Telephone poles began to give way, bringing down tangles of wires. More and more, cars were forced to leave the roads, bumping, jumping, and slipping in mud, to forge new routes across lawns or even far out in fields in order to bypass the wreckage on the highway.

[40]

Just beyond Laurel, two towering trees leaned over the road, falling slowly. A driver stepped hard on the gas and sped under them; they fell in slow motion just behind, blocking the route totally. Others were not so lucky; at least a half-dozen cars were scattered along the road, crushed under heavy trees; at the time there was no way of knowing what happened to their occupants — or whether they were dead or alive.

The few cars still moving crawled through darkened villages; there were no electric lights anywhere. Occasionally one might see the tumbled ruins of houses and barns. Shards of glass were everywhere; roofs were piled up on lawns and streets, and chimneys had disintegrated into heaps of bricks. The wind screeched. Emergency crews pulling away at trees or attempting to prop falling buildings were pathetic in the face of such elemental malevolence.

At Southold, the wind blew every nut off a horse chestnut tree and through the windows of a house; the chestnuts riddled the panes like machine-gun bullets. The ocean moved up into the town; it crawled into cellars; it washed around ground floors; it lapped at foundations.

Russell Owen was one who made that drive from Times Square. "The weary motorist acknowledged defeat," he said. "The objective had been Greenport, five miles beyond, but after hours of nerve-wracking travel through almost impassable roads and fields, the prospect of conquering those last five miles seemed remote. Where well-paved state highway ordinarily lay, the Atlantic intervened, in all its formidable majesty. . . ."

Elsewhere on the north side of Long Island, across which Mr. Owen had driven, dramatic and tragic events of several kinds were in process. In the Port Washington area, something like four hundred craft, ranging from rowboats to seventy-foot yachts, were ripped from berths and moorings when the storm struck at 2 P.M. Seven sloops were carried over a seawall and dropped into the

[41]

swimming pool of the Manhasset Bay Yacht Club. A forty-foot power boat came to rest with its bow inside a grocery store; the water that carried it there also floated a one-ton delicatessen display case.

Ninety thousand homes on Long Island in the Glen Cove area were without refrigeration because the Long Island Lighting Company had to suspend services at its No. 2 plant, only seven years old and one of the most up-to-date in the country.

Near Northport, the First Lady of Brooklyn and the First Lady of the City of New York were stranded in their homes, six hundred feet apart, yet unable to communicate with each other or with the outside world. Mrs. Raymond V. Ingersoll, wife of the borough president, alone in her Duck Island home, was trapped as high water covered her lawn, making it impossible for her to leave without a rowboat. A broken telephone line prevented her from calling Mrs. Fiorello LaGuardia, who was stranded on the second floor of her home at Asharoken, while furniture floated about in the first-floor rooms below. Local firemen finally rescued them, both uninjured.

Robert Pryde, thirty-five, of Oyster Bay, with two companions, was trying to save his forty-foot yawl and decided to beach her at Asharoken. As the boat went ashore, Pryde jumped to the beach side, to make for the land, about twenty feet away. Simultaneously, a sea rolled in. It dropped the boat on him. His two companions got him ashore, and the Northport Fire Department was summoned to bring a respirator. Chief Ray Terry and fourteen men of the department battled for more than an hour to get from Northport to the beach; they had to cut and remove forty trees from the road and, coming to an exceptionally large one at Chesebrough Hill, they transferred respirator and emergency crew to a passenger car that happened to be on the other side of the fallen tree.

After the respirator had been used a half-hour, Pryde was pronounced dead by the coroner, and the undertaker was called to the beach. By the time the undertaker was ready to leave, the rising tide was so high that he could not get off the beach, and he was marooned there until it began to fall.

At Port Jefferson, the 150-foot steam ferry *Park City* left her dock at 2 P.M. for the customary two-hour run across the sound to Bridgeport. Shortly after 4 P.M., when it had not arrived, word was passed that it was missing, and anxious calls were made to Coast Guard stations on the Connecticut and Long Island shores for possible sightings. Aboard were nine crew members and six passengers, including Mrs. George St. John, Jr., of Wallingford, Connecticut, and her two-month-old baby, and Mrs. H. L. H. Fry of New York City.

The *Park City* was having her problems. When she was well out into the sound, the sea became so heavy that Captain Ray Dickerson, a veteran skipper, attempted to turn back shortly after his vessel approached the Middle Ground' Light, but a shift of wind made it impractical to attempt to remain under way, so he decided to anchor.

Then the storm broke upon them, bringing with it dense fog and heavy rain. The seas drove green water over the steamer's bow, gradually filling the hold until the water reached a height of five and a half feet in the fire and engine rooms. This extinguished the fires under the boilers, stopping the steam pumps, which had been operating up to that time to keep the water down in the hold. That was about 3:15 P.M.

"As the gale reached its height, the ship started to drag anchor and we had plenty of worries," Dickerson related, "although the ship was at no time in danger of going down. Our main worry was wondering just where we were going to be blown. The waves kept pounding over the deck and the boat shipped plenty of water."

With the generator knocked out by water below decks, passengers and crew members were provided with lanterns. There were no other lights in the darkened ship. The engineer, Frank Smith, assisted by oiler Percy King and fireman Edward King, worked in water up to their waists in a futile effort to keep the fires and engines going. After the steam pumps failed, all of the crew and two of the male passengers worked on the hand pumps and used buckets to keep the water down.

At 7:30 Wednesday night, the anchor finally caught and held and there they stayed, without heat or food, six miles off Middle Ground Light, through what Dickerson said was "the worst weather I ever experienced in all my sea career and one of the longest nights I can remember." The passengers stayed in the large reception room of the *Park City* or in their automobiles. For Mrs. Fry, it was "a harrowing night. I never expected to get back alive. The crew was magnificent. We prayed and prayed fervently."

The next morning, about 7, the Eastern Steamship Line's *Sandwich*, bound for Boston, reported the *Park City*'s location to the patrolling Coast Guard cutter *Galatea*, commanded by Lieutenant Commander A. W. Davis. It took an hour in the still-heavy sea for the cutter to get a line aboard the ferry and three hours more to tow her to Port Jefferson because she had three feet of water in the hold and was listing heavily. A thousand people were on the dock to greet the ferry after her 21-hour drubbing, and when Captain Dickerson came ashore, he said, "Our chief worry was about Mrs. St. John's baby, but there wasn't a whimper out of the child."

Some babies weathered the storm very well. Mrs. Joseph Gatz of Riverhead was in Eastern Long Island Hospital at Greenport on September 21, awaiting the birth of a child. Her daughter, Shirley Ann, was born at the peak of the hurricane, at 3:20 P.M., and first saw the light of day about the time that part of the hospital's roof blew off. Rain flooded the delivery room where Shirley Ann was born. However, Dr. Hallock Luce, Jr., the attending physician, said she was healthy, vigorous, and totally unaffected by "the inauspicious circumstances attending her arrival."

Some were born in the Eastern Long Island Hospital; some died there. About 5 o'clock on the day of the storm, Emmett Young of

[44]

Southold climbed to the roof of his barn, in an attempt to refasten damaged sections. The roof blew off, pinning him under fallen timber. Dr. George T. Thompson came to the aid of the injured man as quickly as possible but he had to walk from the village because the main highway was impassable. Mr. Young was removed to the hospital early the next afternoon, after the roads had been cleared; he died of internal injuries, without regaining consciousness.

Emmett Young was a graduate of Southold High School, Class of 1914; there were ten members in the class. A classmate gave his eulogy: "Letting the mind roam back twenty-four years ago, there was much to remember in which all of us joined together with a great deal of glorious good fun. There were school sails to Sag Harbor, Fourth Pond, Three-Mile Harbor, the school dances at the parish house, straw rides in summer, big bob-sleigh rides in winter, candy pulls, skating parties, the first Washington trip ever undertaken by any class in school. What a host of good times accompanied those school days.

"Emmett was quiet, with a thoughtful, conscientious mind and fine determination . . . he could always be counted on to fulfill his promise or whatever he had set out to accomplish with anyone. I recall his kind, pleasant smile, his courtesy always to his elders, his fine spirit of friendly helpfulness and his enjoyment, never boisterous, in all that he did in work or play with us. Modest and retiring in many ways, he never failed to implant his own sturdy individual personality upon the character of our group. Emmett Young was a gentleman. . . ."

At Greenport, where the anemometer of the big Vanderbilt yacht *Vara* disintegrated after registering a wind velocity of 91 miles per hour, Herman Ficken, manager of the Metro Theater, became uneasy as the storm crisis came at about 3:45 P.M. He halted the showing of the film and asked the sixty men, women, and children in the audience to leave. The audience filed out in orderly fashion and just as the last one left, the front entrance and the rear of the building were blown in, the roof fell, and the structure collapsed.

Sag Harbor's greatest loss was the spire of the Presbyterian Church, called the Old Whalers' Church. The steeple, 125 feet high, regarded by many as one of the most beautiful in America, was torn off close to the roof and blown to the ground.

Of the steeple and its destruction, Ernest S. Clowes wrote, "[It] had stood for nearly one hundred years. Built in a curious medley of architectural styles, yet harmonious and graceful, it had been a welcome sight to the old whale hunters of eighty years ago, returning, perhaps, after a three-year voyage around the world.

"For three generations, it had dominated by its height and singular grace the landscape of Sag Harbor. In the worst of the storm, a great lifting gust tore it whole and bodily from the church, carried it about twenty feet and then dropped it, a crashing mass of shapeless ruin, fortunately clear from the church, which was not otherwise damaged.

"That great crash, preceded by the melancholy tolling of the bell as it fell, was one sound which people who lived nearby heard above the vast roar of the storm."

As glass was blasted out of windows of many of Sag Harbor's stores, power was cut off, roads were blocked by fallen trees and wreckage, and the breakwater was submerged in the high tide and smother, an upset motorist whose car lay crushed beneath a big, blown-over maple approached a police officer. Virtually in tears, the motorist said, "My car is totally wrecked. It will never run again. Whom can I sue for damages?"

The officer, subject to storm demands from all directions, replied calmly, "You might sue God almighty, but I don't know whether you'll collect."

As bad as all of this death and destruction was, the awful truth of what was happening on the south shore of Long Island was not yet generally known.

[46]

Chapter 4

F ROM L ONG B EACH ON THE WEST to Southampton on the east, there is a thin dune barrier that ordinarily holds back the Atlantic Ocean. Behind it lie usually placid bays and beyond those, the mainland of Long Island's south shore. In the fall of 1938, this dune barrier was well settled; its several colonies of beach homes ranged from modest to pretentious.

Dr. William T. Helmuth of East Hampton wrote, "About three P.M. on September 21, a southeasterly wind reached hurricane force and it rose to a peak about six P.M., at which time, the local barometer reached its lowest point at 28.55.

"An unusually high tide coincidentally also reached its highest point almost at the time of the hurricane's greatest intensity, helping to produce the first, and less gigantic, of the several hurricane waves, called by most people 'tidal waves.' By far the greatest amount of damage was done at this time. When the sea broke through the barrier of sand dunes in hundreds of places, inundating land which had previously been protected by them, many dunes were literally blown away to the northward [and] salt water engulfed the coastal bays and ponds, turning them into open arms of the sea. . . ."

Six miles south of Bay Shore, across Great South Bay, lies Fire Island, with its summer colonies, including Saltaire, Kismet, Fair Harbor, Ocean Beach, and Point o' Woods. In this area, within two hours' time, the barometer tobogganed from a high reading of 29.78 to 27.43. As it dropped, the velocity of the wind mounted from a warm zephyr at noon to a forty-mile-an-hour blow at 1:30 P.M. to a ninety-mile-an-hour hurricane at 3. By that time, Coast Guardsmen at Fire Island station, surrounded by water, reported that the beach was "raging like the ocean." One hundred twenty-seven houses were destroyed at Saltaire, 91 at Fair Harbor, and 29 at Oak Beach.

This is Coast Guard headquarters in Bay Shore on the night of September 21.

The only light in the offices is from candles; there is no electric power. As the anxious, many from New York City, come stumbling up the dark stairs seeking information about relatives who are on Fire Island, they face the gray-haired, mild-mannered Commander William M. Wolff.

"What about Ocean Beach?" they ask. "What about Saltaire?"

Wolff speaks quietly, trying to reassure, "The ice cutter [BA-25] has gone over to Saltaire to help the people in that vicinity. They appear to be most badly off. The ocean has apparently cut through in several places and one is between Saltaire and Fair Harbor. The ice cutter is a powerful boat and will be able to help these people if they need it. The crew over there is also trying to get through by using a tractor on the beach."

The hours pass, with no word from the icebreaker. With power lines down in Bay Shore, it is not possible to contact the vessel by shortwave radio. Efforts to get in touch with her through the Rockaway Point Coast Guard station also have been futile. You can feel the rising apprehension among those who stand there, waiting, especially after word comes through from Center Moriches that Westhampton Beach has been hard hit.

At Saltaire, Long Island, one of those trapped tried to swim to the mainland and was pulled from the water exhausted.

At 11 o'clock, power is restored in Bay Shore. Harold G. Cogswell, chief motor machinist, begins to twirl the dials of the headquarters' shortwave radio apparatus. Out of the first crackles of static comes a hoarse, initially indistinct voice that gradually clears and grows louder. It is Paul Long, machinist's mate aboard the icebreaker. Communication across Great South Bay to the cutter, plunging and rolling in the stormy night sea near Saltaire, has been established.

"BA-25, this is Bay Shore, Fourth District Office. Come in, come in, BA-25."

"Fourth District Office, BA-25 standing by, Bay Shore."

"What is the situation at Saltaire?"

"Conditions at Saltaire very bad. Half the houses are down, two women are lost, about seventy-five people are waiting to be taken off the island."

"Are the people waiting at Saltaire safe?"

"They are assembling in the town hall."

"Do you know the conditions of any other places along the beach?"

"No, but they must be approximately the same."

"Take off all who want to leave. Can a boat leave Bay Shore and go over to Saltaire dock now?"

"No, it would be impossible because of floating wreckage."

"Find out the exact number lost. Try to send someone to the town hall to get the names of the dead women."

"We will get you all the information we can."

The conversation ends. One of the waiting men in the office says to another, "Are you going across the bay?" The other replies, obvious strain in his voice, "Yes. But first I want to hear those names."

There is no sound, no movement in the office as communication is resumed with the cutter. "We have the names of the women who died," the voice crackles from offshore. "We have the names. Mrs. Angeline Bazinet, 501 West 122nd Street, New York. Mrs. Max Haas, 38 77th Street, Brooklyn. Three other persons unaccounted for, no names."

"Good God," one of the waiting men says, "Mr. Haas has been here for hours. He just left in a boat for Saltaire."

At Saltaire, the morning after the storm, a blond girl sat on a box, which rested precariously on a tilted remnant of one of the boardwalks. As Chief Assistant District Attorney Lindsey R. Henry arrived to survey the damage, she stood up and walked over to him.

"Could you assist us in the search for a body?" she asked.

"Of course," he said. "Whose body is it?"

The girl shut her eyes tightly for a moment and then said very carefully and slowly, "My mother's."

Her mother was Mrs. Haas, who, with Madame Bazinet, had clung to a tree as the wind-lashed sea swept across the island. The Haases had just built a new house on the ocean front at Saltaire; on this Thursday morning, there was nothing left where it had stood but wet sand, flat and hard from the ocean's pounding.

Soon after 3 o'clock on Wednesday, the situation on the beaches became critical, especially on that long strip from Shinnecock Bay to Moriches Inlet, where the dunes were mostly low and had at their backs a succession of bays and canals. Clowes noted, "By half past three, [the sea] was breaking over and through the dunes in many places and sometime toward four o'clock, the final catastrophe occurred. Before the onslaught of that terrible tide, itself about ten to fifteen feet above the normal height and crested with breakers towering fifteen feet higher or more, the whole barrier of the dunes crumpled and went down. . . .

"In a few minutes, along the stretch of beach from Quogue Village to Moriches Inlet, there remained of one hundred and seventy-nine summer homes only twenty-six battered shells of houses, of which hardly a dozen will ever be habitable again."

Westhampton, with twenty-eight dead and four missing a month later, with at least one hundred and fifty houses destroyed and a property loss of two million dollars, was the worst hit of all the Long Island communities. The storm dealt death indiscriminately; among the victims were prominent members of the colony along with their servants.

Those who did not die owed their lives to chance, to fortitude, and, often, to being at ease in and about the water from long custom. The sailors and swimmers usually did not lose their heads when they found themselves overboard, although this was no iron-clad guarantee of survival. Moreover, to aid those who needed help, there emerged heroes and heroines, born of the crisis.

[51]

Wreckage of houses swept into piles at Westhampton, Long Island

Agnes Zeigler was the governess of twenty-three-month-old Ann Renée, daughter of the Countess Charles de Ferry de Fontnouvelle, wife of the French consul general in New York. The countess, her daughter, Miss Zeigler, and the family cook were in their Westhampton home.

"About four o'clock, our house began to tremble," Miss Zeigler said. "I was never so frightened in my life. The wind was howling and the water was up to the floor of the living room, having already flooded the basement. I waded through the water to a nearby house, where I found a chauffeur and a maid in the basement. I asked them to come and help us, but they wouldn't, so I went back to the house."

The countess said her first thought was of an earthquake, and when the building began to shake, she knew they could not remain there. When Miss Zeigler returned, the countess bundled the baby in a blanket and the four of them set out to seek a place of safety. They struggled along the beach through water up to their hips; the countess, holding the baby to her breast, had to discard the overalls she was wearing because they impeded her flight; she waded on in the sea and gale, clad only in her underclothing.

Planks, branches, and even doors were flying through the air; heavy boards and timbers swirled past them on the crests of the seas. "It was only by the grace of God that we were not killed," said the countess. Once they looked back, in time to see the big rambling frame house they had left collapse with a roar.

After traveling a half-mile, they reached the storm-battered residence of William Ottman, Jr. The Ottmans were not there, but their household staff was, including Arne Bendicksen, a Norwegian who had been their butler for two years. Mr. Bendicksen, who already had given shelter to twenty other refugees before the countess and her party arrived, took charge of the situation, and assumed responsibility for all of them. His incredible composure strengthened them; so thoroughly was he in command that not one of the twenty-odd in his care even asked him his name, nor did they know it the next day.

Bendicksen sensed that the situation was getting worse. He went upstairs and out through a scuttle to the roof and attempted to signal the mainland; he thought there was an answer but decided they did not have time to wait for help to come to them. Accordingly, he fought his way to the bridge that crossed to the mainland; here he found three husky boys, Stanley Wilson and Charles and Michael Goy, and they returned to the Ottman house with him.

With the four males to guide and sustain, the refugees linked arms and started for the bridge, which, already weakened by the flood, was threatening to break up. Somewhere along the way, the butler's chin had been cut badly and was bleeding, but he made no mention of it.

All of them crossed the bridge safely, and with little time to spare before it was impassable. "I am convinced we were spared because of the baby. Providence looked down upon us through her eyes," the countess said. The Ottman house collapsed as they struggled to gain the bridge.

Westhampton Police Chief Stanley J. Teller and Officer Timothy J. Robinson were credited with saving seventeen people who were stranded in a house occupied by Mr. and Mrs. Henry G. T. Martin. Teller received a call for help from the shore and started along Beach Lane in one of the village police cruisers. On the way, he met Robinson in the other police car and called to him to follow. They got across the West Bay Bridge, had to abandon their vehicles, then half-swam, half-waded the remainder of the way. "It was the worst thing I ever saw," Teller said. "I saw a woman helpless in deep water, with three children, on Dune Road."

They were Mrs. Herbert J. McCooey, her six-year-old twins, Richard and Robert, and her son John, aged nine. The policemen led them to the Martin house, together with the McCooey chauffeur and maid. Already in the house were Mr. Martin and two maids; Mrs. Carl H. Kappes, her daughter, Eleanor, and a maid; Mrs. Frances B. Stebbins and a maid, and an unidentified couple, who had sought sanctuary there.

Wallace H. Halsey, a Southampton civil engineer, who was driving home on Dune Road to avoid fallen trees, was a principal in what followed.

"A young lady at the Martin house hailed me," Halsey remembered, "and said there were several people there and that they had called the police for help. I left my car and started for the Martin house. I met Officer Teller. The storm was becoming more intense by the second. We met an old man on his way out.

"I looked to the east and saw a sea eight to ten feet high was almost upon us. I grabbed the old man and Stanley grabbed me. We were all carried at least one hundred feet. We got our footing. Stanley pushed me and I pushed the old man. We got back into the Martin house through a window.

"The front door had been blown open and we were unable to hold it. So we cut down another door for a brace. The door crashed and Stanley grabbed for me and I hollered for him to get upstairs. I stayed in the angle back of the front door for several minutes and saw three houses and the bathing station go by.

"[I] was about six feet above average high water . . . and had a very clear view of the progress of the seas and tide over and through a low beach. I would say that the seas were about three feet high for a length of one hundred and fifty to two hundred feet, solid blue water coming in apparent regular intervals of about ten or twelve seconds.

"Above these seas, there was a clear space, I would say from ten to twenty feet, above which there was a curtain of white mist carrying much flying debris, passing over with terrific velocity. In fact, the air was so clear, although dark, that I saw several houses break up and disappear.

"A house nearby was breaking up and a piece of it came smashing into a corner of the Martin house. It knocked me down, but I got clear. Then there was a crash like thunder and the next thing I knew I was in seas running over ten feet high, with floating debris of all kinds around. . . ."

Meanwhile, Teller and Robinson led all the occupants of the house upstairs as the first floor and, finally, the second were flooded. They all gathered in a third-floor bedroom, and when water began to seep in there, climbed out onto the roof. Shortly thereafter, an enormous wave knocked the house off its foundations and they were afloat. Three hours later, they grounded at Quogue, having crossed the bay with no lives lost. Halsey also floated across the bay successfully.

And there were others.

The experience of George E. Burghard offers an extraordinary insight into what crossing the bay on storm-driven wreckage meant to hurricane victims at Westhampton.

He and his wife had rented a cottage on Dune Road for the summer, so that he could carry on some radio experiments. For this purpose, he had installed several large poles, two more than 50 feet in height, to support antennae.

The cottage was 75 feet from the top of the dune on the south and 100 feet from the Dune Road on the north. On the west, 100 yards away, was the Coast Guard station, No. 75. In the vacant space between were the radio poles.

The house was well-built, with concrete foundation and wooden bulkheads on the surf side. The distance from the bulkhead to the normal water's edge was 200 feet, making the normal distance from the road to the surf about 150 yards. The dune itself was 8 or 9 feet high. East of the house was the Livermore residence, which was an identical building; between the two houses was a large bath-house. Each house had a boardwalk to the dunes.

There were four people in the Burghard household: Burghard and his wife, Mabel, and Carl Dalin and his wife, Selma. The Dalins were in their mid-sixties. The Dalins took care of the house and had been with the family for many years. In addition, there were two dogs, a wire-haired fox terrier named Bitzie and a cocker spaniel, Peter. The Livermore house was vacant — the Livermores had gone to town for the tennis matches — but their 30-foot power cruiser was fastened to her mooring in the bay, off the dock between the houses.

For the Burghard household, as in many another, the matter began almost routinely.

[56]

10 A.M. The wind was strong from the north, with a heavy sea and sultry weather, but there was no cause for alarm. In fact, the surf was not nearly as high as it had been the afternoon before. The sky was overcast and it was raining slightly.

11 A.M. The wind started shifting toward the east and grew considerably stronger, until at 11:30, it blew almost a gale from the northeast, with heavy rain. It looked like a good northeaster, which was to be expected at that time of year and caused no concern.

Then Dalin reported water bubbling up through the concrete floor of the garage, which was situated under the house on the ground floor opposite the servants' quarters and furnace. Burghard and Dalin went down to investigate and found water coming up in two places. They thought at first it was bay water backing up because of the wind, but after tasting it, they found it was quite salty and decided it must be seawater. Up to this time, no waves had come over the dune, so they concluded it was seepage from the surf through the sand.

All this time, the wind was increasing in strength, and Burghard looked out the window to see if the poles were still standing. The large poles, holding a V-antenna, were in good shape, but the dipole on the 30-foot mast nearest the house was swinging so much that Burghard thought it might be carried away any time. It was raining very hard now, but was quite warm.

12 noon. Dalin saw Livermore's boat start drifting with her mooring, and Burghard called Chief Boatswain's Mate James Ketcham, who commanded the Moriches Coast Guard station about three miles west on the dunes. This was the only station open up to Shinnecock, ten miles east; all the others were closed and No. 75 had only one lookout in the tower; its other buildings were shut. Ketcham said he would come right down and get the boat.

Mrs. Burghard called Mrs. Norvin Green, who lived two miles west on Dune Road, and told her they were not going to the tennis matches, which had been called off. Burghard said later, "We had been planning to go to town about noon, but the storm looked so good that we decided to stay over and watch it. I took my field glasses and watched the Livermore boat, but it soon drifted out into the bay and the rain was so heavy I couldn't see very much."

1 P.M. All this time, the Burghards' radio was going and tuned to WEAF. The Arlington time signals came on and Burghard went to the radio room to set his chronometer, as he did each day. After the time signals, the announcer gave the following weather report: "The West Indies hurricane is in mid-Atlantic." This was said in such a casual way that Burghard paid no further attention to it. He said, "It seemed impossible anyway. The electric power was still on."

1:30 P.M. As Burghard looked out of the sunroom windows, he noticed that the dipole antenna was in bad shape, so he put on his rubber waders and a slicker coat and went out on the boardwalk to tighten up the guy rope, which was fastened to the railing near the dune. When he stepped onto the walk, the wind was so strong and full of sand and rain that it cut his face. Twice he was lifted off his feet, but by crawling along the railing, got the job done and managed to get back to the house safely. He tried to reach the top of the dune and look at the surf, but it was impossible to keep one's footing. He said, "I tried to phone Bill Ottman, who was coming over to watch the storm, and tell him not to come over, because the wind was so strong it would blow his car off the road, but the phone was dead. I couldn't get the operator. About ten minutes later, he called us. Mabel answered and he said he wasn't coming because his garage had just blown into the bay."

2 P.M. Up to now, no waves had come over the dunes, but the wind was shifting more to the east and growing stronger all the time. Burghard judged it to be at least 90 miles an hour. He and Dalin went down to the garage, finding the water about 2 feet deep, both there and in the servants' quarters. Things didn't look

good, but they both thought it would let up very soon and they went back upstairs.

Burghard said, "Mabel had been sitting in the sun porch sewing, with her back to the easterly windows. Mrs. Dalin told her to change her seat, because the windows might blow in. She left, and went into the kitchen to press the dress she had been sewing, but the power was off and the iron wouldn't heat up. Just at this moment, the window where she had been sitting blew out completely and showered glass all over the place.

"The outside screen was still intact, but the sand and rain were filling the whole house. Lucky thing that Mabel left when she did, and I asked her how she timed things so nicely."

He and Dalin got an old door from below and lashed it up in front of the window. The wind was so strong that it was all they could do to hold the door against it. They finally secured it with half-inch rope and screw eyes in the casement. Then they spent some time sweeping up the glass, sand, and rainwater.

2:30 P.M. The wind and rain were increasing, always turning more to the east — in fact, the wind was almost due east by this time. The sky was dark, but the air was still quite warm. Burghard went to the leeward windows and saw that the 50-foot mast to the northwest was leaning at an angle of about 30 degrees. The dipole was still standing, although much bent. As he looked, he saw the first wave come over the dune, right in front of the house. It was all white water, but about 4 feet deep, and with plenty of force. All kinds of driftwood and wreckage came with it, but it was difficult to see distinctly through the sand- and rain-covered windows.

The next wave came a few seconds later, and he saw the bathhouse lifted up in the air and swept around the west end of the house into the Dune Road; he estimated that it moved at about 20 miles per hour.

3 P.M. Burghard recalled, "This did not look so good, and Mabel

said to me, 'Don't you think it's getting serious?' I didn't know what to say, but I thought I would go out and let down the large V-antenna to save the poles. She had been wet from the rain coming through the broken window and had gone upstairs to put on her bathing suit, which proved very useful later."

He told Dalin to go below and get what clothes he could and bring them up to the third floor to the guest room, where he and Mrs. Dalin could spend the night. Burghard helped him with a suitcase and other clothes and then went into the servants' quarters. The water was about 2½ feet deep and all white and swirling like the surf. He went to the rear door, picked up some shoes and other things that were floating around, when suddenly a wave broke through the back door and swept him along the hall. Luckily, the door to the stairway was open and he managed to squeeze through.

He went through the garage, which had 3 feet of boiling water in it now, and got to the leeward side of the house, where the cleats that held the halyards on the V-antenna were located. Just as he got there, a big sea came over the dune and he had to hold onto the pole to stand against it. Between waves, he managed to clear the halyard and lower the V-antenna, but the northwest pole was almost down anyway.

3:30 P.M. After he had finished, he noticed John Avery, the Coast Guardsman who had been on watch in the tower, coming across the meadow. As Burghard watched, the meadow between his house and the Coast Guard station became completely covered by white water, but Avery managed to get through it. Burghard asked him, "Well, lad, do you think it's getting better or worse?"

Avery replied, "The whole dune is going. We'll have to walk for it. I had to leave the tower because all the windows blew out. Is there anybody in the house?"

"Yes, three. Two women and an old man."

"Let's get them moving quick," Avery said. "There is no time to lose."

Every wave was now coming over, and the white water bounded down the slope of the dune like a snowslide. It was then that Burghard realized that the tide had just started to come in. High tide was scheduled for 6:10, E.D.S.T., and if the surf was that high now, where would it be at 6:10?

They went into the house and everyone was quite calm — no trace of panic. Mrs. Dalin kept saying that this storm wasn't as bad as the storm of two years ago, which, of course, was not so, but if she felt that way, it might help matters.

Avery said they would all have to leave the house and try to walk to the bridge, a half-mile to the east. This was their best chance and even if they couldn't make it, the bay there narrowed down to about a hundred feet, which would·be only a short swim at most. Where they were, it was well over a mile across to the mainland. Burghard told the Dalins they had to abandon ship; he gave the old man a pair of boots and sent Mrs. Burghard upstairs to put on shoes — the walking would be hazardous because of wreckage.

"My pet barometer, which I had had for years. was hanging in the radio room not fifteen feet away," said Burghard, "but for some unaccountable reason, I never once during that day consulted the glass. It seems a pity, because I had always wanted to see a barometer go below 28."

The surf was now running through the bottom of the house — all white water. The Burghards went up to the third-floor bedroom to see what they could find to take with them. Strange things happen in such unusual situations. Mrs. Burghard put on a pair of sandals, her lorgnette on a chain about her neck, and her handbag on her arm. Her husband, disregarding his watch, keys, and cuff links nearby, put only two season tickets for the tennis matches at Forest Hills in his trousers pocket, thinking, "I must have these because I have to see the semifinals tomorrow."

Burghard came downstairs. Dalin was coming up from below

with a suitcase and some clothes. Mrs. Dalin was still working in the kitchen, and Burghard upbraided them for not hurrying.

"Do we really have to go?" Mrs. Dalin asked, and her husband said, "Can't I take my car?"

The Burghards had given Dalin a new car early in the summer, and he took great pride and pleasure in it. Both Dalins were reluctant to leave the house; they seemed stunned.

Burghard told them that the cars were useless because the engines had been under seawater for an hour and that, moreover, even if they had not, the force of the waves and the storm wreckage would wash a car off the road and into the bay. He added, "We must leave at once before the house caves in, and try to walk to the bridge."

4 P.M. Mrs. Burghard came downstairs, and picked up Peter. Her husband followed with Bitzie, after telling the Dalins to hurry, and leaving Avery to help them along. When they arrived at the door to the garage, which was the only exit, they found themselves in white water up to their waists and, what with dogs and all, could not get the door open against the tide. Avery came to the rescue and they jammed the door open so it would stay. The Burghards floundered out into the driveway, and Avery went back into the house to hurry the Dalins.

The wind was now due east and blowing all of 100 miles an hour. The driveway was full of holes gouged out by the surf, and each wave brought more wreckage. After several spills, the Burghards finally reached Dune Road, which was a roaring torrent, awash with logs and boards. There, in the lee of the house, they exchanged dogs, because Mrs. Burghard had the heavier one. He took her arm and they walked east along the road to the Livermore fence and hedge, which afforded some protection from surf and debris. They put the dogs on the hedge and waited for the rest of the party.

Avery came out the house leading Mrs. Dalin. He virtually

had to drag her to the Burghards. She was very frightened, and Mrs. Burghard tried to comfort her by telling her to grab a telegraph pole, which she did. All this time, the surf was coming over the dune with every wave and washing into the bay. They had to hold on to one another to keep from being washed away, and to duck the floating wreckage at the same time.

Burghard looked back and saw Carl Dalin walk out of the driveway, get to a fence post on the road behind the house, and sit down. He was only 75 feet west of where they all were together. They called to him, since he was to leeward and could have heard, but he never even moved his head — he just sat there with his head down, looking at the water.

Time was getting short, so Avery and Burghard, with much difficulty, worked Mrs. Dalin loose from the pole and started to walk east. Then it happened. The wind shifted to the southeast and the surf seemed to be lifted right over the dunes to the road where they were standing. Green waves — some 50 feet high — came over, and the surf began breaking on top of them. They resisted the first of it, but then had to get hold of the telephone poles to duck the boards, planks, and timbers. Mrs. Burghard fell a few times, but they managed to haul her out, and the dogs strangely stayed in the hedge. Mrs. Dalin became hysterical and dragged Avery and Burghard to another pole near her husband — who never moved — and took a death grip, screaming and yelling.

4:15 P.M. Burghard said, "Now we knew we could never walk. The wind was southeast, at well over 110 miles per hour. The rain had let up to a great extent, but the sand in the air was terrific. The sky was as dark as at dusk, the atmosphere heavy and warm, and the temperature of the water almost tropical. Avery and I had a council of war, and decided we had to swim the bay. So we told Mabel and kicked off our boots, threw off our coats, and cut off our trouser legs with a penknife.

"I looked at the Coast Guard station and asked Avery if the large

[63]

building, which was two stories high, would stand, suggesting that we might all get in there. . . . He said there was no use trying, that everything would go. I looked toward the Livermore dock, and saw the small boat still tied fast and made a run for it. Just as I reached out to get the painter (quarter-inch line), it snapped like a violin string, and the boat went across the bay at a 50-mile clip. I thought perhaps we could drag the Dalins over and send them off in the boat, but that was that. As I was fighting my way back through surf and wind, a big wave caught the Coast Guard station and all five buildings, the steel lookout tower, and the 100-foot steel mast seemed to rise right off their foundations and were washed into the bay.

"It was a terrible sight, but more so because of the absence of noise. The main building — 60 by 50 and two stories high — hit the bay and smashed to pieces, throwing the lifeboats in all directions. But the effect was that of a silent movie — there wasn't a sound. I had heard stories of the silence of hurricanes, but was always skeptical. Here now I got the full effect. Although only a few hundred feet to leeward, we could hear none of the break-up crash — the 110-mile-an-hour wind took care of that.

"As the station went, I could think of only one thing — the large building would knock down the poles carrying the high-tension power lines, and we, all being up to our waists in salt water, would surely be burned to a crisp. I yelled to everybody, the Dalins in particular because they were right under the poles, to get away, but the chimney of the large building cut all the lines just as clean as a razor blade cuts twine, and left all the poles intact. Of course my warning was silly, as the power had been cut off hours before.

"When I had worked my way back to where Mabel and Avery were standing, the waves were still higher, and the Townsend house, 100 feet east of Livermore's, cracked up and was blown and washed into the bay in a thousand pieces. This made us realize that we had to take to the bay at once, because anything might happen from now on. We decided to go out on the Livermore dock, which was still intact, and lie down and wait for a big wave to wash us, dock and all, into the bay.

"The surf was so strong by this time that it was all anyone could do to keep a footing. We called to the Dalins to follow us, but no response. Mrs. Dalin was screaming and holding to the pole, and the old man was still in the same position, not even looking at his wife. I still think the poor fellow was either so stunned he couldn't move, or had had a stroke. There was nothing we could do, as it was now so bad you could walk only with the wind and water.

"We decided to abandon the two dogs, and put them on the hedge, but at the last second, little Peter looked at me so helplessly that I took him under one arm, and Mabel with the other, and so we virtually floated to the dock, with Avery on Mabel's other side. As we sat down on the dock waiting for a good wave, I suddenly noticed Bitzie, who had swum up all by himself and joined us. We stood up and yelled and waved at the Dalins to let go and float over to us, but no response. Then the thought came to us that they were now in the lee of the house and as neither of them could swim, if the house and poles held, they were safer where they were. Also, we felt sure that this couldn't last much longer, and that when we got over to the mainland we could come back in a boat and get them. It never occurred to us that this was a major catastrophe.

"Just then, the Livermore bathhouse, which was quite a substantial structure, was lifted up by a huge wave and came right at us. Luckily, it hit some poles and cracked up. A beautiful flat piece came right toward us on the dock. Avery grabbed one end and I the other. Mabel, who was perfectly calm, jumped on the center and the dogs followed. Avery climbed on the rear and I got on the front, and waited for the next wave. The wind had driven the bay water across to the mainland to such an extent that for about 200 feet, the bay bottom was dry, but only between waves. When a wave came, which was every few seconds, there was about five to six feet of white water.

"We looked at the Dalins, but they were still in the same position, and we could do nothing. The next big wave was a dandy and we shoved off just like a surfboard and went about 200 feet into the bay, where we grounded. Avery and I climbed off and waited for the next wave, then gave a shove and jumped aboard and we were off for the deep water. Of course we had a little trouble keeping the wave from throwing the raft over us, but we were lucky.

"The wind was still southeast and blowing us toward the Old Moriches inlet to the west. I said, 'Well, lad, we're going to sea.' Avery answered, 'Yes, I believe we are.' Mabel had overheard us and asked, 'What was that?' So we told her we were just having a little sail. The raft we were on was almost submerged and the waves in the bay, at least six feet high, would wash us off with each breaker from the sea, but we always managed to swim back again."

The flotsam following them was very bad. Halves of houses came floating by, with many large nails protruding. Roofs, second stories, which had a larger "sail" area than their raft, passed them like motorboats. It was quite dark and the visibility was low, although the rain was slight; to look back was almost impossible, due to the wind and sand. Several automobiles followed them. The surf picked the cars up, the wind caught them underneath and threw them a hundred feet or more until they finally struck deep water, where they sank out of sight. As far as the Burghards could see, their house was still standing. The air and water remained very warm.

Mrs. Burghard, looking west, saw what appeared to be a motorboat traveling at about 60 miles an hour and said, "There is a boat going after the Dalins." The men had to destroy her illusion; the "boat" was the corner of a house that had grounded and the wind and tide made it look as if it were moving. A huge black fuel tank, 50 feet long and 10 feet in diameter, passed close by. (It was found next morning on the golf course, two miles inland.) Doors flew over their heads, 50 and 100 feet up, and planks 20 feet long were lifted out of the water by the wind and hurled over their heads.

As they drifted into deeper water, their raft began to sink, apparently because some of the bottom of it had fallen off on the way. "Mabel was perfect all the way," said Burghard. "Every once in a while she would be washed off and I would stick out my foot so she could grab it and haul her back to safety." With the gradual sinking of the raft, the dogs became troublesome. Peter was fine, but Bitzie, the wire-haired terrier, climbed on Mrs. Burghard's neck to get out of the water and pushed her head under.

Avery and Burghard found the dogs "a nice little raft," put them aboard, and shoved them out ahead. When they were about 100 feet away, both dogs jumped off and swam back against the 110-mile wind to the Burghards, who pulled them onto their raft again.

Burghard estimated there was 40 feet of water in the channel, and the waves became constantly higher. Holding onto the raft was steadily more difficult. Several times, as they scrambled back aboard after having been washed off, both dogs swam back with sticks in their mouths, in a playful mood, dropping the sticks on the raft and waiting for somebody to throw them. Once, Bitzie was washed off and Peter jumped in after him, towing him back by the ear.

Just as their raft was going down, along came a very large piece of a house, well-studded with nails, but flat. Avery said, "Somebody better get onto that and lighten the load." Burghard, being the heaviest, climbed over and found it so large that both his wife and Avery came aboard, with the dogs. It was big enough so that they could sit above water for the first time since they had left the beach, which was a great relief; there was even a place to brace their feet, which lessened the danger of being washed off.

They were now beyond the channel and the danger of their situation increased. Large chunks of houses, with spikes sticking out, were chasing them on every hand. The two men picked up long

[67]

pieces of boards and pushed the raft around all the big hunks of debris. By paddling and pushing, they managed to get between the houses and roofs and let them all go by to leeward. A flock of ducks appeared, trying to fly against the wind, which was impossible; the birds were blown backward at about 40 miles an hour while flying at full speed.

"By this time," Burghard said, "we could see the houses on Oneck Point distinctly, but there was so much wreckage that we didn't know whether we were going to miss the point or not. We could see Harold Medina's boat across the cut to the west, apparently on her side, on the lawn.

"There was a house on the point just west of Oneck, which we afterward found out belonged to Mr. Steinbugler, and it looked as if we were going to land there. We were still about 300 yards out in the bay but, for the first time, saw people on the front porch — about ten of them. This was a welcome sight and we thought surely they had seen us and were waiting with a drink and blankets to warm us up, as the strong wind blowing on our bare backs had tended to chill us a bit, although the water was still very warm. We all waved to them with a great feeling of relief, but not one of them responded. They just kept milling about on the porch, which was well underwater.

"From then on, we were so busy keeping the wreckage from crushing us that we had no more time to look. The waves were getting higher as we neared the shore, and we had all we could do to avoid things that were washed and blown at us. One huge plank came over with a wave and rode right across the raft between Mabel and me. I was busy pushing off a roof, and she put her hands on the plank, guiding it safely between us, but sprained her wrist badly doing it.

"The wind and waves swept us on, and we finally grounded in a clump of berry bushes about fifty feet from the Steinbugler house. We looked for the people we had seen on the porch, but to our disappointment, they had all disappeared. No one was in sight to give

us a hand — we were all alone again. Avery and I helped Mabel
off the raft. He took her around the bushes; there was about three
feet of water and we had to go quickly as all the houses and roofs
were piling up behind us. Peter swam off and followed them, but
Bitzie grew panicky and jumped on a roof to the east. The roof
floated into the brush about 100 feet away. I called and whistled
to him, but he wouldn't move. I tried to get him, but the wreckage
was coming in so fast I couldn't walk. Then he jumped into the
bushes and although we looked everywhere, that was the last we
ever saw of him.

"I followed the others around the bushes, which were very sharp
and scratched us up badly. But we finally reached the road, which
was three feet under water. After ducking around and over wreckage, we made the fairway of the Westhampton golf course, the
eleventh hole of which was just across the road and high and dry.
Peter came along and joined us, tickled to death to be on land; so
were we.

"A woman came out of the Steinbugler house and waded through
the water to us. She was more or less hysterical . . . , but upon
questioning, told us there were two babies in the house. Avery said
he would get them and I took Mabel by the arm and we started
walking up the golf course.

"On the chart, from our house to where we landed, one point
west of Oneck, is a little over a mile, but we figured that with the
detour, we floated about two and a half miles. How long it took
us to get across will never be known, but I imagine we were traveling at least ten miles per hour.

"The wind had shifted to the southwest by now and was still
blowing just as hard, and boards and things were still flying through
the air. Trees were blowing down all around us, but we were in an
open space on the fairway and in no danger. We looked back at
the beach and I thought I could make out two shadows where our
house had stood, so that we thought the Livermore house and our
house were still standing. This may have been a bit of imagination,

as the people on the Steinbugler porch must have seen everything go on the dunes to frighten them as badly as it did.

"As we walked along, we took account of ourselves. Mabel wore just a bathing suit, but the lorgnettes were still around her neck, and her handbag, dripping water, was still on her arm, with cruel welts showing where the handles had bruised her flesh on the way over. We were both in our bare feet, I with just the remains of a pair of trousers, and our legs bruised and bleeding from many cuts and scratches, but nothing broken, although Mabel's ankle and wrist were badly swollen. Nevertheless, we walked on — where, we didn't know, because we had never been there before. I had Mabel by the arm, but the wind was so strong that several times she was taken right off her feet and I had to pull her back by the wrist. Peter was running about having a grand time."

As they walked along, the darkness lifted somewhat; the sun tried to come through the clouds. The rain had stopped but the wind was bone-chilling. They walked about two miles and, seeing a house over a hedge, finally came out on the main road from Westhampton to Remsenburg. Burghard now knew where he was and said, "I'll go into that house and telephone." The house was unoccupied; even if it had not been, there was not an operable phone in miles.

They stood there, half-naked, bleeding, and shivering in the wind. A woman came out of a house and paid no attention to them, apparently being too frightened or preoccupied to have time for anyone else. A car drove up, and although the driver appeared not even to notice their condition, he asked how he could get to Westhampton. He was looking for his family and had been trying to get there for two hours. They all jumped into the car, including the dog. After trying road after road blocked by trees and downed utility poles, they came at last to Montauk Highway and found a way into Westhampton.

There was no one in sight, and in the center of town, there was at least 6 feet of swirling water, which was still coming up. A man walked by, leading an old woman. Burghard called to him: "Where can we get warm?" The man replied, "Follow me to the Howell House; it has a stove." When they walked in, with bare feet and bleeding legs, some of the people — frightened, because they thought it was the end of Long Island and the water was still rising — asked, "What do you want?" Burghard replied, "We just swam across the bay," and the people looked at them skeptically.

Finally, someone took them to the kitchen, and they stood dripping there before the warmth of a coal range and had coffee and brandy, Peter getting dried out with them.

In about a half-hour, the water in the village, which had risen to 8 feet in Main Street, receded as quickly as it had come. Burghard got some shoes and dry clothes from the manager of the hotel and went to the third floor to look at the dunes. It was about dusk, but from what he could see, there wasn't a house left standing. He went back downstairs, for the first time looked at a barometer and found that at about 6:30 P.M., it was 28 inches. Somebody put disinfectant on the Burghards' cuts; they had a drink and a sandwich.

Immediately after that, Burghard went looking for his friend, William Ottman, and the Dalins, having borrowed sneakers, blue jeans, and a sweater. Main Street was deserted; he walked through the dark, stumbling over wreckage, without a flashlight, and finally arrived at police headquarters. He said, "They were glad to see me, since we had been reported missing. I asked about Bill [Ottman] and they knew nothing. There was no report about the Dalins. Discouraged, I went into the Patio and there found Jack Face, Bill's chauffeur, who told me Bill and the baby and all were safe and sleeping. This was a great relief, so we all had a drink.

"Then I made my way to the country club, which had been turned into an improvised morgue, and there identified the body of C. Dalin. It appears that he washed up on the golf course, right where we had landed, and they found him about 9 P.M. His son, Alvin, was there and we identified his father at about 12:30 A.M.

It was a gruesome business, as there were no lights and we had to look the bodies over with flashlights.

"Of course we didn't sleep after that, and searched for Mrs. Dalin. At 5 A.M., we found her body in the undertaker's. They had picked her up about a half-mile east of where he landed, at 2 A.M.

"By way of aftermath, to the east and west of where our house stood, there is nothing left but sand, where over sixty houses stood before the storm.

"After many days of searching, we found practically nothing of value. The roof and attic of our house was washed up a swale behind the first hole of the Wasthampton golf course about three miles from where it started. Part of the Livermore house landed some 300 feet farther on. The largest radio pole, with halyards intact, was found on the first green of the golf course, and a vest to one of my suits was nearby, 20 feet up in a tree. We found both of Mabel's riding boots, one at least a half-mile from the other. One of my slippers was perched near a Coast Guard lifeboat, a mile inland. Incidentally, there was a piece of shingle driven through the side of this boat with the force of a rifle.

"On the beach where the house used to be, we found part of a loudspeaker, the kitchen sink, a card table on its back, with only one leg broken, Livermore's beach umbrella, and a sweater belonging to old man Dalin.

"Two weeks afterward, they found my briefcase and some papers, checkbooks, etcetera, belonging to Mabel and me, under ten feet of wreckage on the golf course."

On September 24, Coast Guard Commander Wolff at Bay Shore cited Surfman John R. Avery, the lone lookout at Westhampton Beach, for bravery.

As soon as conditions permitted, John T. Tuthill, Jr., editor of the Patchogue *Advance,* went to Westhampton to see his old friend John L. King, editor of the Hampton *Chronicle.* "The town was under martial law; on each street corner was a man armed with a pistol," he wrote. "I reached Main Street and found the *Chronicle* office, but it was closed. The street and sidewalk were thick with mud; debris was all about.

"I peeked through the windows stained with water and saw a sight that wrenched my heart. Desks, typewriters, chairs, books, and other office equipment were all in a heap, covered with mud and slime. A man in plainclothes with a gun on his hip said that on Wednesday afternoon between 3:30 and 4 o'clock, a six-foot tidal wave swept across from the ocean to Main Street and crashed into the business block. He said that Mrs. King, wife of our publisher and friend, had lost her life.

"I went to the beach. At the corner of Stevens Lane and Jessup Lane, there is the home of Mrs. Randall McDonald of New York. It was one of the showplaces of Westhampton. On the south side of the house is a lovely sunroom, surrounded on three sides with glass. The windows there were smashed in, beautiful yellow silk hangings were hurtling wildly in the fresh breeze. The once well-kept yard was heaped with portions of roof, kitchen tables, stove-pipes, mattresses and bottles. Mrs. McDonald was sitting alone in a large wicker chair in the remains of her driveway.

"She invited me to step into her once-beautiful house. Her grand piano, oriental rugs, fine old mahogany chairs, hangings, and other appurtenances were completely ruined. Mud and water were all over the hardwood floors and a heavy tide mark lined the walls, showing the height of the water at its peak.

"She has lived each summer for thirty-five years in that home. She said she was not interested in repairing the damage now, but only wished to go away for a rest and to forget.

"I went back to the village. In the Patio tavern there, I found a small group of young people, members of the summer colony. Two girls in their early twenties were seated at a table, red-eyed, with drinks in their hands, talking to some young men. They had lost their families. One of them had had her entire family swept out to sea in a collapsing beach home. They were a pathetic group. . . ."

[73]

Chapter 5

THE IMPACT OF THE HURRICANE left lasting marks upon the survivors. In 1974, Everett T. Rattray, editor of the East Hampton
Star, reflecting upon the storm, remarked to me, "Five or six years
ago, I was in New York with a man and a woman who had been in
Southampton in 1938 and who were then probably teenagers.
They told me that as it became obvious the storm was of unusual
severity and the water got higher, they came out of the cottage
and went down the back side of the dune to escape.

"They had just reached the bottom of the dune when, as they
put it, they looked up and everything was green. Apparently, this
was the solid green of the sea coming up over, which demolished
the house even while they watched. When they recovered themselves, they had both been carried by this huge wave a hundred
yards, and they landed in the tennis courts.

"Somebody, either of their acquaintance or in their family, was
drowned in this area at about the same time and in the retelling of
it, even this many years distant, they were both visibly shaken and
finally did not want to talk about it anymore."

Southampton suffered heavily along the shorefront. From the
bathing station to the municipal beach, only two cottages remained

standing after the sea swept Dune Road. Among the shattered landmarks was St. Andrew's Church on the Dunes, the scene of many society weddings over the years. The storm left the church in ruins; its south and west walls were battered down and pieces of the organ, pews, and other furnishings were scattered over an area of a mile. An inscription on the church's east wall, which remained standing, lent a touch of irony; it is a verse from the Psalms: "Thou rulest the raging of the sea; Thou stillest the waves thereof when they arise." A stained glass window in the church, presented about a year before by Mrs. Henry E. Coe, in memory of her husband, was discovered intact, frame and all, under a hedge a quarter-mile away.

At Bridgehampton, the farmers were heavy losers; nearly fifty barns went down from Water Mill to Wainscott and north to the line of the Scuttle Hole Road or a little beyond. Potato farmers near the ocean found many acres washed out, washed away, or buried deep beneath sand from the beach. On other fields that had been flooded with seawater, the potatoes rotted soon after being dug. Farmers lost garages, chicken houses, and outbuildings, as well as barns; there were more than eighty places with such losses. An estimated 3,500 trees were lost in the Bridgehampton-Sagaponack-Hayground area alone.

Trees went down everywhere the hurricane struck, but perhaps nowhere was this phenomenon of the storm more heartbreaking than it was to the residents of East Hampton. The elms and locusts that formed an arch a half-mile long over Main Street had been planted before the American Revolution; they can still be seen in the canvases of many important painters, including Childe Hassam and Thomas Moran.

The trees were among the town's most cherished historical landmarks, but when the storm was over, 42 percent of the Main Street elms were gone. From the Hedges Inn on the east side of Main Street to the Methodist parsonage, counting only trees outside private property lines or just on the line, there were sixty-eight down. The Ladies Village Improvement Society had been about to vote on the next year's "tree budget" when the storm intervened.

As in all such disasters, the recollection becomes, at last, purely personal. The late Jeanette E. Rattray, with whom I discussed the hurricane shortly before her death, was former publisher of the East Hampton *Star*, an author and historian who knew and loved her village well.

"It began as a beautiful, warm fall day," she said. "The leaves were still on the trees, children were enjoying their second week at school. At eleven-thirty, a 'year-rounder' who had been listening to a New York weather report, casually remarked, 'Guess we're in for a no'theaster. I better get the rest of the tomatoes off the vines and take down the awnings. Time they were down anyway.'

"Noon came and the sun, having reached its zenith, slowly began its descent, vanishing so gradually behind a wall of ominous gray clouds that its disappearance went unnoticed. By two-thirty, barometers were sinking to new lows and a hundred-mile-an-hour wind was roaring toward the village.

"At six o'clock, all was quiet, but in the early darkness, stunned residents, bewildered by the unexpected turn of events, picked their way gingerly through the mass of fallen elms which the hurricane had tossed around like giant jackstraws.

"Word quickly got around that Dominick Grace had lost his life when a garage had blown down on top of him. The road to Montauk was flooded. The ocean had also broken through at Georgica, carrying with it the Coast Guard boathouse.

"I'll never forget, after a narrow path had been chopped the length of Main Street, how the single line of cars, going at a snail's pace, made it a funeral procession, the funeral of our old trees.

"I will not forget sitting by the light of one candle, with only three sleeping children for company and the little dog who was too terrified to venture out of the front door. I waited until nearly

[76]

midnight for my husband to return from Montauk. Not a sound anywhere. East Hampton was like a city of the dead."

Graeme Elliott, son of Mr. and Mrs. William Elliott and grandson of the late playwright Augustus Thomas, was ten when he observed the hurricane from the family home at Georgica. He recorded his observations in an essay called "The Storm!!!"

"This morning [Wednesday, September 21] I woke and evry body told me it had rained cats and dogs last night. The morning went peacefully, then the wind began to blow very hard, then it got worse. Trees began to fall left and right; the lake has now flooded the ground! Now it's over the gaden fence. The fence on the porch has been knocked down. The windo in the living room is broken. There are waves all over the west side. They break in the garden.

"I just went out to look at the water. The waves are at least four feet tall. One the east side, you can't see six feet around. The living room is a mess. One of the rooms upstairs is flooded. We are complealy hemed in except by water. Vertualy evry tall tree on our six acres is down, we are all in the dining room not one of us are at all injured.

"The wind is trific, the fence fell of the side of the poch, the shurter is slamming. All the chairs on the poch are piled in the heap the water is now under the house. I hate to say what the celer looks like all the logs must be floating.

"Mary just went out trying to keep the shurtter from slamming. I just went upstairs to find that the Kelpy [Bill's boat] has gone. We are all eating life savers — feal fine. Bill is reading Scott. Tom is playing cards and viewing them with the glasses. Mary is very encoraging. The water is going down. The storm continues with unabated furie. The stove is going better than its ever gone. It is now fifteen minnis of six. Sandy is frightened to death. Every time the wind blows the windows he scutels under the nearest furniture. He is sitting in his little bed with Bill scraching him.

"I just went out on the back poch, it smells marvelous. Bill is taking Sandy out on a string. We just sighted land in the garden. The sun is coming out. All the trees except the one we wanted to fell down. . . . We are all going to bed with candles at around nine I'm very sleepy now."

The next day, Graeme had a better opportunity to see what had happened. "The fence around the garden is mostly nocked down," he wrote. "A friend of Marys talked to a man eighty-five years old he said that he had never seen such a bad storm. As I look out my window I can't believe that this is our propertie. Its surtainly a mess. We are now going to realy see the Rodabushes house they surtainly had a much worse time than we did.

"The kitchen is very muddy and awful they said they went straight upstairs and watched the water come up. Step by step sloly but surely the water came up five steps to your waist all the belongings are steren all around they gave us some potatoes then we came home.

"We went through the streets and found these huge trees upruted. The rutes were huge. The back to Halseyes [Halseys'] garage has blown out there is a big tree on the post office. A tree fell on one car and bashed it completely there are millions of trees have fallen. Some of the houses along the beach have roofs blown off. There were sixty refugees in the Beale house from up and down the sand bar."

Elsewhere, Mrs. Chester Browne drove into her garage, went into the house, looked out the window and saw the garage sail into the top of a butternut tree. The cook at Juan Trippe's dune house found bluefish in her kitchen the day after the storm, and at Leroy King's and Forrest Hulse's houses on Egypt Lane, turtles were discovered in the rich mud on the floors after the water had receded. Mrs. Hulse escaped drowning by standing on a table.

From East Hampton to the eastward, it was the fishermen who paid the storm's toll. At Montauk, the hurricane rendered 150 fishermen homeless, destroyed or badly damaged more than 80 good-sized fishing craft, ruined scores of dragnets and fish traps, valued in some cases at $10,000 each, and came close to wiping out the sole year-round industry at Montauk.

About 100 houses were seriously damaged, 6 ending in the pond near the center of town; all power and lights were lost; the storm tore up miles of track along the Long Island Railroad — near Montauk Point, even the roadbed was obliterated — and the community was virtually isolated from the time the hurricane struck until the twenty-third.

Supervisor Perry B. Duryea, who owned the commercial fish depot at Montauk, was in New York when the storm began. He attempted to return, got stalled at Southampton, and finally borrowed a tractor, making his way home along the beach. Arrangements were made to care for the town's homeless in Montauk Manor, the big summer hotel that had been closed for the season, and Duryea sent out an urgent radio appeal to federal agencies and the Red Cross: "Montauk fishing village practically destroyed, number of boats lost, residences destroyed, several lives lost and missing. No water, light or phone connections, fishing industry wiped out. Immediate aid necessary."

Duryea sent the tractor for county help, and the first relief crews came back on it. Supplies, including a truckload of meat and vegetables from the county farm, were rushed from Brooklyn and Bay Shore, and a food station was opened at Montauk's Union News depot restaurant.

Twenty-nine vessels, some worth as much as $25,000, had been blown ashore and since they lay from one hundred to three hundred feet up the beach, the task of launching those that could be made seaworthy again obviously would be major, and expensive. Montauk had been dealt a crushing blow, yet as disconsolate as its residents were, they were principally preoccupied with gratitude for those who had escaped with their lives and grief for those who had not.

[79]

Gene McGovern, a fisherman, had gone into the post office to get his mail. The wind and water came up so suddenly that he was unable to leave the building. As it started to move, he kicked out a window at the back and jumped out. The post office was carried four hundred feet.

Mrs. Gunnar Strandberg, whose husband was employed at the Willard restaurant, was helping him put boards over the restaurant windows when the storm struck. Unable to get back to her house in the village until the hurricane abated, she was greatly concerned for the safety of her two-year-old infant, who was alone there. As soon as she was able, she hurried home. The child was safe and unharmed, but there were three other houses resting against the Strandberg home, and an automobile had been slammed through the wall of the dining room.

The 110-foot schooner *Jean and Joyce*, Captain Lewis W. Vatcher, of Halifax, Nova Scotia, was eastbound, on her way home with a load of coal. Also aboard were Harold Rose, mate; John Kendall, cook; Wilby Cluett, engineer; Gordon Paul and Cecil Kenslow, seamen, and sixteen-year-old Russell Gordon Read, making his first deep-water voyage. When the vessel was struck by what Captain Vatcher later said was the worst blow he had ever experienced in thirty years at sea, he attempted to anchor. Cables to both anchors that he put out parted almost immediately as the full force of wind and sea struck the heavily laden schooner.

At the height of the storm, she foundered off Hedges Bank, Sammis Beach. Captain Vatcher and his crew of six were able to launch an 18-foot dory, and they made the beach safely after a wild and exhausting struggle. They hauled the dory up to dry ground for a shelter, crawled into the lee of it and huddled there for hours, cold, wet, hungry, and just about done in. Fortunately, somebody ashore had observed the loss of the schooner and knew that there were men somewhere along that stretch of storm-pounded beach who needed help if they were still alive.

Leonard E. Bauer, captain of Company No. 1, East Hampton Fire Department, and a crew of volunteers went to search for the crew of the *Jean and Joyce*. After hacking their way through fallen trees and searching a large area of beach, Bauer's team found the men from the schooner, suffering greatly from exposure, under their bottom-up dory at Old House Landing, to the westward of Sammis Beach. The firemen took them back to East Hampton, fed them, and put them up for the night in the Masonic Temple.

Captain Seth Scribner of East Hampton had his trawler *Tacoma* moored to a stake in Fort Pond Bay and was afraid that she would go adrift as the intensity of the storm increased. With Claude Burrows, also a fisherman, he attempted to save his boat, and they were both aboard when she broke loose. Harold Kip was the last to see them, when the storm was at its peak; the *Tacoma* was drifting to leeward in the direction of Gardiner's Island.

In October, Captain Henry Birkenstock found the body of Burrows drifting in Gardiner's Bay. In November, the net of the trawler *Adelaide* hung up on what proved to be the sunken *Tacoma*, not far from Fort Pond Bay. The boat was dragged into the bay and beached; Captain Scribner was not on her.

At nine in the morning of the twenty-first of September, Captain Samuel Edwards, thirty-five, of East Hampton and his crew of three — his brother, Gilbert, thirty; his brother-in-law, Herbert Field, thirty-six, and Vivian Smith — sailed for the west side of Gardiner's Island to lift their fishing traps. They were never seen alive again. Several boats searched for them all day Thursday and Friday following the hurricane and about midnight on Friday, the Coast Guard reported that the body of Samuel Edwards had been found on the beach at Block Island. He was identified by a receipted hardware store bill in his pocket.

In early November, Lewis Fiedler of Greenport was fishing near the Old Fort on Gardiner's Island, and on several occasions the gear he was towing struck something that he could not move; at one time, he had to cut his net clear. He succeeded in bringing to the surface an anchor, with a line attached; it eventually was identified as one that was aboard Samuel Edwards's boat.

The Reverend E. E. Eells conducted Samuel Edwards's funeral service, and one who was there wrote, "Mr. Eells spoke very beautifully of the deceased, of his high character, his courage, and of the pride that his children will feel in his memory when they are old enough to know about such things. He spoke of the risk taken by those who go upon the sea to bring us fish for our table, and of the risk taken by others to provide us with everyday comforts, of how little we appreciate those things until a tragedy like this brings it home to us. Mr. Edwards took an active part in church work here and enjoyed doing it.

"Mr. Eells concluded his address with Robert Louis Stevenson's self-epitaph: 'This be the verse you grave for me:/ Here he lies where he longed to be;/ Home is the sailor, home from sea/ And the hunter home from the hill.' "

The worst tragedy to hit the Long Island fishing industry came with the loss of the Smith Meal Company's bunker steamer *Ocean View*, which sailed out of Promised Land. Three bunker boats — seiners of menhaden, a fish that furnishes oil for the manufacture of soap and which, in its desiccated form, is widely used as a fertilizer — were fishing in the same general area on Wednesday morning, the *Robert E.*, the *Rowland Wilcox*, and the *Ocean View*.

Captain Herbert N. Edwards, Jr., of the *Robert E.* said, "When the glass began to jump, we headed for Promised Land. At two o'clock, by the look of things, I knew we could never make Orient Point. We were making only two knots. So we turned around toward New Haven and ran before the gale for an hour and a half. Seven or eight miles past Faulkner's Island, we hove to. You couldn't steer; she was out of control. I was at the throttle and had the wheel. Did my best to straighten her up, but it was no use until the wind shifted. Then we were off Cow and Calf, four miles east of New Haven. That was about five o'clock. You couldn't see

[82]

the breakwater when we went through it. I just said, 'Give her all she's got,' and in we went. The docks were all submerged; you couldn't find one. We put her onto the flats about six o'clock.

"Nothing would ever scare me now on the water. I know that the *Robert E.* would come through anything."

The *Ocean View* was making for Promised Land with 125,000 pounds of fish aboard; she held on, hammering east into the teeth of the storm until about 3:30 P.M. With wind and sea unabated, Captain William Smith of Fairport, Virginia, considered beaching the vessel on Long Island, but about that time, her crankshaft broke, disabling the engine and leaving the steamer helpless before the storm. The doors were torn off the engine room; everything was adrift. Broadside to the gale and relentlessly battered, the *Ocean View* began to leak badly; obviously she was going to sink, and fast.

Captain Smith ordered the crew to take to the two seine boats; he and sixteen of the twenty-three-man crew got into one boat and managed to get away from the steamer safely. Six others — Roy Griffin, mate, of Shelter Island; Thomas Forsett, chief engineer, Round Pound, Maine; Samuel Coleman, second engineer, Weems, Virginia, and deckhands Elton Smith, David Starvi, and Jeff Hodge, all of Virginia — got into the second boat. In those first critical moments of attempting to get underway, the second boat capsized and those in the first — fighting to stay right side up and afloat themselves — were unable to get to the men overboard in time to rescue them. All six drowned.

Captain Smith's boat went ten miles to leeward, across Long Island Sound; shortly before 11 o'clock that night, they made the beach near Madison, Connecticut, after a final smashing sea swept them, boat and all, over a concrete seawall.

One of those lost at sea was not a fisherman. William Langson Lathrop, seventy-nine, was aboard his 26-foot sailboat *Widgie* in Lake Montauk on September 21. Mr. Lathrop, the son of an Illinois farmer, was a self-taught artist of distinction. In the late nineteenth century, he had moved to New Hope, Pennsylvania, where he became dean of the Bucks County artist colony, which he had helped to found. Eight years before the hurricane, he had built *Widgie* with his own hands, this man who was an academician of the National Academy of Design, holder of the Webb Prize of the Society of American Artists and numerous other honors, and whose works hung in the permanent collection of the Metropolitan Museum of Art, the Carnegie Institute at Pittsburgh, the National Gallery, and Phillips Memorial Gallery at Washington.

He became an ardent sailor. Although his best known works in the various museums are landscapes, once he took to the sea, marines became his favorite subjects. A friend wrote, "Since building the boat, he sailed the little craft tirelessly, sometimes being absent for a week or ten days before his family heard from him. He sailed alone along the seaboard, anchoring from time to time, to sketch. The grandeur of the ocean in a storm appealed to him particularly."

Two fishermen in a boat anchored near the *Widgie* — whose own craft was slammed ashore, thus escaping a similar fate — said that when the hurricane broke, huge waves carried Mr. Lathrop's boat to sea. His body was not in the wreckage that eventually washed ashore.

The grim communications traffic concerning bodies — trying to locate the missing and identify the found — was beginning. "To Corporal William Brockman, State Police, Montauk: Body of a man, apparently a fisherman, washed ashore at Block Island and a child's body has been found at Moonstone Beach, South Kingston, Rhode Island. The man was six feet tall, weighed about one hundred and eighty pounds, was bald and clean-shaven and bore no scars or discernible tattoo marks. Wore brown khaki pants and a brown denim shirt and was barefoot. Portions of an inner tube wrapped around his ankle. In his pocket were a brass padlock key, a pocket knife and a portion of a pink celluloid comb. . . .

"The little boy found was between 36 and 37 inches tall, weigh-

[84]

ing forty pounds and was between two and three years of age. His hair was medium brown, inclined to be wavy. His undergarments were of white cotton, bordered at the neck and bottom with very fine lace. The underwear reached to the neck with fine embroidery stitched down the center of the garment. He wore a dark blue suit with white pearl buttons and green jacket with white celluloid, saucer-shaped buttons. The jacket was lined with black cotton material and bore no labels."

The message was addressed to Corporal Brockman because Montauk was to windward, in terms of the hurricane.

Not all of Corporal Brockman's news was bad. There was the situation of the *Ruth R.*

Captain Dan Parsons owned the *Ruth R.* and her skipper was Captain Charles Landry, who had worked for Parsons eighteen years. The boat, 41 feet long, of 16-foot beam, and drawing 6 feet, had been built twenty-nine years before by Percy Tuthill of Greenport, and she was considered one of the most substantial vessels operating out of Montauk.

On the day of the hurricane, the crew of the *Ruth R.* was off Culloden Point, working on a fish trap. As the wind increased, Captain Landry signaled for his crew — Cleveland Noels, Wilfred Fougère, and Joseph Guyetche, who were working in two trap boats — to come back aboard the sloop.

Before the men could get to the vessel, Noels's boat had capsized. Swimming to a stake a hundred yards away, Noels clung to it while Fougère and Guyetche fought to reach him against a wind that had by then reached hurricane proportions. They were forced to row ashore and hastily bail the water out of their boat — a heavy sea had half-filled her — before they could reach Noels to pick him up. Gaining the side of the sloop, the three leaped aboard, making fast their painter — which proved to be a futile gesture. The wind immediately smashed the boat against the *Ruth R.*, shattering the smaller craft. Left without either small boat, the four men now had to fight for their lives aboard the sloop; she was their only hope.

With her engine hooked up to the last notch in an effort to keep her head into the wind's eye and to stem the thrust of the rushing flood tide, the big sloop nevertheless was forced steadily toward Gardiner's Island. Driving rain made it impossible to remain on deck or to see a boat-length ahead. With the island close at hand, they finally got two anchors down; the wind shifted almost immediately and snapped both cables. An effort to start the engine again proved futile; water had gotten to it.

Now they were adrift and helpless, having neither power nor anchors; they were being driven with the full force of the hurricane in the general direction of Block Island. The sloop was not leaking, but she was taking aboard hundreds of gallons of rainwater. With their clothes soaked, suffering from exposure and fatigue, and in constant danger of capsizing as they drifted broadside to wind and sea, the crew — without heat, food, water, tobacco or matches — pumped continuously all night to keep the *Ruth R.* afloat.

They were adrift for eighteen hours before they sighted Block Island. Then they managed to get the engine started, and tied up in New Harbor at 9 o'clock Thursday morning. There they found that thirty-five out of fifty fishing boats were wrecked and the village shattered. Yet from what was left, they obtained food, a dry, one-burner gas stove, and they ate, grateful to be alive, praising as only seamen can the virtues of the boat and her builder that had made survival possible. Few relationships are closer than those between men and boats who have cheated death together.

Back in East Hampton, Captain Parsons knew only that his boat and her crew had been swept out to sea during the hurricane; over the hours, he had maintained a constant vigil, knowing very well that each passing hour made it more likely that the *Ruth R.* and all aboard were lost. From every source, the terrible casualty figures were mounting; Parsons was haggard and worn by anxiety.

Finally, it was Friday, and it was State Trooper Brockman who reported to Dan Parsons: "The *Ruth R.* has been sighted. She's on her way home."

Parsons found the news incredible. Even when he first saw the sloop, inbound, he thought his eyes were playing tricks on him. It was not until he threw his arms about Captain Landry, tears of relief streaming down his cheeks, that he accepted as fact the survival of the crew of the *Ruth R.* — something little short of a miracle. In fact, a miracle without qualification.

While man struggled to survive on and about Long Island, so did other creatures. Dr. William T. Helmuth, of East Hampton, has left an invaluable record of his observations during and after the hurricane:

"Nearly at the peak of the storm . . . flocks of small passerine birds were occasionally seen squatting in groups upon the ground, poorly sheltered behind whatever wind breaks they could find. . . . They clustered in the lee of the wind breaks in wedge-shaped formations, the bases of the wedges pressed closely against the protected barrier, the apices consisting of long 'tails of birds' trailing away to leeward in Indian file.

"Provided such crouched wedges of birds remained flattened upon the ground, their beaks heading into the wind, they seemed safe enough, but in the case of one group of chipping sparrows which my son and I saw, the birds unluckily attempted to move elsewhere. As soon as they tried flight, most of them were at once whisked away downwind, becoming a part of the rest of the miscellaneous airborne debris of broken branches, rooftops, planks, barn doors, sand, spray and leaves. A few of the birds, however, promptly hurled themselves to the ground and thereby saved their lives.

"Another observation of flying birds was told to me later by a gentleman whose house stood upon a small rise of ground overlooking a pond, beyond which lay the coastal dunes and then the ocean beach. When the wind shifted to the southeast, the first of the gigantic hurricane waves, a wall of water fully thirty feet in height, broke through the dunes and into the pond. A flock of many herring gulls had apparently sought shelter from the gale in the lee of these dunes, but the birds were forced into flight by the inrush of sea water and at once 'collided,' so to speak, with the virtually solid stream of wind above their former shelter.

"The flock was instantly blown to fragments, some of its members being dashed down into the water, but the majority of them were hurled forward by the wind, to pass directly over the house in which the observer was standing. He told me that most of the gulls had suffered either broken or dislocated wings, to judge from their shattered and disheveled appearance. . . .

"Before the peak of the storm and while the wind blew from a northeasterly direction, an adult mute swan, a species feral on Long Island, had evidently been blown against the end of an already broken limb of a tall post oak, which grew only a short distance away from the shore of a pond frequented by swans. This bird's great body had been transfixed by the sharp-pointed broken bough and then whirled violently about it as an axis, so that the swan's left wing had snapped and had been torn from its attachment to the sternum.

"The whole pinion, including the left scapula and coracoid, had been wrapped so many times around the branches that the carcass could not be disengaged without cutting away the tendons. Later, when the wind swung to southeastward, the whole tree blew down, but the swan remained impaled upon the branch."

On the morning of the twenty-second, Dr. Helmuth commented, "The true oceanic debris was piled in mounds and drifts at considerable distance inland, often, indeed, in pitch pine woods and scrub oak thickets where it had been swept by the inrushing sea waves. Even telephone wires, if still remaining in position, were festooned with strands of seaweed and at times, with fragments of fishermen's nets. Often such seaweed-decked wires were a quarter-mile or more from the ocean beach.

"Flooded cellars and the porches and living rooms of houses equally distant from the seaside held marine mollusks, crabs, and occasional salt water fishes. With this material, one often found both fresh water and terrestrial forms of life, as well as large quantities of inorganic debris ranging from Christmas tree ornaments and corsets to expensive radio sets, crockery, cook stoves, cushions and bathtubs. Deep in one pitch pine grove a large tin bucket stood upright on a patch of sea sand and in the bucket, which was about half full of water, floated the drowned bodies of three Norway rats.

"Only at Montauk Point itself, where steep bluffs largely prevented oceanic matter from being washed far inland did the truly marine flotsam accumulate upon the shore itself but its quantity was incalculable and one could wade knee-deep in stranded mussels, moon shells, surf clams, crabs and lobsters without ever setting foot upon the underlying shingle. Doubtless many other organisms were buried in these heaped-up piles or in or under the twisted and knotted snarls of kelp and sand.

"Tons and tons of this sort of stuff rotted on the beaches or had been buried beneath enormous masses of clay and earth from the chewed-out cliffs. Wherever the cliffs were not so steep, the withered grass and low, leafless shrubs along the coast seemed to blossom into twinkling white efflorescence which was caused by innumerable small white feathers of birds. . . ."

On the day following the storm, Lieutenant Theodore Harris of the Coast Guard flew the length of Long Island for eight hours; his job was to spot bodies and report their location.

From the air, the coast of Long Island presented a scene of unbelievable wreckage and desolation. There were roofs floating without walls, walls without roofs, and whole houses adrift. There were a thousand small boats capsized, cast upon the land, or pounded to pieces against the shore.

Pat Grady, who was in the plane, said, "At Ocean Beach, 300 houses were crushed and scattered about. At least 100 houses had been demolished at Fair Harbor and about the same number at Saltaire. There were about 40 houses largely inundated at Little Cap Tree Island.

"Approaching Westhampton, the land had the appearance of a child's room on New Year's Day, with all his toy houses and automobiles broken and warped. At least 100 automobiles were washed up in inland waterways and will be searched for bodies. We flew low and even from the air, pathetic scenes were visible as families searched in what was left of their homes for their possessions or for the dead.

"At Moriches Bay, we began to see the dead — the body of a man clad only in shoes and socks was lying face down on a sand dune. The wind had blown off the rest of his clothing. . . ."

There is one aspect of this storm which literally picked up the water of the sea, tore it into shreds, and flung it across the land so that there was no separating driving rain and salt spray that was extraordinary: the noise.

"Despite all the destruction," Ernest S. Clowes recalled, "few people heard anything but one sound: the voice of the storm. It was like nothing else, although it could be analyzed into three parts; the lowest on the scale was the deep bass of the sea, the highest was the shout of the wind through the trees, rising at times almost to a scream. Between them both in pitch and exceeding both in volume was a steady, almost organ-like note, of such intensity that it seemed as if the whole atmosphere were in harmonic vibration. No sound rose above it. It was something one not only heard, but felt to the core of one's being.

"A woman whose house was literally barricaded by fallen trees said afterward, 'I never heard one of them go.' "

Book III

Connecticut

Chapter 6

AS THE HURRICANE BELTED ITS WAY NORTH, those in its path continued to be generally unaware of what was coming, because it imposed upon areas already devastated a tragically effective pattern of isolation. Communications, by land, sea, phone, telegraph, or teletype, were mostly wiped out in those areas which had most to communicate; the system fell apart piecemeal, and even where electric power or telephones still functioned, the information coming out of places battered by the storm was fragmentary and confused. In communities worst hit, even if anyone had been able to piece together what had happened, the transmission of news was low on the priority list of what needed to be done.

So, in New Bedford, and a hundred other cities and towns, as yet untouched, the day drifted on, not greatly different from a hundred other days. How much difference it would have made if we had known immediately when the hurricane first blasted Long Island how savage it was is difficult to say. Some might have left low-lying sections; others would have ignored the warning, but once the storm reached the Northeast, there wasn't that much time left anyway.

There are those now who will tell you that it felt all day as if something in the way of weather might happen, and it did, but you just don't pick up and run every time the atmosphere makes your ears feel peculiar and storm clouds are low enough to sit on your hat. Looking back, I think principally it is as well in instances of massive disaster that one does not know everything at once. There are limits to what the human creature can comprehend and bear in a hurry. I suppose it was as well that we did not know then what had befallen Long Island. Nor did we know that Connecticut was next.

On Saturday, September 24, three days after the hurricane, the New York *Herald Tribune* reported on Page 1 that author Elmer Davis was missing from Mason Island, off Mystic, Connecticut. Actually, he wasn't; he did, however, share with thousands the extraordinary experience of being forced to accept the reality of the hurricane.

"When the wind began to blow about 2 o'clock Wednesday afternoon, most of the inhabitants of these parts were convinced that it was only the traditional 'line storm,' the three-day blow that comes every September when the sun crosses the equator," Davis said. "Even as the wind rose and its tone changed to the ee-ee-ee that well-read persons recognize as the mark of the hurricane, even when the rain came in horizontal sheets, and tightly closed windows began to leak streams of water, traditionalists insisted that this couldn't be a hurricane because there never had been a hurricane in these latitudes. . . .

"And then all at once in a thousand households, the argument stopped and everybody began to nail up all the doors and windows and hope that with all the air shut out, the wind would not take the whole house along in one piece. With every window, every door fastened as tightly shut as you could get it, you sat in the living room and watched the shingles on the garage roof ruffle up like a hen's feathers blown in the wind and then, one by one, tear off and whirl away. You saw nearby trees slowly lean over and go down; you listened to the crash of breaking windows; the steady

[94]

ee-ee-ee of the wind, you felt the floor waving under you like a shaken carpet."

When the sea rose 14 feet above normal at Mason Island, Carolyn Wilson, a former Chicago correspondent, looked up, while trying to plug leaks in her wall, to find the ocean at her door when it ought to have been one hundred yards away. She had to get out and tried to take her cat with her, but he refused to go, so she kissed him a dolorous good-bye and swam a half-mile over drowned shrubbery to high ground.

Y. E. Soderberg, the etcher, opened his house to relatives who had to abandon their own, but presently the water was three feet deep in his house and the family had to seek refuge in the second story, watching all the ground-floor furniture floating away out of the windows. Herbert Stoops, the New York illustrator, living a scant half-mile from the main highway, had to climb over seventy-nine fallen trees when he made his way out the next morning.

But it was not until the Mason Islanders plodded over the shattered causeway to the mainland, seeking food and candles, that they learned what the hurricane had done to Connecticut.

It was in the New Haven area that New Englanders began to realize the magnitude of the storm's impact upon their natural heritage. Five thousand trees lining the city's streets were destroyed and as many more damaged so extensively that they had to be removed. At least a sixth of the city's trees were gone. They had proved especially vulnerable to the wind because heavy rains preceding the hurricane had left the ground like a filled sponge, weakening the turf holding down the roots. Tree Superintendent Fred Eaton predicted it would be twenty to forty years before the city looked as it had before the hurricane.

It was the loss of the trees that prompted H. I. Phillips to write his eulogy, "The Hurricane's Wake," in which he commented, "Here, where the lordliest of trees stood, all is waste and desolation, a scant company left to stand out gaunt and broken, like the remnants of a lost battalion. . . . The glory of the years is gone, the beauty so long in building is vanished in the twinkling of an eye. The legions of the ages along this road have met destruction. This is the crime of the years, the tragedy of generations."

It was five years later that the U.S. Forest Service in Willimantic was able to announce that the last of the hurricane timber in Connecticut had been sawed and salvaged, and to close its office there.

And there were the rampaging rivers, already bursting from days of rain. It was at Hartford where man and river fought their fiercest, most prolonged, and most costly battle; the roily, swollen Connecticut provided disastrous counterpoint to the hurricane.

Howling out of the southeast at four in the afternoon, an 80-mile-an-hour wind, the highest ever recorded in Hartford, spread death and destruction, ripping off roofs, toppling buildings, uprooting trees, disrupting traffic and communications, shattering brick walls, and tearing up fences, which one resident described as "floating in the air like paper." Rain was driven through the city in great sheets, and the *Courant* noted that "few people ventured on the street to brave the wind; at times, their feet were whipped away from under them. . . ."

The clock in the Old State House stopped at 4:10. Pigeons, unable to fly with their beaks to the wind, were smashed against the windshields of automobiles. Store windows buckled in the wind and shattered. Simultaneously, the Connecticut River was rising at the rate of 4 inches an hour; by midnight on Wednesday, it had reached 24.7 feet and was expected to crest at 28 feet by Thursday noon. As rain continued to spill out of gray skies, the residents of the lower East Side stolidly watched their old river foe lapping upward to threaten their homes and their well-being. They made their preparations. Chairs and couches were taken to second floors. Pictures were removed from the first floors. Clothing was packed in case evacuation became necessary.

One woman on Potter Street said, "I was born in a flood and so was my mother. I lived here during the 1936 flood. I'm not afraid.

They come every so often." Bushnell Park became a watery wilderness; by night, the lamp-post bulbs glowed like floating Japanese lanterns. But the critical points as the rain-swelled Connecticut rose were at the dikes.

From Hartford's Travelers Insurance Company Tower at noon on Thursday, the view presented a stark contrast.

Overhead shone a benign September sun, and a hazy blue sky dotted with white cloud puffs. Below, the landscape had two faces. One of them complemented the sky. West, southwest, and northwest lay a landscape full of calm and peace, mellow in the mood of early autumn. The other half of the horizon was menacing, and from north to south there stretched a scene of desolation.

The inexorably rising Connecticut River seemed to lie within its banks as it rounded the bend near Windsor, but then, like the contents of a broken paper bag, it sprawled in unsightly disarray over miles of lowlands. The brown, swiftly moving flood, thick with its freight of half-submerged trees and the wreckage of Wednesday's hurricane, stretched from the new concrete Windsor Street extension on the west to the distant meadows of South Windsor on the east.

A few strings of freight cars, temporarily abandoned, stood in the vast lake which covered the freight yards north of the city. To the east of the Willimantic railroad bridge, a foundationless building squatted in the flood, and a long line of coal cars held down the East Hartford trestle.

The entire western section of East Hartford, with the exception of the boulevard, lay inundated by river waters, which had crept to the sills of first-floor windows. Several scores of dwellings, a school, and an apartment house were cut off entirely from the rest of the town, and there was no sign of life about them. Prospect Street, north and south of the boulevard, was the "beach" of a rapidly advancing shoreline. The pier and the gasoline pumps of the Hartford Yacht Club had gone down the river at 9:45 A.M., carrying with them a private craft. Other boats, huddled in awkward clusters, were flanked by driftwood in the upper branches of trees which stood where the river's edge had been only a few days ago.

Memorial Bridge was covered with black crawling lines of slow-moving cars and trucks; the urgent blare of automobile horns below the Travelers Tower indicated the anxious feelings of the drivers, pushing toward the remaining route to their homes east of the river.

A deserted barge loaded with scrap iron, perhaps bound for some foreign war, stemmed the river's current; once it had been berthed alongside the dock at the foot of State Street. Now it was more than 100 feet from dry land.

Here and there in the streets between the Travelers main building and the western rim of the flood, the scars of Wednesday's storm were apparent. The yellow boards of roofs whose shingles had been ripped off by the hurricane and the white jagged points of shattered tree tops reminded one acutely that the city had barely had a chance to draw its breath after the impact of one catastrophe before it was being forced to face another.

There was a reassuring sight in the southeast, where Brainard Field, a pale green oasis, stretched dry and unscathed, protected by its wide encircling dike and by Colt's dike to the north, which, while its durability was in doubt, still held back the river to this moment.

Reporting from what he called, with wry humor, the "East Side Gulf," T. H. Parker patrolled those city streets where deepening water was forcing the people to leave. "The National Guardsmen standing along the road stopping traffic halfway down all streets leading toward the river; neat, new uniforms; night sticks twirling at the end of rawhide loops, and each man with a pint of water in a hip flask while uncountable millions of gallons flow by at their feet," Parker wrote.

"A sign at Grove and Market streets barely above water, reading 'Stop: Through Traffic.' A motorboat being rowed by a man making little progress. And a skiff tied to a sign: 'No Parking.'

"The grandstand seats afforded by window ledges of tenements on side streets off Front. Women yelling down and children shouting back up. A man seated on a doorstep wearing a yachting cap, watching a four-year-old child fish with a string hanging from a twig. A Police Department boat run up on the asphalt shore with youngsters clambering in, quarreling shrilly for a place on the bow.

"Talk is of business, small business in distress. 'Everything gone. Couldn't get it out. We thought it wasn't coming up so high. Well, how much did you lose? 600 cases? 1,000? You asked me, I'd say 1,000 cases.'

"Trucks disappearing down warehouse alleys amidst loud blowing of horns. 'Get the hell out of the way. Don't you see we got to get in there and get that stuff out?' Same trucks reappearing, crammed with goods and being chased by a man trundling a hand dolly. 'Wait! Wait! You gotta take it this time or it's no good by the time you get back!'

"Water, water everywhere. In the kitchen. In the parlor. In the bedroom. Rowboats tied up to porches. A church dismantled. St. Anthony's on Market Street, ruined two years ago, and recently remodeled in such outstanding interior design as to be described in *Liturgical Arts*. Everything taken out; altars, pews, lined in rows on the sidewalk. The fixtures taken to safety from water already running in. Children sitting in the pews, laughing and playing games. Nothing left in the church but the floors, walls, ceilings, and pillars. A novena begun this morning and then canceled, and all hands, clerical and lay, turning to to carry out every last object. Water pouring down a flight of steps into the church and disappearing with a sucking sound down the drain pipes. . . ."

All day, tensions over the flood increased. When the relentless upcoming of water caused street after street to be inundated, and hundreds to be homeless, predictions of the crest changed several times and always to a higher figure. Boat patrols were set up and took many to safety. Workers in threatened industrial plants, fighting against time, moved millions of dollars' worth of property to higher ground.

And now began the struggle by 1,200 WPA workers, World War I veterans, college students, and other volunteers in the southeast section of the city to save the homes of 5,000 and to protect the semi-industrial area, where two-thirds of the $6 million damage occurred in the flood of 1936.

This is Thursday night:

A thousand men crack their backs to keep a million tons of water out of the south end of the city. A hundred trucks slam over the pitted, pitch-black roads. They dump bags half-filled with sand along the Colt and Clark dikes, raising the low spots, stopping up the street ends.

Under the hiss of flares, a hundred crews grunt to throw the fifty-pound sacks in place. "Place 'em right; pack 'em carefully," the foremen shout.

On the land side, there is furious work, shouting, din, and sweat. On the other, no haste. Just the river, leisurely climbing up and up, seeping through, no more noise than an occasional, ominous lapping. The water creeps up over the 33-foot mark. Three square miles of a city is imperiled; if this army of a thousand is defeated, if the dikes go out with a roar for the second time in two years, the whole of that three square miles will be the scene of flood, devastation, tumbled wreckage, and ruin.

From Springfield, Massachusetts, where the river has been at a standstill for three hours, comes bad news; the water is rising again. In Hartford, the American Red Cross headquarters, already caring for 1,500 evacuees at six relief stations in the city, is notified by the city government to prepare for 3,000 refugees, ordered to evacuate their homes in the area back of the dikes south of Sheldon Street and east of Main Street. Some go fearfully; some debate going; some have to be forced out of their homes.

All during the evacuation, the diking goes on. The people may not be gotten out in time. Even when they are moved to safety, there are still millions of dollars' worth of property, thousands of

One of the sandbag dams at Hartford, Connecticut,
that held back the swollen Connecticut River

homes and businesses to be protected, if protection is possible.

A crest of 34.5 feet is predicted for sometime Friday morning. At Springfield, the upsurge of water accelerates to a rate of one-tenth of a foot an hour. U.S. Army Engineers say there is only a fifty-fifty chance that the Hartford dikes will hold.

All night, the engineers roar in automobiles along the dike areas from Commerce to Sheldon Street to Wawarme Avenue, evaluating the constantly changing situation, ordering quick countermeasures against the creeping waters. As early as 9:30 P.M., the two most critical spots are obvious: the junction of Sheldon and Sequassen, near the Colt Firearms Company office, from which the battle against the water is directed, and at Sheldon and Commerce; here at the low levels of these street ends, the river makes its major threat to overwhelm the city's south end.

Sandbags are piled, quickly, surely, with tireless haste, into the depressions made by the low roadways. A triple row for a foundation, and then a single row. Bag upon bag, a slender buttress, half a bag wide against infinite pressure of water. Where the water does not simply press, quiet and deadly, it seeps, and by 11 o'clock, small streams ooze from the sandbagging, trickle across Sheldon and spill into the gutters on the sharp declines of Sequassen and Commerce, the perimeters of the great three-square-mile area that is menaced.

It is more than a mile over pockmarked roads to Brainard Field airport, where a roaring digger throws up earth at the "burrow" and sweating men shovel it into bags. Squads of trucks are backed to the spot, and none waits to be more than half-filled. Time is precious. A few bags can do a lot of good if rushed to vital spots. The trucks bound over roads as black as the inside of a pocket. They dodge between red lanterns and shoot by trooping workers en route from one bad spot to another. The workers scuttle out of the way, their electric torches flashing, as they make their way past holes in the road and tangles of tree branches sent down by Wednesday's storm.

Slam-banging into the lower end of Sheldon Street, the trucks slow down into single file and as they pass the laboring crews, the foremen cut them out as needed. With shouts, they are guided up close to the sandbag walls, the dump body rises with a roar of gears, the bags of sand slide to the ground and without stopping to lower the dumpers, the trucks charge down the side streets and off to the pit for another load.

After each clatter that announces the arrival of a truck, after the noise of unloading, silence once more falls over each crew, broken only by an occasional order barked by the foreman. These men work without talk, in part because they were hours ago tired enough to rest, yet there is no time for rest; they work tensely, but without excitement, to bag up each dangerous spot, higher and higher. They work swiftly but with deliberation and care; one sack out of place and enough water might seep through to start the fatal breach.

When each truckload of bags has been laid, they walk back and forth over the tops of the bags, settling them into place; the foreman watches with a critical eye; this bag needs readjustment, square that one up. Now the water is rising at the rate of two-tenths of a foot per hour. Opposite the Colt office and about twenty feet beyond the dike there is a white post nearly covered with water. It is a stake marking the 35-foot level. There are 800 men working in this area; the call goes out for 200 more. Thomas F. Foley, local WPA representative, is the man in charge of the battle. Sleepless and with a sprained right ankle, he answers a battery of phones in the Colt office, patrols endlessly between the Commerce and Sequassen weak spots, receives half-hour readings from the yellow-chalked post in the swollen stream just beyond the soaked sandbags, and is grimly noncommittal.

Beyond the stake, the murky expanse of rampaging river stretches away into the dark. Some small buildings can be seen dimly in the flickering lights, water halfway up to their single-story roofs. The water makes no sound, and as you look over the top of the sand-bagging, it hardly seems to move. It is a sullen river, brown with churned-up earth, and the smell of oil rises from it.

There is some little talk to break the silence when the reserves arrive, with truckloads of shovels. They line up on the porch of the Colt building, waiting to be assigned to gangs. From the dark, there is a loud halloo from some distant foreman, calling for trucks. The wind off the water is cold; it is more comfortable to stand near the flares — at least they give an impression of warmth. By midnight, the water has reached to within a few inches of the tops of the bags in some places and 200 nearby Legionnaires are trying to persuade remaining residents to leave and to assist those who are willing to go.

At 10 o'clock Friday night, the Connecticut River gave up its fight. Reaching a height of 35.1 feet, it began to recede. The U.S. Army Engineers, who had taken over direction of the defending forces, under Colonel John S. Bragdon of Providence, reported that the first recession of the water had been noted and that the level was then 35.09, a drop of 1/100 of a foot. By midnight, the reading was 35.02. The little army, blistered and exhausted, watched by thousands, including the refugees, and prayed for by thousands more, had won the "Battle of Colt's Dike."

It was not until Sunday, when all danger was past, that Mayor Thomas J. Spellacy disclosed that an emergency plan had been set up to dynamite the Clark dike along Brainard Field and the South Meadows at the moment that the Colt dike or its long Sheldon Street emergency sandbag extension gave way. The theory was that if the sandbagging effort had not been successful and the water had broken through, the force of the pent-up river, unless relieved by immediate creation of another outlet to the south, might have swept away the Colt factory buildings and all other structures in its path. City officials anticipated it would have torn oil storage tanks in the area from their moorings and slammed them against the South Meadows generating plant of the Hartford Electric Light Company, and hoped that the dynamiting would have prevented this.

In all of this time of crisis, the most extraordinary phone call received by the Hartford *Courant* — one among a bombardment of hundreds made by those concerned about roads, property, missing persons, and the state of the Connecticut River — came Wednesday night as the city lay shocked and battered after the hurricane. "Can you tell me," the caller asked, "on what date the blizzard of 1888 occurred in Russia?"

Claude Adams lived on River Road in Cromwell. He had been operating a party boat out of New London for five summers and was well known to Hartford area saltwater fishermen as a competent boatman. His craft was *Wanderer*, 36 feet overall, with a

10-foot beam, a raised deck forward, a small deckhouse amidships (and under it, an 85-horsepower engine) and a large open fishing cockpit aft. Compared to a good-quality stock boat of equal size, *Wanderer* was about twice as heavy, and with corresponding staunchness, and "I was glad of it," said Mr. Adams, after he rode out the hurricane in her in Long Island Sound.

If it had not been for the Connecticut River flooding, *Wanderer* would not have been on the sound that Wednesday. But the Adams home at Cromwell was almost on the river bank, and as the water there began to creep steadily higher, his family sent for him, knowing that a roomy and able boat would be a great help if the house were inundated — something that did, in fact, happen a couple of days later.

The trip from New London to Cromwell was normally a routine affair for Adams, and so he asked a next-door neighbor, Ray Hudson — who had never been on a boat before — to accompany him, "just for the ride."

They left New London about 12:30 in the afternoon. The weather had been nasty all morning, with a rising easterly wind kicking up increasingly uncomfortable seas outside. Mr. Adams had a sailor's misgivings about starting out at all, but he and *Wanderer* were much needed at home.

After a half-hour underway, with the wind freshening steadily, visibility had decreased to almost nothing, and *Wanderer* was picking her way by compass alone. Mr. Hudson came in handy; with the boat virtually standing on her head with every sea that swept beneath her, the compass was swinging wildly and uselessly in its gimbals — it did not hold steady long enough for Adams to check his course. Mr. Hudson dutifully hung on with one hand and steadied the compass with the other; this was his principal job for the next several hours and, landsman or no, he was of stout stuff, for he never once panicked and he did not get sick, perhaps being too busy to do so.

Very soon, it became impossible to see more than a few feet

ahead. The wind whipped the water and carried it in solid sheets from the crests of the seas. The forward hatch, normally open to let light and air into the sleeping cabin in fair weather, finally was loosened by the battering and carried away. It pulled its stout fastenings through the hard wood like a knife going through warm cheese. This was a grim thing, for by now *Wanderer*'s bow had to be swung into every wave to give her the best chance to stay afloat; allowing her to be struck other than head-on would risk capsizing. With her forward hatchway gaping open, if she decided to "take it green" — if her bow was slightly slow in raising on the giant seas and solid water poured down into her cabin — that would be the end.

Somehow or other, due in combination to the skill of the man who had decided what the lines of her bow ought to be and to that of the man who stood, rocklike, at her wheel, squinting into the smother, easing, guiding, and feeling her needs in every minute of the battle, *Wanderer* shipped only rain and spray. Plenty of both, but nothing solid.

The worst time was off Hatchett's Reef, about five miles from the mouth of the Connecticut. It was here that the motor began to skip. Adams knew what the trouble was right away. The force of the hurricane had atomized the flying spray into such fine particles that they went through the tiniest crevices under forced draft; in so doing, they had soaked the ignition wires. The wires had to be dried, and in a hurry; if the engine stopped, they were likely done for.

He yanked up the engine hatch and played the fire extinguisher over the wires. The carbon tetrachloride in the extinguisher, being extremely volatile, evaporated and took the moisture with it. The engine kept going.

"We didn't expect to make Saybrook," said Mr. Adams. "We didn't even expect to stay on top of the water. We couldn't see a thing. Even if it wasn't for the spray, it seemed as if we were always facing a wall of water. When we rose to the crest of a sea, there always seemed to be a higher one beyond."

"How could you see the jetty and the breakwater at the mouth of the river?" he was asked.

"We couldn't. We must have come in to the east of the jetty."

East of Saybrook jetty is a treacherous shoal, virtually impassable under normal conditions. Thus, for *Wanderer*, the giant storm waves which provided water enough for safe passage in areas ordinarily dangerously shallow were a salvation. Adams estimated the seas ran twenty feet high as far up the river as the Saybrook–Old Lyme railroad bridge.

"How high were they outside?"

He replied, "I could tell you and be telling the truth, but anyone would call me a liar, and I wouldn't blame him if he hadn't been there. But I do know this. Under the East Haddam bridge, there is a clearance of twenty-four feet to the water. My masthead is only thirteen feet high. As we passed under the bridge, a wave lifted *Wanderer* and snapped the mast off clean. Figure it out for yourself. The bridge is fifteen miles upriver from the sound and that was a couple of hours after the height of the gale."

As they made their way upriver, they could see the devastation ashore, both wrought and being wrought. "I saw the wind pick up some trees," said Adams, "and I mean pick them up, too, not just blow them down." The gale was now easterly and at right angles to *Wanderer*'s course. For several miles, she was heeled over so far to port that her propeller was breaking water constantly.

Just below the entrance to Hamburg Cove, they saw a big motor cruiser, apparently a survivor of the Essex Yacht Club fleet, making her way into the comparatively sheltered water. Adams thought it might be a good idea to head more toward the sheltered side of the river, too. But suddenly, he saw the cruiser's deckhouse crumple and blow over the side like a wad of paper. He kept *Wanderer* where she was.

When they finally made fast in Cromwell, Adams found that the trip from New London had taken more than eight hours, compared to the usual four and a half. *Wanderer* had burned 80 gallons of gasoline; she usually consumed 15 to 30 on the trip. Aside from the lost hatch and the mast, she had come through without a scratch.

Mr. Adams assured Hudson that the chances were against subsequent boat trips being as uncomfortable as his first.

"I don't imagine *you'd* like to go through that again, Mr. Adams," somebody said.

"No, I don't think I would."

"And I imagine your wife was surprised to see you."

"Yes, she was," said Mr. Adams.

And some remember the hurricane for other things.

In Harwinton, an apple tree on the property of Frank Fredsall was uprooted as the storm reached its peak, but later in the day, when the wind shifted to a westerly direction, it pushed the tree into an upright position again, where it remained, still standing, a couple of days later.

Matthew Strong of East Hampton, Connecticut, caught a five-pound bass with his hands in the middle of the town's Main Street, which at the time was under two feet of water.

Actress Katharine Hepburn was at the summer home of her parents, Dr. and Mrs. Thomas M. Hepburn, at Fenwick, when the storm threatened. With other members of the family, she waded through the rising waters and reached safety about an hour before the Hepburn home, as well as most of the others nearby, was blown to pieces or washed away.

Wind and water were cruel in the small communities. On September 20, Glastonbury's reservoir gave way, buckling under flooding from heavy rains. On the following day, the community was struck by the hurricane winds, which witnesses described as "taking a peculiar twist, circling vertically, and creating vacuums." The

First Congregational Church was torn to pieces; its four walls exploded outward and its spire, the tallest in town, tumbled into the wreckage.

More than one hundred houses in the town were blown down. Police Chief George C. Hall said he saw several tobacco sheds lifted up into the air before they fell apart and dropped into the ground; he emphasized that they were not flattened by the wind, but picked up and dropped.

At Middletown, the wind pushed the hands of the clock in the steeple of the town hall inside the clock face. At the state hospital, 2,000 inmates became panic-stricken when the hurricane blew off part of the roof; sheets of metal and attached rafters, some in pieces 15 feet square, were lifted from the roof and blown as far as 150 feet. All available doctors, nurses, and attendants were called into service to quiet and reassure the patients until the wind abated.

William Coleman's Middletown farm was an especially tragic target. A tobacco shed, icehouse, and garage were demolished, the top of a brick silo was torn off, twenty-three of a herd of twenty-seven cows were killed when the dairy barn collapsed — all men of the neighborhood worked for hours freeing the bellowing, wounded survivors from the wreckage — and upstairs in the main house, windows were blown in where Timothy Coleman, eighty-three, the father of William, lay seriously ill. The elder Mr. Coleman had to be moved downstairs, where he died several hours later.

In Cheshire, Patrick Joyce, fifty-eight, the father of five, was killed shortly after 4 o'clock on Wednesday afternoon when a blast of wind hurled him against the side of a brick building in the yard of the Connecticut Reformatory, where he had been employed for nearly twenty years. Joyce had been sent out into the yard with a message for an inmate; shortly after, his body, which had sustained severe chest, head, and internal injuries, was discovered at the side of the building.

Mrs. Carl Carlson of Branford was driving toward Guilford; her car was halted in a line of traffic during the hurricane while a tree was removed from the highway. She picked up a book from the car seat and began reading when another tree crashed down upon her car, killing her instantly. The book she was reading was *Gone with the Wind*.

Stafford Springs (population 5,500) was typical of many of Connecticut's towns, hit by both flood and hurricane. Undermined by flood waters, Tuesday, when Buck's Dam let go, then knocked down by wind, Stafford Springs was getting its provisions Thursday night chiefly by way of a single-plank bridge, 20 feet long, 8 inches wide. No word came out of the town after the storm Wednesday, and almost no one could get out of it Thursday, but a visitor got in.

"The borough has its main street through Haymarket Square caved in," he reported, "its railroad station foundations washed out, its railroad bed bordering Main Street scooped away, factories undercut, and sections of several highways carried away.

"As incoming goods, ordered before the town lost its telephones, trains, mail and wire service, began to pile up at Barlow's store, west of the break in the road, it was decided to try to bridge the torrent that poured through the gap. Just one plank in width, precarious to cross, the bridge was serving its purpose Thursday night. With power off, bakeries in the town could not provide bread. Bread made up many of the loads carried across the plank.

"Before the hurricane hit, the borough had been flooded. Its Main Street ran with five feet of water in some places. Never had this happened since the Stafford Hill reservoir gave way back in 1877. All over Stafford, no one could smile or laugh Thursday, in the face of all the wreckage.

"St. Edward's Church, made widely known by the late Rev. Felix J. O'Neill, the poet-priest of New England, had shingles blown from its roof and trees toppled at its doors. Father O'Neill spoke of 'fair Stafford — the gem of the vale' in some of his poems and told of its beauty Today, it is a horribly-battered beauty. . . ."

The story of the storm over a broad Connecticut River area — including Suffield, Hazardville, Enfield, Scitico, Somersville, and Somers — was the story of the tobacco sheds, all of them filled with the year's crops. In Somersville and Scitico, twenty-four sheds were knocked down within an area of two square miles. They looked as if they had been stepped on. Five out of five down was the score of the gale against the tobacco sheds in one spot in Scitico. Four out of seven was the most damaging hit in Poquanock, where the sheds also burned; charcoal was burning in many of the sheds full of drying tobacco that were destroyed, and the helpless owners watched the buildings go up in smoke after going down in the wind. On the day after the storm, not even the owners would give an estimate of damage, although for the area, for the tobacco lost alone, $2 million was thought conservative.

In the inundated South Windsor Meadows, eight men who were working in tobacco sheds were stranded by high water. Charles Davis left his companions in water up to their waists and swam for help. Early Thursday morning, State Troopers Robert Erdin and Joseph Saksa, in a motorboat, were able to reach the marooned men — four of whom were clinging to the bottom of an overturned boat — and rescue them. The sheds in which the eight had been working were leveled.

When a steeple toppled on the Poquanock Congregational Church, Edward Barkal, next door, saw it. The steeple came to rest along the ridgepole of the church. Barkal was asked what he thought when he saw it happen. "Didn't think anything at all. Just ran," he said. He ran from the barn into the house. Then a tree fell on the house and he ran out into the yard again. When he saw no more trees could hit the house, he went in.

In Windsor Locks, a very old man sat looking at two fallen trees on his lawn. "My grandfather planted them," he said.

[111]

Chapter 7

For New London, it was holocaust: hurricane, flood, and fire combined to leave hundreds homeless and jobless, the city in ruins, with damage estimated as high as $4 million after a destructive interlude of several hours that constituted the greatest disaster in the history of eastern Connecticut.

The hurricane, sweeping up the Atlantic coast at an unprecedented rate, struck about 2:30, "taking the entire city and all of the suburbs in its wanton will" for a period of four hours. The storm tore away roads and beaches, wrecked wharves, tossed vessels, large and small, high and dry onto the shore, washed out railroad tracks, ripped off roofs of houses and industrial buildings, uprooted trees, knocked down poles and wires, smashed store and house windows, razed barns and other outstructures, and carried away bridges.

The Thames River and Long Island Sound broke over their banks along the entire shorefront, while flood waters from inland rivers, brooks, ponds, and lakes rushed down upon the city from several directions. Within minutes, the ordinarily placid Thames was a maelstrom and the Sound a tormented sea. In both river and sound, pounding waves came piling in; wharves collapsed beneath eight feet of flood water, tugs, barges, and yachts were driven from

*New London, Connecticut, burns. Most of the
five-masted barkentine Marsala in the foreground*

their berths and moorings, slammed ashore, holed, sunk, and left in shambles, their stacks and wheelhouses just above water, their masts poking skyward at grotesque angles.

The 300-foot five-masted barkentine *Marsala*, training ship of the American Nautical Academy — a school for merchant marine officers — was moored in the stream off the Custom House wharf. She had down a ten-ton anchor with 680 feet of chain on the starboard side and a port anchor of eight tons and 540 feet of chain. Despite this substantial ground tackle, the big ship started to drag, placing her in grave danger because of her size and the relatively confined area. With her master, Captain Oliver Bohld, her chief officer, Commander George Terry, and seventeen midshipmen aboard, the *Marsala* drifted toward the Shaw's Cove railroad bridge, a helpless juggernaut before the withering blast, a threat to the craft to leeward — some anchored, some adrift — and facing the prospect of being seriously damaged herself, either by collision or grounding.

Somebody on a beleaguered yacht, trying to hold on with anchor down and engine all ahead full, saw her coming, got his anchor up, and steamed to windward of her, in the nick of time. Nearing the railroad bridge, the barkentine seemed certain to collide with a barge up against the trestle. But the wind shifted and swung *Marsala's* stern about, so that she cleared both the barge and a tugboat seeking a haven there. The training ship finally fetched up off the Chappell Lumber Company wharf, where her crew succeeded in making her bow fast to one dock and her stern to another. Here, she inadvertently blocked the offshore end of a large slip between the wharves in which were trapped thousands of board feet of lumber washed overboard, which otherwise would have gone to sea.

Captain Bohld, who had experienced a number of hurricanes at sea (where he would much rather have been, with desirable maneuvering room) never had experienced one in port before. He said the glass went down to 28.22 and that it was "mainly by the grace of God" that no serious damage was done to his command, or to other craft or structures, by his big ship.

What *Marsala* did not do, a huge derrick lighter did. The lighter broke loose from the dock of the Merritt, Chapman and Scott Company on Pequot Avenue; driven rapidly by surge and wind, it became an instrument of destruction in the lower harbor.

It first struck Marsters' wharf, carrying it away completely and sinking eight or ten vessels there, including several cruisers, a couple of schooners, and two large water and supply craft owned by Silas M. Marsters. The huge lighter, formidably constructed, next swept away the long wharf of Burr Brothers, together with gasoline tanks and other equipment, and sank a number of other vessels berthed in slips there. In a final gesture, it destroyed St. Germaine's wharf and piled up on the shore near the Coast Guard training station, close to Fort Trumbull.

By 3:30, the official anemometer at New London registered wind of 98 miles an hour, at which point the wind cups of the instrument blew away. A party from the steam yacht *Cythera* — Second Officer O. C. Erickson, Federico Barbuto, Leonard Kelly, Carl Soderstedt, and Henry Thorsen, aided by Patrolman George McCaskey and Alvero Aguiar, a young repairman — hastily put together their own volunteer task force. In motorboats and skiffs, buffeted by the storm, wet, cold, and hard-pressed, they rescued the stranded from houseboats in Shaw's Cove, took people out of flood-swept buildings in Bank Street, and labored for hours in behalf of strangers to whom they also were strangers. An adult male, described as an amnesia victim of the storm, was admitted to New London's Lawrence Hospital. Insofar as I am aware, this was the only total memory loss officially attributed to hurricane experience, although many were so traumatized that they were unable to recall the details of what happened for several hours.

One man died on the waterfront. Ingvald Beaver was a crew member of the barge *Victoria*, the roof of his quarters started to peel off. The sea at that time was pounding with great force off

Vessels sunk and piers shattered

at New London, Connecticut

the Custom House, where the barge was lying, and Beaver got on top of the cabin in an effort to tie down part of the roof. Before he could secure it, another blast carried it away, and he was last seen reentering his living quarters.

Fire broke out in the stricken city at 4:30 P.M., in a business section near the waterfront; water, flooding the building of the Humphrey-Cornell Company (wholesale grocers), short-circuited electric wires. The blaze raced in several directions and within a few minutes a conflagration that raged for hours and completely destroyed more than a dozen commercial buildings and houses was in progress.

Under the command of Fire Chief Thomas H. Shipman, every available piece of fire apparatus in the city was called out to fight New London's worst blaze since that September day in 1781 when the British under Benedict Arnold burned the city. It was a roaring pyre that sent aloft billowing black smoke clouds and an ugly orange glare visible for miles and threatened with annihilation a flaming quarter-mile of the community's business section. Firemen, floundering in deep water, struggling against a gale that blew the streams from their hoses back into their faces, turned desperately to the battle, soon realizing that New Londoners must save their city themselves.

For efforts to obtain assistance from nearby communities proved fruitless. All telephones were out and it was impossible to contact the fire departments in Westerly, New Haven, Norwich, Mystic, Noank, Old Lyme, and Niantic. Many volunteers who started by car found the roads blocked by uprooted trees and felled poles. Others finally managed to get to the Jordan and Oswegatchie stations of the Waterford fire department, and both of these companies sent their apparatus and crews. It was impossible to get to the Goshen or Quaker Hills fire companies and later, when equipment started from these units for New London — their fire fighters alarmed by reflections of the blaze in the night sky — they found the roads impassable and had to turn back.

The fire rapidly consumed the Humphrey-Cornell structure and the Sisk Building; it swept through the big Putnam Furniture Company and on to a grain store, a second-floor factory, the office building and lumber yard of the F. H. Chappell Company. Next to fall was the woodworking shop of the Nasetta brothers. At this point, the sparks, flying on the wind in showers, carried the fire into Bank Street and set Thompson's garage ablaze, and a building in Tilley Street, directly behind the garage. More sparks flew over the entire area and set fires on roofs of several buildings on Tilley, Starr, and Pearl streets.

Then the wind shifted, probably saving more houses on Tilley Street from destruction, but causing the blaze to spread to the building of the Plaut-Cadden Company. Within a matter of seconds, the entire structure, with its huge stock of furniture, was aflame. Despite efforts of the embattled fire fighters, the flames then spread farther to destroy the hardware store of Eaton and Wilson Company. Firemen went aloft on the buildings, dousing persistent roof fires. It was feared at about this time that all the buildings on one side of Bank Street were doomed, and Chief Shipman and his aides were prepared to dynamite buildings in the path of the blaze in an effort to halt its deadly march.

Suddenly, the wind shifted again, sending the fire back over the blackened path it had already traversed. This wind shift and the fact that almost torrential rain for hours had thoroughly soaked the buildings and the stricken area prevented the fire from assuming far more serious proportions. At about 11 that night, the blaze was under control.

As the clouds of rank smoke hung over the fire area, New London was placed under virtual martial law; National Guardsmen, with pistols and helmets, sailors and Marines from the submarine base, Coast Guardsmen, and soldiers from several Army vessels moved into the darkened city. Veterans, Legionnaires, and platoons of Boy Scouts assisted the weary policemen. Electric power was gone, telephone calls on the few lines still available were limited to three minutes, and the Western Union office had a double line of waiting customers that extended out into the street. Slabs of twisted metal roofing, piles of wood, glass, and other debris littered the main streets, and the burned waterfront area was roped off.

The fire alone caused $1 million worth of damage; in addition to the buildings and their contents, at least twenty vehicles, including trucks in two coalyards, were destroyed. As late as Friday — two days after the storm — many burned buildings still smoldered and firemen were overhauling the coal piles of the Central and F. H. and A. H. Chappell Coal companies to get at the flames that burned deep within them.

Of all that befell poor New London, one of the most awe-inspiring sights created by the storm was provided by the 190-foot steamer *Tulip*, thrust ashore by wind and storm tide near the U.S. Lighthouse Service wharf, in the rear of the Custom House. On September 22, New England officials of the Bureau of Lighthouses informed H. D. King, commissioner, in Washington: "The principal casualty so far reported is that to the lighthouse tender Tulip, 1,057 tons, which was driven ashore at New London, as per attached telegram [received from her]: 'Tulip driven ashore northeast side of dock at New London, nearly broadside, with bow across railroad track. Attempts to float unsuccessful, apparently will roll over at low tide. Have sent entire crew ashore.' Unable to get in touch with New London. Am proceeding there by rail. (Signed) Yates."

Tulip's grounding was observed by few, but thousands came to see her (her bow was on the eastbound tracks of the New York, New Haven and Hartford Railroad) and to watch salvage operations that were started on the fourth day after the storm. The task was at once taxing and delicate. Black-hulled *Tulip* was heavy; she was also resting on her port bilge and there was always a possibility that any effort to pull her free would roll her over, as her commanding officer had noted in the telegram.

George W. Tooker of New York, salvage officer for Merritt,

The lighthouse tender Tulip *across the railroad tracks at New London, Connecticut*

Chapman and Scott Corporation, was in charge of getting her afloat, and he set crews to work night and day cutting a waterway in which to launch her. They dredged 5,000 yards of mud, sand, and rock to shape a basin about 15 feet deep near the lighthouse wharf and 20 feet deep farther out, to accommodate her stern, which was closest to the water.

At 5 o'clock in the morning of October 7, the floating operation began, with the wrecking steamer *Willet*, the tug *Alert*, and the big derrick *Commodore* on hand. Lines were made fast to the

Tulip, whose portside ports were battened, in case she should roll over, and the *Alert* took up the slack and churned the waters of the basin near the wharf. *Willet* set up a steady pull on the line offshore and cables creaked through block sheaves on the *Commodore*. *Tulip* moved, ponderously; her bow came free, and suddenly, she was on an even keel for the first time since the storm. The *Alert* whistled a blast of accomplishment; *Commodore* moved out to take stern lines passed under *Tulip* and made fast to the lighthouse steamer on the shore side to get a better pull. The stern was still on the bottom, but not for long.

Salvage officer Tooker's signal was as shrill as a football referee's. *Commodore* piped a note of instruction to *Willet* and there was the steady, deep throb of straining screw against the sea. *Tulip's* stern was free; she was afloat, and the lighthouse steamer *Hawthorne* nearby sounded several joyful and fraternal blasts of her whistle.

New London would survive, even though some on the eve of the twenty-first had described it as "facing ruin"; it would float again, just as the *Tulip* did. John Calvin Goddard commented on his city's ordeal, "A storm has the merit of being dramatic. Acts 27 is called the best elocutionary passage in Scripture, the shipwreck of St. Paul. 'And when they had taken up the anchors, they committed themselves unto the sea, and loosed the rudder bands and hoisted up the mainsail to the wind, and made toward shore. And falling into a place where two seas met, they ran the ship aground; and the forepart stuck fast and remained unmovable, but the hinder part was broken with the violence of the waves. . . .'

"This storm was all of that, with a flood and fire thrown in. It was full of the picturesque. A house was lifted bodily across a pond, with one ferry passenger aboard and the lady emerged unharmed. A freighter in New London harbor was lifted bodily and set upon a wharf.

"When short circuitage set fire to Thames front property, the engines could not reach it because of wreckage in the streets and scores of distant houses were fired by flying cinders.

"The word 'calamity' comes from 'calamus,' the reed,* which indicates that our cue is to bend likewise to the storm. We would go further and say, let's get the benefit first of all of the nobility the flood and hurricane brought out. Lives were freely offered in behalf of the imperiled. One little girl even swam, with death threatening in every stroke, in order to get food for her stranded family. Perhaps greater catastrophes are sent to certain souls in order to bring out their noblest possibility. Emergencies make charities emerge, and of every kind. . . .

"Another teaching of our calamity is the bringing into prominence the worth of our common blessings. When the lights went out and we resorted to candles, we learned anew the luxury our books had been to us. The power goes off, the phone shuts up, the daily paper fails to reach our aching void and we learn that we need each other far more than we commonly allow."

Harrison McDonald of Lafayette, Indiana, traveling by train, saw New London immediately after the storm, although he had had no intention of doing so. He left Albany at 8 o'clock Wednesday morning on the Wolverine, bound for Boston.

"We got to Springfield [Massachusetts]," he said, "and they told us there was a washout and the train had to be rerouted. So we started off for Hartford, creeping very slowly, with the water lapping around the tracks at various points. We made it all right, and started off for New London. Within about three miles of the town, at 3:15 Wednesday afternoon, the hurricane and flood stopped us.

"The engineer, a smart fellow, pulled ahead to a sharp curve in

* Actually, it doesn't, but the advice is good.

the track and stopped there. He figured the curve of the cars against the wind would help us and I guess it did. I don't think the train could have stayed upright if it was broadside to the wind and in a straight line. A pullman car weighs sixty-seven tons and as it was, the cars were rocking from one track to another — not just shivering and shaking, but literally rocking.

"The Yankee Clipper pulled up behind us and we spent the night there. We were comfortable and had plenty to eat, but the trains ran out of water and finally they were passing coals from the engine back to the dining car in order to get a fire and quick food.

"The next morning, we were taken into New London in buses. The first thing we were given was a card from the National Guardsmen warning us not to drink water or to pour milk without boiling it. The first store I saw was a five and ten cent one. It had been flooded out, but one counter had been set up on the sidewalk and they were selling candles only. We walked down to the business district and found the firemen still pouring water into the smoldering embers.

"Parents were crowding the newspaper office and police station in search of schoolchildren. They had been missing for sixteen hours. They told us that school had let out just before the flood. By then, it was a hopeless hell for them. One man had managed to get forty girls out of his factory after the wind had lifted the roof of it and a moment before the flood and fire had hit it. Another had several missing from his factory still and the factory was gone.

"I was standing at the desk in the Western Union office when a young schoolgirl came in. She was looking for her younger sister, who had not been heard from since school let out the afternoon before. The clerk said they had no report on her. A moment later, a businessman came in. 'Can I get a wire through to New York?'

" 'No,' said the clerk.

" 'Well, I don't suppose it's essential' he said. 'I'd just like to let

[124]

my company in New York know that they haven't got any New London factory any more. It's not a problem of damage, but one of complete abolition.'

"They had no electricity, no lights, no heat, no power of any kind. There was also no accurate estimate of the dead and missing. The editor of the New London *Day* said 100 summer cottages were swept to sea in five minutes at Ocean Beach."

At least one vessel sought without success such sanctuary as the port of New London offered in the hours after the storm. Mr. and Mrs. Frank F. Douden of Guilford, Connecticut, were aboard.

They had spent a couple of days visiting Mrs. Douden's relatives on Long Island, in and about East Hampton. On September 21, they had planned to take the Port Jefferson–Bridgeport ferry in the morning and go to their summer cottage at Madison, Connecticut, to stay overnight. Instead, they decided to stay over for a drive to Montauk in the morning and to take the ferry from Orient directly to New London. The vessel was the *Catskill*, Captain Clarence Sherman of Shelter Island; it sailed from Orient at about 1 P.M. Wednesday, with eight passengers, including the Doudens, and three automobiles, one of which was theirs.

The steamer was about three-quarters of the way across the sound when Captain Sherman, a ship handler of ability, realized that the increasing intensity of the storm would make it dangerous to try to get into New London harbor. He put the vessel about and butted back into the heavy sea and wind toward Long Island, continuing to steam beyond Orient. At 6 P.M., he gave the orders for all hands to put on life preservers, having decided they would have to spend the night on the Sound.

There they stayed, pitching and rolling. Faulkner's Island light, which they could see, gave them mixed feelings of frustration and relief. On the one hand, it was a staunch beacon of hope, but on the other, its presence did nothing to improve their situation. To the Doudens, watching it through the long dark hours of the storm, "the cheerful thought occurred that if we were washed ashore, our bodies would be easily identified."

Early the next morning, the *Catskill* steamed into New London. Because of the flood and fire, there was no dock left on either side of the harbor at which the passengers could be landed. Captain Sherman decided to try Groton, and there was finally able to tie up at a coal dock. When the lines were secured, passengers and officers stood in a close circle and sang ("With teary voices," said the Doudens) : "Praise God, from whom all blessings flow;/ Praise Him, all creatures here below;/ Praise Him above, ye heavenly hosts;/ Praise Father, Son, and Holy Ghost."

Once ashore and in their automobile, it took the Doudens from 7 A.M. to 12:30 P.M. to find clear roads and pick their way through blocked roads to their home in nearby Guilford. And the final chapter of their experience was still to come: as soon as they were able to get to their beach cottage at Madison — where they had planned to spend Wednesday, rather than on the ferry — they discovered that it had been reduced to a pile of kindling.

Off Saybrook, the ten members of the crew of the lightship *Cornfield*, which marked the approach to Cornfield Reef, also spent some bad hours on the Sound during the storm, but under even more vulnerable circumstances. The lightship was not only duty-bound to remain on station; it was without propelling power and could not have got out of the weather even if given permission to do so. Those aboard agreed that the principal reason there were no casualties and little damage during what they described as "a trip through hell" was because they received ample warning of the storm and were able to secure everything before it struck.

The crew let out more chain on the huge mushroom anchors, secured all windows and ports, lashed doors, doubled the fastenings on boats and such deck equipment as could not be moved below, and then got inside under cover.

From then on, for about five hours, the 197-ton, 115-foot steel vessel was under water almost continuously. When the wind was at its worst, she was hove down onto her beam ends until it appeared that she was about to capsize. Then the massive seas struck her. She quivered from stem to stern; she rolled, tossed, and plunged like a porpoise as waves of tremendous height rolled completely over her. The vessel — her bow pulled down by the weight of the anchors, which were dragging — was more submarine than lightship.

In the cabin, the men had resigned themselves to their fate — whatever it proved to be; there was nothing they could do to influence the outcome, and to have ventured out on deck would have been to ask for death. They knew that the longer the storm lasted and the longer they dragged anchor, the more likely it was that one or both chains would snap. If that happened, the vessel's head would no longer be held into the wind; she would wallow to leeward, broadside and vulnerable, until she fetched up on rocks or beach. If the chains held and the pounding of the sea damaged the hull, the lightship might well founder or roll over. No one aboard would survive in either case.

At last, the mushroom anchors took hold again on a sandy bottom, and shortly thereafter, the storm blew itself out. The seas subsided; the crew came out on deck. Dented steel plates and smashed skylights testified to the force of the battering the vessel had received. "Landmarks on the Saybrook shore previously used to determine whether the lightship was on station had been obliterated," Acting Captain Stanford L. Tukey observed, but it was eventually established that the vessel had been blown two miles west of her assigned position.

Captain Tukey's landmarks were among thousands that were "obliterated" on all the Connecticut shores. A resident of Westbrook wrote, "This community is back where it started fifty years ago. Beaches, cottages, pier, and shore are all in a total wreck. . . . At Grove Beach Point, only three cottages are left standing and they are beyond repair. At Little Stannard Beach, where there wasn't even the protection of a seawall, the cottages were washed out and then smashed against the beach stones."

When the storm had passed in Hartford, the water was still coming in on a rising tide at Westbrook, and at Stannard Beach, it began to threaten the cottages. As the cottage of Morrison W. Johnson at the east end of the row began to shift on its foundations, Mark Holbrook put out in a rowboat to bring the occupants ashore. Mrs. Johnson and her friend and housekeeper during the summer at the beach, Mrs. Ada Dickinson, got into the boat, but as Mrs. Dickinson climbed in, it capsized. All three were thrown into the water. Holbrook clung to the cottage, but the two women were swept away; their bodies were found at 4 the next morning by searchers combing the long, littered shoreline.

To the west, at Little Stannard Beach, warnings and rescue boats got most of the occupants of the cottages to safety before the buildings collapsed into the water. Westbrook postmaster Paul Wren went to the beach at 3 Wednesday afternoon to urge his aunt, Mrs. Sarah Mathers Wren, seventy, and her daughter, Mrs. Ella F. Remmert, forty-six, to leave their cottage. They declined to go, apparently believing that they would be safe. That is the last time either was seen alive. The sea gullied out the underpinnings of the cottage and swept it away; no trace of the building ever was found. The bodies of the two women were found in a nearby swamp, and it is not known to this day whether they were swept to sea in the cottage or were caught by the storm waves while trying to reach high ground. The fact that Mrs. Wren had her pocketbook in her hand suggested the latter.

Mrs. Louis Higgins of Plainville and her sister, Mrs. George McCleary of Longmeadow, Massachusetts, were at Grove Beach. Mrs. McCleary had closed her summer place for the season, but there were a number of things she wanted to do to fix up the house for the next season, and she thought that an extra week of fall at the beach would be an interesting vacation. They had been at the shore since Monday, and although Tuesday's weather wasn't much, there was nothing alarming about it.

Wednesday afternoon, when the wind rose, they saw screens of nearby cottages flying past. Then the tar roof of a garage "traveled like a magic carpet" overhead. Still they remained in the house, which showed no sign of collapsing, although Mrs. Higgins said, "It shook a little."

They went to the front of the cottage, looked out the window, and saw the first great wave pound over the breakwater. The sea, hissing and frothing, encircled their house. "Come on, Mae," shouted Mrs. McCleary, "we are getting out." They grabbed their pocketbooks and ran out the back door, past the garage which held Mrs. McCleary's car, to the Somerset cottage on the far side of the road that runs parallel to the beach. Debris flew through the air as they ran through the water.

From the porch of their new sanctuary, they watched the storm wave come across the Sound to the beach. They had hardly reached the Somerset cottage when the houses on the shore began to fall.

"We could see the wave between the wrecked cottages. It was forty feet high, just like a moving mountain," Mrs. Higgins said. "It would swallow up everything. When it struck the beach, it broke, and moved over the tumbled houses and surrounded the cottage in which we were. Men came in boats and rowed us to another building which was on a bank.

"I thought that the end had come. There were nine persons in the cottage to which we had fled. No one talked. We just stood staring at each other as the houses on the shorefront came down. No one screamed. We just looked at each other."

"Well, Mae," said Mrs. McCleary to her sister, "if we go, we go together."

They watched with set faces the destruction of Mrs. McCleary's seven-room summer home, "blown into thousands of pieces" thirty minutes after they had run out of it. They saw the fifteen-room cottage next to it collapse into the sand and water, watched the sea smash it to splintered junk and wash it away. They slept that night with their clothes on in the cottage on the bank.

The next morning, they went to look at the debris and stood on the spot where their cottage had been. "I couldn't find anything," Mrs. Higgins said. Mrs. McCleary said she saw a sideboard, but although there was lumber from other buildings there, none of the wood from her home was in evidence anywhere. Thursday afternoon, with the help of two men, they dug out Mrs. McCleary's car, which rested in four feet of sand; remarkably, it ran, and on Friday, they started for Plainville.

Near Clinton, they saw a man with a truckload of milk in a brook in a gully. "How did he get there?" Mrs. Higgins asked.

"I haven't the slightest idea," Mrs. McCleary said.

When Mrs. McCleary left Mrs. Higgins to return to Springfield on Saturday morning, she invited the latter to return with her to Grove Beach in October and to spend another vacation in a new cottage there next summer.

"I told her that the next time she goes, I won't go," Mrs. Higgins said. "She can go alone."

Mrs. Orris B. Norman was in Old Mystic. "Being from Florida, where hurricanes are not too uncommon, I laughed when I sat down to observe what I thought was a peach of a windstorm," she said. "But I didn't laugh long.

"I had just started my afternoon stint in the Old Mystic post office, where I was also postmaster, janitor, and clerk, and when the window blinds began to bang, I tried to steady my jittery nerves by reading a magazine article.

"I reckoned the stone building, more than a century old, with walls about two feet thick, was the safest place in an affair of this kind. But I soon changed my mind. Believe it or not, the building began to rock perceptibly and the desk began to jump. That's about the time I got hysterical and decided it was time to close up. I fastened the window blinds and called my dog, Patsy.

"Just as we stepped out the front door, the big elm tree in front of the house fell with a resounding crash across the telephone wires, snapping a brand new pole. That's when I realized we were really in for something.

"Patsy ducked back into the post office unobserved. I made a mad dash for my house next door. On the way, I observed that most of the panes were gone from the attic windows, and I started up there to close the blinds. I found my brother, Ray Lord, frantically trying to nail the french door in my bedroom, which had blown off its hinges, to the door frame. And I stopped to hand nails, to count nails, and to assist him.

"We then went to the attic, and he tried to nail a piece of linoleum over the attic windows, but it was useless. We had to abandon that when the blinds in the kitchen began to bang and window lights began to shower down like ripe apples, letting in the wind in full force. It gathered up the oilcloth on my kitchen table, wrapped it around the crockery in the middle of it, and dashed the whole business to the floor, breaking all the dishes, and leaving a nice slippery mess, which tripped us up as we tried to rush around.

"The wind blew in a broken pane in my back door, and I grabbed a strip of linoleum and held it there while my neighbor, Mrs. Freeman, nailed it fast. It stopped the wind from that angle. Meanwhile, Sidney Freeman, her son, and my brother had tackled the kitchen window, but were unsuccessful in tacking linoleum to it until they brought wooden strips from the cellar to hold it.

"Just about that time, the blind broke loose on the east living room window and half the window lights in that broke out, letting in a gale of wind that nearly blew us out of the house. I rushed to the attic and brought down a couple of storm windows, which miraculously fitted the opening, and with our combined forces, we managed to nail one fast.

"About that time, I missed Patsy. I looked and called to her and started to search, but high water distracted my attention, and I got the gang together to save what we could out of the cellar while we could. We went down and put everything of value in a high place and I resumed my hunt for my dog.

"In the meantime, I rescued my black cat from a precarious perch about six inches above the rapidly rising waters in the basement. I finally decided Patsy was locked in the post office and would drown. So I waded in water breast-deep to see if I could find her. I broke out a window pane and called to her but no answer, nor could I see her in the swirling waters inside. I could see miscellaneous effects of the office, however. (After the storm was over, my brother rescued her unharmed, but tired from swimming to save her life.)

"My older brother, Ben, came home in a rowboat that evening. My husband, Constable Norman, when he arrived home Wednesday night, said he had been driving a bus along the streets of New London and a large telephone pole had fallen across the roof of the bus, denting it. He and his passengers took refuge in an automobile agency office. He walked home from Mystic, where our car was flooded in front of the car barn, in company with four large yachts. After the excitement was over, I keeled over in a dead faint in Mrs. Freeman's kitchen. I guess the excitement was too much for me.

"The next morning, everywhere I went, I saw faces full of misery and despair, as people who had barely been hanging on and trying to get along the best they could surveyed incalculable damage to their properties. I heard many stories of a miserable night spent in roofless and sometimes wall-less houses or how they had taken refuge with neighbors in the night. I saw parents who had spent the night worrying about children who had not returned from school. I saw people worrying about relatives and friends they could not communicate with and about whose safety they feared. I saw barns flattened to the ground. Hardly a barn was left standing in the whole village. Hen coops and other such light buildings never were found.

"The streets were strewn with broken elms and other trees, many of which I had to crawl over or under in order to get through. I went up and surveyed the ruins of the Baptist church. It was unroofed during the storm and it will take thousands of dollars in my estimation to repair and make it the beautiful building that it was. The church, founded in 1706 by Timothy Wightman, was the oldest of its denomination in Connecticut.

"I took a picture of the home of Mrs. Nellie Davoll, which had the entire sides blown away. On the way back down Route 84, I stopped and talked with William E. Congdon. He had just finished building a garage on his filling station property. All that was left was a stack of kindling wood. Across the lot, one side of his barn was covered with what was left of the rest of it, including a brand new tractor and his winter supply of oil and alcohol for his filling station."

And near Mystic, Mrs. James E. Stark, in attempting to fix a window of her home during the storm, was struck by a piece of flying glass that severed her jugular vein. She bled to death.

On his wild ride up the Connecticut River to Cromwell, Claude Adams had had an inkling, but little more, of the catastrophe that had befallen the yacht fleet at Essex.

Walter Rowe was there; he told how the popular yachting center was gale-battered, lost two of its captains who tried to save their commands, and counted its damage in hundreds of thousands of dollars when its fleet of fine sail and power yachts finally lay at the bottom of the river.

"A fleet of well over 100 boats was assembled at Essex before the storm swept the river clean," he wrote. "Many of them had come from other ports, as Essex offers a landlocked, safe harbor under most conditions. A large fleet of schooners, yawls and cutters were anchored in the river awaiting the Off Soundings Club's annual fall rendezvous and cruise that weekend.

"As the barometer started its downward trend, the various owners and their captains gathered at the Essex Yacht Club. All hands knew that it was September 21, the date of the autumnal equinox and expected some kind of a blow. Extra anchors were put out and mooring lines were doubled up. The anemometer showed a velocity of only thirty-five miles an hour, when the barograph line suddenly took a precipitous dive. E. V. D. Wetmore, harbormaster and owner of the Essex Paint and Marine Company, where most of the yachtsmen make their headquarters, warned everybody to take their boats away from the slips at the dock.

"The winds began to pipe up but nobody believed that in less than an hour a velocity of 75 miles an hour would be registered. Yachts unable to leave their moorings or slips were, without exception, sunk or severely damaged. As the barometer dropped to 28.5 in a nosedive, the group of onlookers abandoned their position in the yacht club building. The power was off, and the anemometer was not working. But the wind backed, from the east to northeast, and it reached a speed of 65 miles per hour. All of the big boats were apparently holding. (The little sailboats anchored off Thatch Bed Island were the first to break loose and go ashore.) Then the glass showed a further drop to 28.3 and the wind blew harder. It whipped the tops of the waves off in solid sheets and the fleet was almost obscured from viewers as it began to rain.

"Someone shouted through the rain and water. It seemed that the entire fleet of boats had broken loose. The wind was blowing at least 80 miles an hour and this tremendous velocity, plus an unprecedented rise of six feet in the depth of the water in three hours, simply lifted the boats and their moorings off the bottom. The sailing vessels were burying their cabin tops under bare poles as they plowed toward the Essex shore. One of the first boats to hit was Stanley Hart's motor sailer, *Ka Ja Mui*, which steered a miraculous course through the docks to fetch up against the float of the Dauntless Club. In a few hours, this boat was standing on its nose high up on the lawn of the club, hopelessly entangled with Clinton Allen's schooner, *Friar Tuck*, and Winthrop Warner's once trim cutter.

"Commodore Hubert Toppin's fine schooner *Blackbird* crashed against the bulkhead of the Dauntless Club and sank instantly, so that only the top of her mast was visible. By this time, the barometer measured its low point of 28.02 and the wind reached its top velocity, which was believed to be well over 90 miles an hour. The large express cruiser *Tarra*, with young Buell Hemenway, son of the owner, aboard, parted all its mooring lines, and came crashing into the creek, where the many small dinghies were tied up. By one of those strange quirks of fate, *Tarra* (over 70 feet long) tried to cross the dike and fetched up on the mud, saving her from complete loss. When the wind moderated late in the evening, they were able to swing her around and actually tied her to the upstairs porch of the Essex Yacht Club.

"Dr. Earl Carter saw his 40-foot cruiser break loose and then perch herself on a spile, where the boat hung at a perilous angle all night. Richard O. H. Hill's cutter, *Lucky Star*, was one of the last boats to break loose. But when it did, it came roaring against the bulkhead that makes Everett Dickenson's slip, with the beautiful express cruiser *Phoenix*. The bulkhead soon gave way and the *Phoenix* sank in less than a minute, the *Lucky Star* on top of it. Henry Harrington's ketch *Lenita* landed on top of this mess and nothing could be seen of *Phoenix* and *Lucky Star* but the tops of their masts.

"As the center of the low-pressure area moved over, the barometer began to rise, and the wind died down for a few minutes, only to come back from the southwest with renewed intensity. The shift of the wind to an exactly opposite direction is typical of hurricanes, but it was unexpected in a climate where tropical disturbances are

[135]

unknown. Boats that had been safely beached from a northeast gale were now exposed to the new wind and were suddenly righted and blown off to the Lyme shore.

"The largest vessel in the fleet, William Gould's big staysail schooner *Lascar* II, landed high on the beach of North Cove. This boat landed so hard after being swept onward before the 80-mile wind that she actually jumped up and over a sand pile.

"By 7:30 P.M., when high water was reached, the crest was within four inches of the all-time high established in the 1936 flood. A freight lighter tied up to the dolphin of the Standard Oil Company just before the storm started. It was the good ship *Let's Go*, often seen on the river. The vessel was loaded with manure. At the height of the hurricane, the captain rowed ashore, holding a kitten under his coat. And the load of manure was abandoned to its fate which, fortunately for the waterfront, was a safe one, as the freighter hung onto the spile."

The two who were lost from the Essex Yacht Club fleet were both knowledgeable and competent. Nils Ek was skipper of the 48-foot cruiser *Marpo*, owned by David Post, Jr., of Hartford. Ek had the cruiser moored well out in the river off the wharf of the Essex Paint and Marine Company. About noon on Wednesday, he went on board after getting the storm warnings and made everything ready for a bad blow. As the gale became more severe, he started his engines to hold the boat against the wind and take some strain off the mooring line.

Nearby, Harry Fiske's new 80-footer *Wachusette* was lying to a mooring. Her captain was on leave of absence and her steward, Walter Brundage, together with another young man, Barrett Dolph — both inexperienced in handling large boats — boarded the craft in hopes of being able to do whatever was necessary. Captain Ek hailed them, told them to start their engines, and to run up river if conditions got too bad. They both said later that Ek was in the best of spirits and evidently had no fear of serious trouble.

About 3 o'clock, the *Lascar*, which was unmanned, broke loose and bore down upon the *Marpo*, forcing Ek to cut his mooring line. He then started up the river. Almost immediately afterward, the line of the *Wachusette* parted and Brundage and Dolph, with both engines going, also headed up river. After some minutes, they passed Ek on the *Marpo*, which did not seem to be making much headway. Captain Ek gave them a signal to go on up and waved his hand that all was well. That was the last time he was seen alive. The young men kept on, and how they made their way into Hamburg Cove and safety, bringing their boat through without a scratch — Brundage, at the wheel, was not expected to know how to handle a yacht — was one of the wonders of the storm.

Captain Milton Dixon on the *Admiral* at the Essex Boat Works watched the *Marpo* as she came upriver, but he saw no one on board and supposed that she was unmanned. She passed the mouth of North Cove and disappeared in the storm. She was next seen by members of the crew of the Essex Boat Works as she came crashing upon a row of spiles driven to form a bulkhead on the side of the boat works property next to the river.

Colin Campbell and Charles Harrison were both sure that they saw the boat as she struck the bulkhead and that she hit it with such force that it broke her open. The water lifted her off and again threw her onto the bulkhead, this time smashing open everything abovedeck. Neither saw anything of Ek. They rushed out into the storm and pulled ashore pieces of wreckage, including the *Marpo*'s dinghy, so that they had absolute proof of the identity of the boat.

After striking the bulkhead two or three times, the craft disappeared, and no trace of her was found after the storm. She is presumed to have slid off into deep water and probably was carried far downstream underwater. Whether Captain Ek fell overboard or had gone below to determine what was wrong with his engine will never be known.

Ernest G. Bushnell, who had long experience with boats, was in charge of a 30-foot cruiser belonging to J. C. Edwards of Chester; he died after danger from the hurricane was past.

He kept the cruiser at a small pier running into North Cove at the foot of Little Point Street. Alarmed by indications of an unusual storm, Mr. Bushnell, assisted by his brother, Edwin, got out extra lines and made everything as secure as possible. The boat rode out the storm without injury, despite the fact that great trees were knocked down near where she was moored and a summer house on the Bushnell place only a short distance away was blown from its foundation.

After the worst of the storm was over, about 6 o'clock, Mr. Bushnell came ashore. He had fallen into the water and he went home to get dry clothes. He returned to the pier about 6:30 and went on board the boat again. Apparently he feared that the storm was not entirely over and he decided to take the cruiser out into the cove and anchor it where there would be no danger of its being blown ashore.

He started the engine and was seen by Mrs. Edwin Bushnell heading out into the cove. Warren Roberts and a companion in a schooner moored above Dauntless Shipyard on the east side of the North Cove channel saw Mr. Bushnell cruising about in their part of the cove, saw him throw his anchor and apparently go overboard with it. They went immediately to help him, but failed to find him. His anchor rode was not attached to the boat and they concluded he had either slipped and fallen over or the line had fouled around his leg and pulled him over, or he had had a heart attack. The boat swiftly disappeared in the gathering darkness. About an hour later, it was found by William Suda, who lived at the head of the cove, a mile or more away. The engine was still running. Mr. Bushnell's body was found in a mass of wreckage floating in North Cove not far from the spot where he went overboard.

At Stonington, the marine disaster was of another kind, for the fleet there was commercial, not pleasure. Of the Point Judith–to–

[138]

New London fleet totaling one hundred fishing craft, employing 650 men, only three boats were working immediately after the hurricane and they were fishing so that the families of the boatless — whose vessels had been blown ashore or sunk — could eat.

As late as October 7, a waterfront observer reported, "One of the most touching examples of the brotherhood of the sea is enacted here each day when the fishing smack *Gloria* returns from the fishing grounds and distributes food free of charge to the mothers and families whose source of livelihood and whose homes, in some cases, were swept away by the hurricane.

"The sturdy *Gloria*, owned by Dinny Seidell, is the only smack working since the storm drove the Stonington fleet of fifty-two craft ashore. Some boat crews consisted of four heads of families. Fortunately, the *Gloria* was in Bridgeport being overhauled on September 21. Fisherman Rodney Singer was the only man able to ride out the storm at Stonington Harbor without going ashore."

Captain John W. Smith, president of the Southern New England Fishermen's Association, to which the one hundred boats belonged, said, "Every night, half of the town comes down to the wharf to get a mess of fish from the *Gloria*. The other townspeople, as well as the fishermen, take it for the asking." He said that what fish were left over after the housewives had taken their dinners home was shipped in the usual course to the New York market but that "up to now, there hasn't been enough surplus to think about."

"Isn't it unusual for a man to give away his source of livelihood as Captain Seidell is doing?" he was asked.

"Oh, the fishermen are that way," answered Smith.

It was about five days later before a big New York lighter, obtained through efforts of the Red Cross, raised George Grogan's *Louise* — the first of the Stonington fleet that went to the bottom or aground to be salvaged. It was some time after that before the port received the "jacks to lift our boats and good greased timber to slide them overboard" for which Captain Smith called on the federal government, and even then they had to replace all the shore-side gear, including the barrels used for shipping fish — which had been swept back into the woods.

In New Haven, an Associated Press writer concluded sadly, "The greens and commons of New England will never be the same. Picture postcard mementos of the oldest part of the United States are gone with the wind and flood. The day of the 'biggest wind' has just passed and a great part of most picturesque America, as old as the Pilgrims, has gone beyond recall or replacement.

"Gables and cupolas, quaint and flavor-giving to a New England smacking of Revolutionary memory, are smashed and twisted in tragic array. Modern and outmoded textile mills that once gave New England its lifeblood have been blown into eternity. Depressions came and went, but it took wind and tidal wave to exterminate much of industrial New England.

"Great elms on the town greens of Connecticut, and all of New England, patient old trees that waved as saplings over Washington and his fellow revolutionaries, are reduced to kindling. Old New London's waterfront is a shambles worse than the sacking wrought by the British of Revolutionary days. The port where . . . whalers unloaded smelly cargoes is clogged with wreckage that had the trim lines of ships only four days ago.

"Modern resorts all along the coastline, playlands of high and low in the most populous area in the United States, are vanished. The average New Englander, thankful to escape death or injury, picked his way homeward tonight through debris that poses a strange new life to him. New structures that will rise out of the devastation will take a form totally foreign to the New England history. The remaining semblances of the old are bound to rate more pricelessly as antiques, as symbols of the struggle that built the war-impoverished colonies into the world's richest nation.

"New England's Revolutionary-rooted antiquity has been razed by the greatest nature-dealt disaster in its history. Heretofore, as Mark Twain said upon becoming acclimated to his hilltop home near Hartford, after a Missouri-spent boyhood, 'This part of the country has never had any weather, only samples of it.' The 'real thing' in weather, when it finally arrived, found New England's old buildings substantial with age but flimsy of substance, unable to withstand the terrific onslaught."

Chapter 8

IT WAS IN THE STONINGTON AREA that the most extraordinary railroad incident of the hurricane occurred.

The Bostonian, a regular Shore Line express, left Grand Central Station in New York City at noon on Wednesday. After the storm was over, the New York, New Haven and Hartford Railroad issued a statement late on Wednesday saying that all its trains had been accounted for. In fact, one of them had not. The Bostonian thus was officially "lost" for the time being, although Connecticut's Governor Wilbur L. Cross said later that even if he had known of the company's announcement, it would have been "humanly impossible" for contact to have been made immediately with the area in which the Bostonian was located.

Three days later, on September 24, the New York, New Haven and Hartford Railroad issued the following statement: "Upon arrival at Stonington on September 21, No. 14 stopped on signal from the tower man at that point on account of the train ahead. Windows of the tower had been blown out by the hurricane and water had reached the level of the track. Engineer Harry Easton got out of his engine and walked over to the tower to find out what conditions were and before he could return the 1,000 feet to his engine,

Fishing vessels lie beside the New York, New Haven and Hartford Railroad's stranded Bostonian at Stonington, Connecticut.

water was already waist-deep from the tidal wave, which was driving up.

"Meantime, the track under the rear cars had started to give way. The crew were making every endeavor to get the passengers moved up to the forward cars. Some passengers, however, insisted on opening the doors and jumped into the rapidly rising water, fighting their way to higher ground. In the meantime, wreckage driven by the hurricane crashed against the train and broke some of the brake apparatus, making it impossible to release the brakes of the rear car. All of the passengers were thereupon moved up into the head car and then William F. Donoghue, general chairman of the Brotherhood of Railroad Trainmen of the New Haven system,

[143]

working shoulder-deep in water, succeeded in uncoupling the head car from the rear of the train.

"The engineer then pulled the train ahead through the water and wreckage until he reached dry land. Telegraph wires were down across the engine and as he forced his way forward, the engine pulled down pole after pole, and forced a house from its path which had been thrown upon the tracks by the wind and water. But the engineer kept his throttle open until the place of safety was reached.

"Only last night when a complete report was available was it revealed that a checkup found one passenger and a pantryman of the dining car missing. Their bodies were subsequently recovered." The statement named the victims as Mrs. William B. Markell of Hartford and Chester A. Walker of New York.

There were others who knew many more details about what happened, although no one asked them and to this day, the essential published account is the statement issued by the railroad.

The media were overwhelmed by the proportions of the total catastrophe; first-person stories never were obtained and whereas they might have been in the aftermath, had nothing else occurred, the threat of war abroad quickly diverted journalistic attention elsewhere. As it happens, however, the Bostonian's conductor and dining car steward are still alive. With their help, it is now possible to reconstruct the full story.

Harry Easton of West Haven was engineer of No. 14, and although he and his train crew never received any medals or national acclaim, the facts suggest that what they accomplished under great duress, through coolheadedness and professional competence, prevented a far greater loss of life. Considerable credit also is undoubtedly due to many of the passengers, who remained calm and who assisted others.

Easton was at the throttle at 3:20 P.M.; wind was clocked in the area as high as 120 miles an hour; his train had been struck by numerous storm-driven vessels, including a schooner, as well as by heavy flotsam. At that point, the railroad — hampered by crippled communications systems that soon failed completely — was ordering all its trains to halt.

Just west of Stonington, taking a battering from wind and sea, Easton braked his train to a stop when he saw a "red block" set against him in the signal tower. He was careful to pull the train to high ground before he halted it.

Easton said, "I had been running over rails that were underwater at various points and had been proceeding with extreme caution." Anxious to ascertain the reason for the stop signal, Easton, accompanied by his fireman, D. C. Horan of Guilford, left the engine and walked toward the signal tower, an estimated five minutes' distance. Meanwhile, the flagman had gone to his post at the rear of the train.

"As we started to walk around a curve," Easton said, "we saw another train that had been stopped, apparently by bad conditions of the road. We knew that the Boston and Albany road was using our right-of-way and were doubly anxious about the 'red block' for that reason. Seeing the other train ahead, we turned and started back for our engine. We had taken but a few steps when water was up to our ankles. A few more steps and it was up to our knees.

"You can get some idea how fast that water came up from the fact that we started running and before we got to the engine, the water was above our hips."

Reaching the engine, they observed that the three rear cars of the train were listing toward the Sound. The tracks were being undermined by the surging water; the passengers had to be evacuated quickly from the rear cars, and if any part of the train was to be gotten out of there, it had to be accomplished swiftly.

Joseph C. Richards of West Haven was the conductor. "The rear of the train was on the bridge trestle," he recalled. "The heading of the train was at the signal at the old water tank, alongside a tennis court. The water was so high that boats from everywhere, Narragansett Bay, Westerly, were coming in and slamming against the train. A big yacht landed on a bank opposite the trestle; that was a good 150 yards from the normal low-water mark.

"I went through the train, warning everybody to move up ahead. I told Johnny [John P. Cooke of North Haven, dining car steward] to get his crew out of there, out of the dining car. As I notified those fellows in the kitchen, Chester Walker went out the side door on my left. He headed for the highway about a quarter-mile away. I watched him swimming in the water. He got almost halfway there and there was a timber floating. It must have been eight by ten. It hit him in the back of the head, in the base of the brain, and he went down and never came up."

"In one coach, there were some prep school kids, and they wouldn't move. They didn't take the thing seriously. I ripped open an emergency case and got an ax. I threatened to pin 'em with it if they didn't move. They got up and went into the car behind the baggage car. Some headed for the tunnel. The water was waist-high then. They were smart; they went on the side so that the wind was blocked by the train, so they made it."

Easton added, "By this time, the water was shoulder-high on the slope on which the train stood on the rails. Passengers were leaping in terror from windows, doors, and platforms into the water. The train crew yelled to them to get back into the train and forced all the passengers forward. We packed all the women and children we could into the engine. The rest of the passengers were packed into the front car."

Richards resumed, "I had heard the brakes go into emergency [which locked them]. A big timber hit the air hose and the whistle hose and that put them in emergency. I heard air escaping from the train, bubbling in the water. I saw the Oriental [the parlor car at the end of the seven-car train] tipped, as I pushed on through. We had to turn off the air to get pressure enough to move the train to high ground. Five minutes more, with the way the water was rising, and it would be impossible.

"Bill Donoghue was there and I said, 'We got to cut this train off,' and he said, 'I'm younger than you' and he jumped into the water. He had to turn off the air so we could build up air pressure to move. In water up to his chin, he turned the air off and pulled the pin [uncoupling the locomotive and first car from the remainder of the train]. I reached over and grabbed him as he come up on his belly on the vestibule." (One eyewitness described Donoghue as "finally emerging half-strangled, after prolonged submersion at the rear platform.")

Cooke said, "When Joe [Richards] started moving the passengers up front, he said to me, 'When we're ready, I'll tell you,' so we kept up the dining car, putting the tablecloths on and that sort of thing so that the passengers passing through wouldn't get panicky. Then Joe came in and he said, 'Get that little Irish ass of yours out of here!' The dining car was third from the last on the train. When we started to walk out, it had begun to tilt."

Richards added, "We had about a dozen in the dining car and two of them objected strenuously because they had paid for their meal and hadn't finished it. I said, 'Get out or I'll throw you out.'

"This will show you the force and the weight of the water against the train. As that tidal wave came, it was about ten feet above the roadbed. The weakest spot was on the trestle. When the trestle was hit, it weakened the spiles and tipped the cars over, and behind the last car, there were no rails, no ties, and no roadbed.

"When I first got off the train at that tennis court, the water was chest-high. The train blocked the wind for me. There was a garage with a Cadillac automobile in it. I noticed when the wind hit it, it shattered the garage to splinters. It raised the car thirty feet in the air and slammed it into hard dirt upright; it went into the ground past the hood.

"We had 252 passengers. About eighty got off the train because progress was slow in moving up to the head car, some didn't know how to open the doors, and others panicked when a boat hit the side of the train. It was a dragger and it hit three times, starting at the engine tank." ("It hit the dining car and scared the hell out of me," said Cooke.)

Richards continued, "I had about 160 people in the [head] coach on top of each other. I gave the engineer the signal. His firebox was cooled off in the water and he didn't have much fire. But he had steam enough to move the engine and the one car to a lumber yard, about 250 feet, to higher ground. We went ahead, against the signal."

In addition to the uprooted utility poles, which Easton's engine dragged along until the wires snapped, he found a house in his way, deposited on the tracks by the flood. He edged his locomotive gently up to the structure and nudged it slowly aside; as its sills cleared the rails, the house toppled over and vanished into deep water.

Many on the Bostonian were students returning to school; nearly two dozen were bound for the Fessenden School, and under the guidance of their faculty member, Roderick Hagenbuckle, these ten- to fourteen-year-olds aided each other and assisted others as well. One boy was swept away by the rush of water, but was quickly hauled to safety by Hagenbuckle. Other young men bound for Noble and Greenough and St. Mark's were described by passengers as very helpful.

Mrs. Auguste Richard of Hewlett, Long Island, and her daughter, Elvine, seventeen, a pupil at the Beaver Country Day School, were riding in a pullman car, one of the three that were left careening by the washed-out roadbed.

"After the train left New London, we became aware of danger," she said. "Trees had been felled along the route and as the train went over a causeway, we saw the water pounding angrily on both sides. The train trembled like a bicycle inexpertly ridden."

When the train was halted at Stonington, the passengers were informed that a 40-foot schooner was on the trestle ahead. Mrs. Richard and other passengers, sensing added danger, suggested that they all move to forward cars. She said the engineer advised the women to jump to safety.

"An elderly, well-dressed woman who stood beside me jumped into the swelling water," recalled Mrs. Richard, "and I saw her disappear. We threw our coats, hats, and purses into the water, then my daughter and I jumped. The wind churned the water into a whirlpool; there was a strong undertow. I think we had to swim about three hundred yards. Some of the time, water was over our heads, but occasionally, we were able to walk."

Her daughter was struck by a floating tree limb and fractured her leg as they swam away from the flooded cars; they were assisted in escaping by Stephen Glidden, sixteen, of Dover, a pupil at Noble and Greenough, and by Edward Brown, a student at the Massachusetts Institute of Technology, fellow passengers. Mrs. Richard said women and children "clustered like flies" on the engine as it moved toward high ground and that she saw Harry Easton rescue a woman and child and place them safely on the coal tender.

Edward M. Flanagan, chairman of the Providence Democratic City Committee, and Mrs. Flanagan were sitting in the diner. "We got as far as the trestle west of Stonington where the water was hurling boats and houses up against the side of the train. The roof of a house crashed into the side of the dining car. The train stopped where it was, right on the trestle, and everyone was ordered to go forward," Flanagan said.

"The people then began to grow panicky and even those in charge of the train appeared panicky. As the water began to beat against the train, we were ordered off. We walked the trestle up to the locomotive but could get no farther because of the rush of water. Passengers clung to the cables, engine wheels, and everything else they could get hold of. Some of them were finally swept away. I saw them go with my own eyes.

"My wife held onto me until a powerful Negro took charge of her and left me to take care of a little boy who was on his way to a private school in Massachusetts. I had never seen the boy before. Some of the women climbed into the locomotive. The boy and I hung onto the wheel of the locomotive. Finally, I was able to join my wife.

"When the storm began to abate, the engineer started the train after we climbed aboard. We reached the far side of the trestle, pushing boats, telegraph wires, and other debris ahead of us. When we reached Stonington, we got off the train and the people of the town opened their homes to us. . . ."

Mrs. Milton Smernoff of Brighton and her three-year-old son, Jerry, had boarded the train at New Haven. "The wind was blowing furiously and it was raining even then," she said. "The train held up in New London, but continued on with additional cars. Waves dashed against the train as we struggled along near the water and debris hammered at the sides of the cars. As windows began breaking, the conductor asked us to go over to the left side of the train to avoid injuries from flying glass and debris, which was hurtling into the car.

"Entering Mystic, water covered the tracks, and boats tossed onto the tracks with the fury of the storm bumped against the train. Passengers were asked to move into the forward cars as one of the rear ones was listing dangerously. The waves became so high that it looked as though we were about to ride under them rather than through or over them. More of the coaches began to tip as the hurricane lashed the water, and the engine slowed down gradually and finally stopped.

"The conductor ordered us to leave the train, to step into the three or four feet of water that engulfed us. Some jumped into the raging water and attempted to swim to shore; others waited fearfully, thinking it safer near the train. A man took my small son in his arms and we started to wade through the water, which nearly reached our waists.

"Biting spray lashed our faces and surging waves tugged at our legs. The man carrying Jerry fell into a hole and they both went down. An engineer noticed their plight and went to their rescue. It was a furious gale that swept over that exposed strip of railroad bed and some who attempted to get to shore lost their lives.

"As we came back into the cab of the train, I noticed the rear car tipping over. Trainmen detached the rear cars to save the rest of the train; all that was left was the engine, tender, and one coach. The engineer tried to start the train again, but debris blocked the way. A huge wave driven on by the gale swept the track clear and we moved slowly for a few hundred feet and stopped again. This time, we were all told to leave. Since we were only about fifty feet from shore, we made it safely into Stonington. I lost all my baggage, but I saw too much to mind a little thing like that."

Conductor Richards said, "I stayed with those people on the vestibule [of the coach that was hauled to high ground] until the wind died down. I had the dining car crew with me. I asked, would they walk out with me and get what supplies we could from the dining car to relieve the passengers. So Johnny [Cooke] and the dining car crew volunteered to go back with me. We saw the rear parlor car, the 'Oriental,' was tipped on its side on the trestle; the car was full of water and the windows were smashed. I found a carton of brandy on the train to take back to the people."

"It was Martell's," said Cooke.

"I found Chester Walker under the weeds," said Richards, "when the water receded at that point. And there were two big vessels on the highway."

Cooke and his crew succeeded in getting a fire going in the dining car and made five gallons of coffee and a hundred sandwiches. They started back to the coach full of passengers.

"Just before we got to the high ground," said Richards, "this fellow Nicholas Pridges [a member of the dining car crew] had hold of a bag of emergency food over his shoulder and he stepped in a hole. I was behind him. It was just getting dusk when he went down. He hollered and he had this tablecloth full of stuff, but he never let go of it. I got under his armpits and he came up. We got back to the coach and my shoes were white with salt, my pants were ripped. We passed the booze around in the car.

"If we'd been five minutes later in turning off the air to get pressure enough to move the train to high ground, it would have been impossible to do it. And if we'd stayed where we were fifteen minutes longer, a good many of those people would have been drowned. A lot of lives would have been lost. I guess the whole operation, from the time we stopped for the signal and I went back to the rear end, until we got the one car to high ground took about twenty-five minutes."

Most of the passengers eventually straggled into Stonington in a body and went to the Town Hall. Stonington was equal to the situation.

Selectmen Ralph P. Wheeler, Elvin B. Byers, and John J. Donohue, Town Clerk Fred J. Moll, Tax Collector Joseph Law, Assistant Town Clerk Ann Ward, social worker Mary Shannon, and just about every occupant of the town hall offices turned to to aid the refugees. James Lynch, the town hall caretaker, went below to start the furnace, and residents in the area made sandwiches and took several of the stranded passengers into their homes.

The Westerly *Sun* reported that "emergency measures were used in securing coffee, cans of meat, and bread and soda from the Cutler Street A & P store." Conductor Richards elaborated, "When I went walking uptown, I met about fifteen men [who were among the passengers]. They had broken into a store. They kicked the door down and took canned groceries to the church."

The church was St. Mary's and the pastor was the Reverend Patrick J. Mahoney. "We hugged each other," said Cooke; "I had been his altar boy." Father Mahoney ordered St. Mary's Hall opened as a refuge for the passengers and accommodations also were set up there to feed them. A hundred blankets stored in the hall for distribution to the needy were given to the elderly members of the group. And so they were fed, and given a place to sleep — some sleeping on floors, some on benches and some even on the stage in the Town Hall.

Eventually, town officials, Stonington residents, and Father Mahoney were showered with telegrams and letters of thanks from the grateful. One said, "We would all have died from exposure had it not been for the generosity and timely aid of your town officials and kindly citizens," and John O. Dozier of St. Louis, Missouri, another of the passengers, commented, "When the train was finally abandoned, I joined other men in a mad scramble along the tracks, fighting the gale and water and expecting every minute to be swept off. When I reached the Town Hall, I thanked God for helping us. And I thanked Him again for giving us such men as your Mr. Wheeler, Mr. Moll and others to care for us."

Book IV

Rhode Island

Chapter 9

In New Bedford, by mid-afternoon of September 21, there were both the signs and sense of an inexorably deteriorating situation. Overhead, there was a torn and anxious quality about the sky as it marched, each hour more swiftly and more wetly, up from the south. In the tops of the most exposed trees, their branches still heavy with green, thousands of leaves turned inside out in the increasingly frequent gusts, pale undersides layered to windward and swaying wildly. Between sharp squalls, driven white and silver across the bay's dark waters, were intervals of uneasy quiet, less relieving than like a hammer suspended. I remember seeing a gray squirrel upside down on the trunk of an elm as big around as a barrel. The fur on his tail was blown all the wrong way. He twitched, scuttled, and smelled the wind. He was looking for something substantial to hole up in.

The city dripped and waited without knowing it. Above the great four-square stone buildings that knew Hetty Green's ancestors and the whaleman with a gold ring in one ear, buffeted gulls cried their anxiety, and a twisted thread of smoke from the galley stack of a lobsterman whipped flatly to leeward. The docks were puddled and the puddles rippled with wind. In the wharfinger's shack on Pier 3,

Old Man West opened the door a hair. "Gettin' dusty," he said, and closed it.

The weather smelled and felt increasingly uncommon. It brought a sense of apprehension as fundamental as that of the gray squirrel's. But New Bedford would have to wait.

Now it was Rhode Island's turn.

When it was over, the topography of the Atlantic seaboard from Watch Hill to Point Judith had been materially changed. Westerly and Charlestown alone had lost 659 homes, and the old Westerly High School building on Broad Street had been converted into a temporary morgue where the bodies — eventually, more than one hundred — were brought for identification. Part of what happened was described by residents of the Charlestown-by-the-Sea area as "a tidal wave, from sixty to seventy feet high, that came entirely without warning, coming over the beach and washing everything before it."

Watch Hill, on that Wednesday, was totally oblivious to danger. The late Charles F. Hammond, publisher of *Seaside Topics*, who was responsible for collecting and preserving invaluable first-person accounts of some of those who survived in this area, recalled, "The shops were open and many cottages still occupied by those who loved to stay into the fall. The morning had been mild and hazy, with a brisk breeze blowing. Many went bathing as usual and remarked how warm the water was. Mrs. John McKesson Camp was hostess at a luncheon on the rocks at Weekapaug and her guests gathered at about one o'clock and noticed only that the sea looked restless and spoke of a strange yellow light over it."

Deterioration of the weather thereafter was rapid; it was blowing wildly by 2 P.M. Some remarked on unusual pressure in the ears. Rain became torrential. Man-made things started to break.

"Forty-two persons were still in the houses on the Fort Road when the final act of the tragedy was reached," Hammond wrote. "Fifteen were killed, twenty-seven survived after their houses were

[158]

*A strip of sand, a few telephone poles were all that remained
at Fort Road, Watch Hill, Rhode Island.*

demolished by the monstrous seas and they were swept to the Connecticut shore. Thirty-nine cottages on the Fort Road were destroyed, in addition to the yacht club, beach club, and bathing
pavilion. The yacht club split in two, and a piano came flying
twenty feet into the air like a big bird."

Herbert Greenman was putting winter shutters on Mrs. Ridley
Watts's cottage when the storm broke. Trapped in the house as it
was being beaten to pieces by roaring breakers, he was saved only
by its complete disintegration, for the roof had settled on him,
breaking his ribs. Thrown into the bay, he saw a rag doll in a
bathtub, its legs rising and falling with the wind gusts. The sight
was so ludicrous that he shouted, "Old girl, if you can make it, I

can!" And he did. The doll was found next day and given to Mrs. Greenman because it inspired her husband to make the effort that saved his life. The Greenmans named it "Hurricane Sue."

In the Geoffrey Moore home at Watch Hill were Mr. and Mrs. Moore, their children, Geoffrey, twelve; Anne, ten; Cathy, eight, and Margaret, four; a relative, Miss May Doherty, and three family employees, Andy, Loretta, and Nancy. Immediately after lunch on the day of the hurricane, Mr. Moore became ill. He slumped in his chair and Mrs. Moore recalled, "He had a bad pain under his heart and his look frightened me. We got him into the living room and onto the davenport. I couldn't feel his pulse until I had given him a stimulant. I called a doctor."

The physician ordered rest in bed for three days and Mr. Moore went to bed. A short time thereafter, the hurricane was upon them; Mrs. Moore said that "tons of water were being hurled against the house" and she saw a nearby house blown over. She did not say anything, but the children had seen it, too, and they began to cry, saying that they did not want to die.

"I told them that they would not die," Mrs. Moore said, "but that they might have to swim. Margaret and Cathy still cried, and Margaret said that she didn't want to swim. I asked them if they didn't want some milk, to take their minds off what they had just seen. They refused, but I took a sip, and so did May. May knelt down and started the Rosary. I knelt, too, for a minute, and we all tried to respond, but I could not stay on my knees; there seemed to be too much to be watching out for."

Jim Nestor, eighteen, member of a neighboring family, arrived at the Moore house breathless and clad only in underwear. "Where are the rest of your family?" Mr. Moore asked, and Jim replied, "Gone." The Moores echoed, "Gone?" and then the full horror of what was happening struck them and they felt they had small hope of surviving.

Mr. Moore told everybody to stay together, no matter what happened. They decided to stand between the Green Room and the hall, hoping that the door casing would help in case the house came crashing down upon them. May prayed aloud as she clutched a picture of Christ. Cathy went to her mother and said, "Mummy, if I *must* die, I want my rosary." Mrs. Moore found a little blue rosary in her room across the hall and wound it around Cathy's wrist because it wouldn't fit over her head.

Cathy was quiet after that; Margaret, with her hand in her mother's, said nothing, and they stood there, awaiting the inevitable. Mrs. Moore recalled, "Loretta asked me if I didn't want my pocketbook, but I told her it didn't matter, material things just didn't count anymore. I told everybody to take off his shoes, in case we had to swim.

"Jeff [Mr. Moore] said good-bye to me, but I told him not to give up yet. I asked him to watch out for Cathy, Jim to watch out for May, and Andy to take care of Loretta and Nancy. I said I would take Margaret. Geoffrey and Anne, I knew, could take care of themselves better than any of us. I put coats and life preservers on Margaret and Cathy and one on May. I could find only three. I told everyone, particularly the girls, to grab onto some large floating object if they found themselves in the water.

"There was no panic. We all prayed constantly, sometimes silently and sometimes aloud. We just waited for the next move that would decide our fate. Suddenly, the house began to collapse beneath us. We ran, together, and like lightning, down the hall and up the stairs to the third floor — and just in time; the second floor had gone down like an elevator, only with a sideways motion."

They gripped the third-floor stair railing for support. At the foot of the stairs, there was ocean where the girls' room had been and some pink curtains washed out of the linen closet. They could see pieces of the seawall and foundation being hurled about below them; Andy called out for them to keep away from the stairway because that would go next.

The cruel fact was that they were trapped. Overhead, there was a V-shaped roof and they had nothing with which to break through it. At each end, there were windows; when they were shattered, the place would be flooded. Beneath them, the floor threatened to give way at any moment. Anne said, "Now say it, Margaret, say it after me, 'Oh my God, I am heartily sorry.' "

"I am heartily sorry," said Margaret.

"For having offended Thee," said Anne.

"For having offended Thee," said Margaret; and so they continued, through the Act of Contrition, and the adults, observing the children facing death so gallantly, were inspired to keep up their own courage.

They finally decided to make a break for it. Mr. Moore smashed the bathroom window and a torrent of water poured through the jagged hole. Anne said, "Shall I go, Daddy?" and he replied, "Don't go, Anne." Just at that moment, the roof blew off the maid's room nearest them and they made for it; it was the best raft in sight, with two iron pipes sticking up through the floor to hold onto. Mrs. Moore grabbed one pipe, sitting down and holding Cathy. Mr. Moore sat with his leg around the other pipe, taking Margaret in his arms. Cathy held his other knee. May sat between Mr. and Mrs. Moore, holding his arm, and Anne held onto him from the back. Geoffrey and Andy sat in front of Mrs. Moore, and Loretta, Jim, and Nancy clung to those who had something to hold onto and to the floor.

"The huge waves washed over us," said Mrs. Moore, "and we had to cling for dear life. The prayers never stopped. May continued aloud; the children didn't say a word. As we were the last house to go, there was nothing around us but our own wreckage, and by the size of the waves that broke over us, we thought we were headed for mid-ocean. A part of the house stayed with us, and we watched between waves the furniture wash out of the cook's room. I kept my eye on the mattress of one of the beds, thinking if we were washed off the raft, I would try to put Margaret on that and she would float all right. Geoffrey said he saw sharks following us. The wall of the cook's room acted like a sail for us and helped speed us along."

After a while, Mr. Moore saw telephone poles in back of them and realized they were in the bay, which was good news. Mostly, the waves were not breaking over them anymore, although they washed wreckage up on the raft, which Andy and Geoffrey kicked off. They passed the Dennison Rock buoy — that meant they were more than halfway across the bay — and from somewhere within the roof peak of the house, they heard the family parrot (which Loretta had let out of her cage when they fled to the third floor) say, "Hello, Polly."

The floor was beginning to buckle. "I wouldn't have given two cents for my chances of swimming ten yards in that water," said Mrs. Moore, but land showed up in the hazy distance. As they got closer, it proved to be Barn Island; their raft swung into a cove and finally was close enough to a shore covered with wreckage for them to jump off. Shoeless, they stumbled through bull briars and blackberry vines. Beside a stonewall, they found the remains of an old barn which had collapsed with hay in it; the haystack and the wall provided some protection from the wind that was still bending trees to the ground.

The light was fading fast and they were very cold. Andy and Jim went to see if there was a chance of getting off the island, for normally there was a narrow strip of shallow water on the north side. But they found only a torrent at least a hundred and fifty yards across. They were marooned.

"We decided to settle down for the night," said Mrs. Moore. They scooped out hollow places in the haystack and pulled down hunks of the briary, scratchy stuff to cover themselves as well as they could. Mr. Moore, already blue with cold because his woolen shirt had shrunk so that it no longer covered him, stayed up to act as lookout. On one of his trips to the top of the haystack, he saw flashlights on nearby Osbrook Point, which cheered them briefly

[163]

but although they called and called, no one replied, and finally the lights disappeared.

"The stars came out and the wind died down," said Mrs. Moore. "We could only watch the sky and listen for the sound of a motor and stamp our feet to try to keep them warm. We thought we did hear a motor and I acted as cheerleader and led two long 'Helloooos.' We heard an airplane go over but couldn't see it.

"We called out intermittently all night long. Of course we did not know that the catastrophe was so far-reaching. We thought that only the Fort Road had gone. We saw the reflection of a fire in the sky and thought it must be in Stonington, but it turned out later to have been New London. As the night wore on, I became certain that some of us, perhaps all of us, would have pneumonia. I couldn't see how anyone could be so cold and not have serious results.

"It seemed ages before we could be sure that the stars were really fading and the sky was taking on the uncertain appearance that precedes the dawn. Large black clouds appeared at intervals, sending down a deathlike chill among us and making me fear another hurricane. There must have been at least ten of these clouds, until it seemed to me we were so cold it would be humanly impossible to survive.

"The sun came up, and Jeff and Geoffrey started to walk around the island, a slow and painful procedure because of thorns and wreckage. The rest of us got up and exercised a little, laughing to see that we were all covered with dirt from the hay and our eyes and teeth stood out from the blackness of our faces. Our wet clothes looked as if they had been through a mud puddle. The children were much amused and said, 'Look at Mummy; she is always so clean, but now she is the dirtiest one of us all!'

"Geoffrey found a mirror in the wreckage and sent signals with it, as the sun was now shining brightly. It wasn't long before a shout went up that a boat had been sighted. It was Mr. Scott, who had come up in his fishing boat from Avondale to look for us. We picked

[164]

our way quickly down to the shore and waved wildly to him. He sent a rowboat in for us, and it took three trips to get the eleven of us to his boat. He and his helpers gave us their windbreakers and sent us down into the cabin, where the warmth from the engine seemed heavenly."

As they soon observed, a strip of sand and a few telephone poles were all that remained to mark the place that had been known as the Fort Road; everything that had meant so much to them over the years was gone. Incredibly, not one of the Moore family was ill as a result of the experience; no one had so much as a cold.

In retrospect, Mrs. Moore observed, "During the whole thing, no one lost his head. We were all calm. The first thing we did when we reached the haystack was to thank God, who in such a miraculous manner had saved our lives.

"We were all most uncomfortable during that endless night, but no one complained. The children were marvelous. They had had no supper and when Margaret woke in the morning — she and Cathy had slept a little — she asked what we were going to have for breakfast. When I said she would have to help herself to a little hay, she only laughed and was very cheerful about the whole thing.

"I sometimes feel that we have had a preview of the end of the world. We certainly saw how easily it could happen and in such a short time. For some, it was the end of their earthly existence; it might easily have been for us. We experienced every sensation except that of actually leaving this world, but that was not in the pattern of our lives. We shall never forget the feeling of helplessness, in the face of the elements let loose. We who have been through this hurricane, I am sure, have gained a deeper, richer, more complete outlook on life than we ever could have otherwise."

At Misquamicut, the hurricane spent itself in swift death and desolation. Hundreds of cottages were smashed and their lumber piled up in neat windrows like wheat in a newly mown field.

The speed at which disaster struck was breathtaking. One young man loaded his family into the car just before the tidal wave struck their summer place and headed up Winnapaug Road. He kept the car moving as fast as he could. The wave, an estimated twenty feet high, tossing telephone poles and houses before it, was less than a stone's throw behind the automobile. He went forty miles an hour, with the wave still gaining, creeping nearer the car every second. At fifty miles an hour, the foam-topped, curling wave was moving closer. At fifty-five, as the higher ground was approached, the vehicle managed to hold its own, although the water was no more than a few feet from the rear tires. Finally, the car and its occupants reached the Shore Road and safety — at a mile-a-minute clip.

Some who might have been expected to survive did not; some who might have been expected to die did not. A dozen women from Westerly's Christ Episcopal Church were having a picnic at the Lowry cottage, Misquamicut; Mrs. David Lowry was a member of the group. Just before the storm broke in full force, they moved to the cottage of William D. Wells for safety. It was washed away and all the women perished. Their pastor, the Reverend G. Edgar Tobin, had to leave the picnic early to attend a funeral; it probably saved his life.

In the same area, two babies, each about a year old, were placed on floating wreckage by their parents, who stayed with them, holding them fast as the wind blew flying fragments of boats and houses past them. Both infants safely crossed the turbulent inland sea that was normally Brightman's Pond; one had breathed in a great deal of water, but emerged fine after brief hospitalization, and the other did not have so much as a sniffle.

Assistant Fire Chief E. L. Reynolds, a Misquamicut real estate dealer, said, "It started from the east and suddenly shifted to the south and sent a tremendous wall of water over the beach. I didn't have five minutes' chance to get into my car. People on the beach were laughing and joking, trying to put up shutters and fasten windows to keep curtains from getting wet. They thought it was lots of fun. Then suddenly, before anybody knew what happened, their homes were under twenty to thirty feet of water. Some of the houses just blew up like feathers. I saw one leap seventy-five feet into the air and collapse before it hit the water.

"I succeeded in rescuing six persons, including my father, who is seventy-five years old. Then the wind picked me up like a balloon. I was forced under the waves. Scores of cottages, meanwhile, were carried over the shore to Brightman's Pond. Later, we found twelve bodies in that pond. Debris went over land and pond and wound up over there by the state highway, almost two miles away."

Alfred H. Chapman, a nationally known trapshooting expert, his mother, and four other women narrowly escaped drowning when they were caught in an automobile near Weekapaug. After his own car stalled, the Chapman party, including Mrs. Mary Chapman, Mrs. Noyes Main, and Miss Betty Hoxsie, were offered a ride by Mrs. Louise Vardilos. "We proceeded along Atlantic Avenue until her car also stalled," Chapman said. "The wind was blowing harder and the water was rising steadily. A large section of a roof struck the car and turned it around, jamming the doors on the left side.

"I let the older women out and they got to the driveway of a nearby cottage. They hung onto fallen telephone cables and several times were almost blown loose. In the meantime, Miss Hoxsie and I crawled out of the rear window of the car and grabbed some swinging telephone cable. We swung hand over hand along eight lengths of cable connecting poles— Miss Hoxsie became tired and I carried her on my shoulders — until we reached a high pole above water." Chapman and Miss Hoxsie perched on the top crossbeams of that pole for more than seven hours waiting for the water to recede; at one in the morning, they were finally able to join the other women, who had spent the night in blankets on the cottage terrace.

Joseph T. Grills was the proprietor of the Oak Inn at Misquamicut. "I was sitting in the front room when four boys came in from the golf course to escape the wind and rain. They parked their car beside the big barn in the rear. All of a sudden, there was a terrific blow," he recalled. "The house shook like a person with the ague and two minutes after it hit, the barn caved in.

"Lou Collins and Tex Ledwidge were the next visitors. They had waded in from the shorefront and were exhausted. While I was getting coffee for them, Joe Christie of North Stonington stumbled in and fainted in the middle of the floor. I gave him a shot of brandy and he got down on his knees and started to pray.

"Then I happened to think of my pony in the barn. So we all went out to rescue him. While we were putting on his bridle and trying to get him out from under the wreckage, the roof blew off the inn. None of us realized how bad it really was until we saw the houses floating over the sandbar across the pond and breaking up in the meadows.

"I waded out to the first floating house in the darkness and who do you think was in it? My own brother, Henry, his wife, and three children. We dragged them all to safety, then Tex, Joe, and I started to go from house to house. Tex put a rope around his waist and tried to rescue Mrs. Kate Main. She was leaning out of the top story of her home, which was coming in fast. Tex grabbed her hand and tried to pull her out of the window. She said her foot was caught inside. He pulled again, to try to get her foot free, but a big wave caught her house, rolled it over, and it fell to pieces, and she went down with it. We yanked him back to the roof we were on."

Sylvester Regucci was a handyman at Misquamicut; when it began to breeze, he secured some boats that were lying at the dock. Then he went home to join his wife; they were both fifty-five, and they lived in a two-story house at 10 Winnapaug Road, about seventy-five feet from the ocean front.

During much of the storm, they were in water up to their necks, but they thought their house would hold, even though they saw all the others going. It was, in fact, the last to go; at about 3 in the afternoon, just when they thought they were going to make it, a big house came floating by and bumped theirs off its foundation. Standing in the water inside their home, they grasped a small statue, a replica of the gold Notre Dame de la Garde that stands at the harbor of Marseilles, and prayed.

The sea ripped away the first story of the house and flung the second story, with them (and their two dogs, Teddy and Lucky) in it, a mile back from the shore. The building landed along the shore road and Mr. and Mrs. Regucci were the only ones found alive in any house struck by the storm along Westerly's eight-mile beach front. Seachers pulled out crushed bodies of storm victims within fifty feet of their newly located home. The only family casualty was Teddy; he survived the hurricane, but died of exposure. "When we prayed, the water went down," said Mr. Regucci. "It was the prayers that saved us."

When they finally touched bottom, watchers along the road shouted to them and they waded ashore, where their milkman found them, and gave them refuge for the night. Later, returning to their wrecked house, they discovered looters had stolen $250 from a bureau drawer, but Mr. Regucci said, "At least we are alive."

His brother, Edward, who found shelter with them in what was left of their home, was owner of Misquamicut's Roseland Inn. "I haven't been able to find a shingle of my inn, but I found my dog alive even though he was shut in the inn when the storm hit," he said.

And James Hamilton, struggling through the remains of the storm-struck houses in search of a missing ten-year-old boy, found first a toy drum and then, not far away, the body of the boy.

The Weekapaug Inn was located thirty feet from the ocean shore. William Wheeler, forty-nine, watchman; Leon W. Bliven, sixty-four, carpenter, and Edward E. Billings, forty, plumber, were closing the inn for the season on September 21. As the weather deteriorated, Mrs. Ella O. Rewick, forty-one, who lived nearby, went to the inn for shelter and a short time later, Lawrence C. Miller, fifty-one, a retired farmer, also made his way to the building.

When the storm seas rolled across the beach, Billings, trying to get to higher ground, walked seventy-five feet from the inn, was blown off his feet into water already a couple of feet deep, and clung to a pole. His legs were badly bruised and he was suffering from shock. Miller succeeded in getting him back to the inn.

The water rose twelve feet above normal high tide at about 6 P.M. The basement of the inn was flooded, and its southeast and southwest sections were wrecked. The storm cut a channel connecting the ocean and Quonochontaug Pond, which isolated the inn. Those in the damaged building were surrounded by knee-deep water; they knew that high tide was due at 4 to 5 in the morning, and they feared a return of the storm and the collapse of the remainder of the inn.

For four hours on the evening of the storm, Henry M. Morris, twenty-seven, a five-foot-six, 170-pound carpenter who was a senior Red Cross lifeguard, with others had been aiding hurricane victims in an area a mile from the inn. With Morris was his nineteen-year-old brother, William; Patrolman Arthur Kingsley and Lieutenant George Madison of the Westerly police; Walter Marshall, Edward Green, and two brothers named Clark.

At 1 in the morning of September twenty-second, this group was standing on the road leading to Weekapaug Beach from the Shore Road. They observed a candle flickering weakly in one of the inn windows and ran toward it, discovering that the storm-cut channel and another similar breachway of surging water east of the inn had left the shattered building on an island.

The west breachway, on whose western bank they stood, was seventy-five feet wide; wadable water in the channel extended four feet from each bank, and elsewhere in the channel, the depths ranged from eight to ten feet. The tide was falling, and in this channel there was a current toward the ocean of 8 to 10 miles an hour; scattered debris also was surging in the same direction. The wind was still blowing 25 miles an hour and visibility was poor, because of heavy mist.

Morris and the others walked to the channel bank; they had a couple of flashlights and they attracted the attention of the group within the inn, all of whom came to the east bank; they were frantic and shouting in desperation to be rescued.

Kingsley, a former seaman, who engineered the rescue, said, "We called a huddle. We tossed a mattress in the channel to see its strength. The mattress disappeared the second it touched the water. We decided that was no place for a boat."

Morris, although fatigued from previous exertion during the evening, offered to swim across. He removed his clothing, except his trousers and jacket. "We got a rope that was just barely long enough to reach across," said Kingsley, and they tied a loop of it loosely around Morris's chest, with a life preserver at his back. Kingsley instructed him that if the rope should break or those on the bank should lose their grips, he should get hold of anything he could and that if he should drift to the ocean, he must swim east or west in an effort to find a rock to which he could cling.

Morris entered the channel and started swimming southeast as hard as he could. Because of the current and mishandling of the rope, he was pulled under the surface of the water briefly after he had gone thirty feet. He was then hauled back to the west bank, where he removed his jacket. Entering the water again, he struck out for the east bank; the group on the west shore payed out line and walked slowly south, keeping abreast of him; because of the strong set of the current, he had to swim considerably more than a hundred feet before he reached the east bank.

The rope then was tied around Miller's chest also, two feet ahead of Morris. The two walked fifty or sixty feet north to allow for the current and entered the water; as the group on the west bank hauled on the rope, Morris and Miller drifted southwesterly, Miller holding to the rope with both hands and Morris holding with one hand and stroking with his free arm and his legs to preserve his balance. They were pulled to the west bank after having drifted southerly about thirty-five feet during the crossing. Morris was aided to the bank; he removed his trousers, which had hampered him, re-entered the water, and once more swam and drifted across to the east bank, while those on the west side payed out the line to which he was attached.

In this fashion, Morris aided Wheeler, Mrs. Rewick, Bliven, and Billings in getting to the west side of the channel. While rescuing Bliven, who was hampered by his hip-length rubber boots, Morris was submerged briefly, and at the conclusion of the fourth trip, he said he was very tired. Kingsley offered to make the last trip, but Morris said he was better able, because of his weight and experience. After the fifth and final trip across, Morris was so exhausted that he had to be hauled out of the water; his shoulder had been struck and bruised by flotsam, and he was assisted to an automobile and taken to the hospital, where he remained until the following day.

Although declining to discuss the affair (Morris said afterward, yelling down from a roof he was working on in Bradford, "It was to be done and I just did it; that's all. See the other fellows"), he did concede that on the last trip he forced himself to act and that his greatest anxiety was that the rope might break with the double weight. The "other fellows" who hauled on the rope, as well as those who were rescued, were unanimous in their view that Morris accomplished the feat at great risk of life, and one of the policemen, commenting on the endurance required, especially because of the cold and cutting wind, said he would not have attempted it. Morris was awarded a Carnegie Medal for Heroism.

In Westerly, it was some hours after the storm before the extent of the tragedy and destruction in the nearby shore resorts was learned, piecemeal. Survivors told of a tidal wave forty feet high that mounted from the ocean, struck broadside against the houses and swept them from their foundations. Louis J. Rossi, Town Engineer, brought back some of the first definite reports from Misquamicut; houses from the beach, he said, were piled up in the fields.

Because of fallen trees across the roads, it was impossible for nearly two hours after the hurricane's height to get to the beaches, but as soon as relief workers did get there — the wind was still blowing freshly — they began to find bodies among the acres of litter. At daybreak, the proportions of the catastrophe were first realized; Misquamicut had been wiped out. Only a desolate space remained, broken by what was left of the Atlantic Beach Casino, the Wigwam Hotel, the Pleasant View House, and a handful of other damaged structures.

As scores of the dead were taken to the temporary morgue in the Westerly High School, state police got in touch with Leo R. McAloon of the State Embalming Board by radio, the only communication available. He appealed to James Heffernan, president of the Rhode Island Funeral Directors Association, who rounded up two emergency crews. The first crew of ten, including McAloon, a Pawtucket undertaker, worked by day; they were relieved at night by a team of five organized by Heffernan. As soon as the bodies at the high school were identified, they were taken to funeral homes for embalming.

This is how the morgue looked to a resident of Westerly:

"Where once gay, laughing students prepared themselves for their life's work, dazed, weary relatives look over row upon row of white-sheeted bodies for signs of their loved ones. The old Westerly High School, only a few months ago the cradle of education, is now a huge coffin of death; it is the morgue.

" 'Where is the morgue?' You can hardly take a step down the street in Westerly's business section without being asked that question by some anxious friend or relative. You point to the high school.

"It is strange that school buses used to drive up the long concrete drive to the vine-covered building and now hearses are going in and out of the yard. A few are forced to wait while they remove their gruesome load, smashed bodies of mothers, fathers, sons and daughters.

"Inside, Coroner Herbert Rathbun, bearded after long hours of toil, affixes tags to those identified. Some, you can't identify. The same sea gulls that point out to searchers the location of bodies have pecked at them until they are unrecognizable. Those identified are taken away.

"Westerly's five undertakers long since have run out of embalming fluid; more has been rushed from Providence. The toll of death will run up to more than one hundred, but people display a marvelous type of courage. Sometimes you have to rush to support a tottering husband who has just lifted a sheet to find the black and blue remains of his wife. But mostly, people just stare. No tears, just stares."

William A. Cawley, reporter for the Westerly *Sun* (which staggered into print on September 23 with 5,000 copies printed on a hand-fed press after its plant was flooded and its power lines and pressroom motors crippled) finally was able to write the story in New Haven on that date.

"I reached the outside world today after witnessing the scenes of horror and desolation that came in the hours after a tidal wave hurled miles inland by a hurricane engulfed Westerly, Rhode Island, my home town," Cawley reported.

"When I left at four o'clock this morning, there were seventy-four dead and almost one hundred missing. At Misquamicut Beach, where ordinary people from all New England come to spend their summers, all that was left of a colony of almost five hundred homes, stores and markets were the gaunt skeletons of five cottages. I saw summer playgrounds of rich and workingmen alike turned into debris and heard the cries of friends and neighbors struggling on the rooftops of homes swept out to sea. Some I later counted among the rows of dead; others I never expect to see alive again.

"There were heroes among them. Alvin Mawson (twenty-three years earlier an outstanding baseball and football player at Stonington High School), one of my closest friends, dashed into the turbulent waters from safety on shore to reach his wife, trapped in their home on the ocean front. Alvin's body was found yesterday; his wife is still missing.

"My prayer was among others that went up from a band on shore for Ralph Bliven as he held precariously to a flimsy raft with one hand and clutched his eight-month-old baby with the other. I heard his cry of anguish as his mother and sister were dashed from the same flimsy raft, as he was helpless to save them. He and the baby were saved. . . . '

The nation first knew the tragedy that had befallen the Westerly area because of Wilson E. Burgess and George "Bill" Marshall, two amateur radio operators.

Telephone and electric service were inoperative, trains were halted, and highways blocked. Burgess, clerk in a local store, recalled, "When the power failed, I was still at work and, thinking there might be some use for the machine [his radio equipment], I gathered together a bunch of dry cells and a large storage battery and other bits of equipment.

"I ran into Bill Marshall, another ham, at the police station, and together we carried the equipment up Granite Street hill against the storm to my home. We were able to borrow a South County truck to carry some of the equipment, but that only got halfway home before the way was blocked.

"We managed to rig up a haywire aerial in the storm and finished this job just about dusk. Since we had no power off the street lines, we had to practically rebuild the set for the dry cells and storage battery power. Marshall returned to his home and picked up parts of his set to substitute and we finished putting the thing together

[175]

in the dark with candles. Then, under low power, we sent out our QRRR distress signal by code."*

The Westerly *Sun* reported, "The two Westerly youths completed the job of wiring and putting gadgets together and then the machine began to crackle and spit sparks out into the murky atmosphere. Out through the ether went shooting for all listeners that dreaded signal — QRRR, a pause and then again, QRRR, the dots and dashes informing the world for the first time that the worst disaster in its history had struck this town. . . .

"It was picked up by another ham in New Jersey and he in turn hooked them up with Hartford, headquarters of the American Radio Relay League. Thus was started the chain of messages which brought relief and rescue workers by the hundreds into this stricken town. . . ."

One of the first messages was to national headquarters of the American Red Cross. Burgess said, "They didn't believe us at first in Washington, but we made them realize what we were talking about. . . ."

The two youths became the official means of communication for the Red Cross and this was the beginning of a fifty-six-hour vigil for them; they stayed by their machine for two and a half days, sending out more than 1,100 messages. Some were calls for assistance — funds, food, clothing, volunteers, medical supplies — some were to notify friends and relatives of death, injury, or miraculous survival; others were to ask for the National Guard, or for more undertakers, or more embalming fluid.

It was Burgess who sent the first newspaper story out of Westerly after the hurricane, an account written by four Providence *Journal* reporters. The dispatch went initially to an amateur operator in Chevy Chase, Maryland, then to the Associated Press in Washing-

---

* QRRR, not in the International Code of Signals, was the official land SOS call, for emergency use only, of the American Radio Relay League, West Hartford, Connecticut.

ton, next to Woonsocket via the AP, and it was taken from there to Providence over the highway.

Burgess was given the Paley Award, the highest honor possible for an amateur operator, for his extraordinary public service.

As was the case everywhere the storm struck, the blow to the farmers was a bitter one. Lafayette F. Main, whose Starlight Farms were in North Stonington, wrote to Westerly: "I suppose you would like to know how things are up here. All my beautiful orchards are ruined. What is not blown out by the roots is ruined. It blew down two barns and unroofed the other buildings. All the blinds on the house are gone and several windows and piazzas and part of the forest is leveled. Elm trees as large as barrels are all up by the roots. And two small children got in just in time or they would have been killed.

"Edna, who attends Norwich Free Academy, did not come home, and I hope and pray she is safe. It is too bad after all the hard years' work to lose all in a few minutes. If you could see the mess, you would shed tears. Everything is gone."

George Durfee, the lighthouse keeper at Latimer's Reef, finally got to Westerly on September 30 and told what it was like out there on the pile of rocks in the middle of Fishers Island Sound.

Durfee was out there with his first assistant, George Doig, and they had no warning of the approach of the storm, because they had no contact with the mainland. When it first began to look like a good blow, however, Durfee went outside the 58-foot structure and secured their two 14-foot boats (their only means of getting ashore) and other equipment, as well as he could. It was a futile gesture. The water rose 30 feet above the high-water mark and carried away the boats, the storage shed on the dock, which contained reserve supplies, and even moved rocks that provided a foundation for the building.

The light shuddered and shook with the impact of seas that

were at times 30 feet high. These waves picked up boulders that Durfee estimated must have weighed at least ten tons; every time one hit, the keepers thought the end had come. The storm door on the top of the building blew away and the heavy steel shed for collecting drinking water was carried off. Many of the steel plates struck the building, cutting deep gashes in the masonry as they were blown away. But the masonry held.

On the first floor, the kitchen was flooded and everything in it went afloat. On the windward side, the window was carried away by the storm, so Durfee opened the window on the leeward side and allowed much of the water that poured in to pour out. As it did, however, the sea carried off the kitchen table (which was smashed to splinters), parts of the stove, and large quantities of supplies.

Through it all, the keepers kept the bell going from 2 to 6 that afternoon and had the light functioning perfectly through Wednesday night, although at midnight they had to clean the mercury on which the light floated because shaking of the building had caused oil to leak down onto the mercury surface.

Despite their ordeal, Durfee and Doig did not realize the extent of the storm until the next morning when they trained their glasses on Napatree Point and the adjacent coastline and found them wiped clean.

The Westerly Sun, its columns still reflecting the shock of its readers, nevertheless noted that "there was general complaint that the Weather Bureau failed to give advance notice of the storm, but this is partly untrue. For in Tuesday's papers, the hurricane sweeping up toward the Florida coast was featured, with the prediction that the whole Atlantic seaboard might be affected, should there be a change in the wind. In fact, several local schoolchildren told their teachers on Wednesday morning that a hurricane was on the way and they were curtly told to 'sit down and forget that foolish talk' as reward for their pains. The teachers, like everyone else, felt 'it can't happen here.' "

The massive changes in the landscape, in numerous instances, restoring beach and water to relationships that had existed many years before, moved Amy Lee Spencer to write a poem called "Sea Flood," in which she took note of "the strange new salt ponds formed after the storm in Rhode Island. . . ."

> *Across ten thousand years, they seek their own*
> *The unforgetting, long quiescent seas*
> *The rose that reddened where salt grass had grown*
> *Man's puny tenure in the roots of trees*
> *Inexorably, relentlessly denied*
> *Before the awful memory of the tide.*
> *Oh never think that waters will forget*
> *A refuge where they fled the hurricane*
> *Stanch up, pave over, block their path and yet*
> *Their storm need finds the hidden place again*
> *Through long-lost channels to a vanished bay*
> *Past death and shipwreck, they will find their way.*

And finally, William A. Batchelor of Woonsocket, former police commissioner of that city, was alive because he refused to obey the doctor's orders. The physician warned Mr. Batchelor that his health would not permit him to make the trip from his summer cottage at Misquamicut to his home on Oakley Road in Woonsocket. Mr. Batchelor decided that his guess was as good as the doctor's, so he went home to Woonsocket on Tuesday, September 20, and felt no worse for the trip. On the following day, his cottage was swept out to sea.

Chapter 10

HOWARD C. BARBER, Class of 1899 of Brown University, was a native of Rhode Island, born in Hope Valley; in 1938, he was a resident of New York, where he was a home relief investigator. He had a summer home at Charlestown, to which he had been coming seasonally for more than a quarter-century. On the day of the hurricane, he was there with his wife, Mabel, and two friends of long standing, Mrs. Sarah E. Stearns, seventy-three, and her daughter, Miss Pauline Stearns, fifty-one, both of New York.

"We were not particularly looking at what was happening," Mr. Barber said, "although we knew it was flood tide and thought it was time for it to recede.

"I looked out of the window and saw the next-door house washed away and our steps go with it. I told my wife we better pack some bags and get out. My wife, a very determined and dependable woman, packed two bags and went out and sat in the car.

"I went upstairs and told Aunt Sadie [Mrs. Stearns] that we had better go. We came downstairs and Aunt Sadie and Polly [Miss Stearns] went into the kitchen and I stepped into the living room.

"Just then, the floor gave way and I plunged toward the cellar and was pinned by a piece of timber. Polly screamed and I told her,

'I'm pinned. I guess it's all over.' With each wave breaking over my head, I thought I was gone.

"I think the water must have accumulated on the floor, however, for another wave came along, the floor sank, and I was shot out as from a gun into Charlestown Pond. I grabbed a plank and then a telephone pole. I don't know how long I was there. My watch stopped at 5:10. I have found out since that my wife's watch stopped at five minutes of ten. I'd like to know whether she lived until that time or whether the watch kept right on running.

"Finally, I was on the grass on the other side of Charlestown Pond. I crawled a long distance and then dropped, exhausted and nearly frozen. Then I saw a little house nearby and managed to reach it. I found four matches in the house, built a fire with timber I found outside, stripped myself, and dried my clothing.

"My skin was torn from the top to the bottom of my face and hung right off [he also had a severe gash on his left leg] and I thought, 'I've got to get to the hospital.' After a long time, I went out and walked and crawled through rocks, brambles, and a barbed wire fence until I reached the Green Hill, Charlestown Road. There I was picked up by Harold W. James of Edgewood, who was an angel to me. He wanted to take me to the hospital, but I first must let them know at Charlestown that I was safe, so he drove me there and we told Ben Gavitt, and he took me to the hospital."

The same huge wave that freed Mr. Barber from the timber that pinned him swept all three women who were with him to their deaths. He said, shocked with sorrow, "I'm living on borrowed time. My escape was miraculous. If you find any other word to tell of it, let me know."

In the aftermath at Charlestown Beach, the survivors tried to adjust; they were numb and confused. A woman who lost her home said, "I don't see how anyone can ever build on this beach again." A man nearby was trudging drearily through the sand with a kettle cover and a handful of knives and forks which he had retrieved from the adjacent marshland. This was all that he had left to show for a $9,000 furnished home. But he said, "I have my wife and daughter. And I owe thanks to my daughter that both she and Ma were saved from death. About half past one, my daughter told her mother that she felt uneasy and thought they'd better start back to Providence. That uneasiness brought them to me safe and sound. I have thanked God for it a thousand times already."

Another said, "There came one walloping big wave out of nowhere. It appeared to tower over the highest building and we were washed for miles, it seemed, before the water subsided and let us down. It took only a few minutes to sweep the beach clean."

The Rhode Island fishing villages of Jerusalem and Galilee were devastated, despite the breakwater that was designed to protect them. Almost without exception, the long row of houses between the road and the shore opposite the public parking ground were destroyed, most of them so completely that hardly a sliver of wood remained. Nor was it possible to find the wreckage of them in the salt pond beyond. They had vanished as thoroughly as though nothing had ever been there. Only the beach and the stones remained, with here and there, pools of salt water. In many places, the road was buried beneath the storm-swept sand.

Fire Chief Walter E. Shannon of South Kingstown, one of those who helped in the rescue work during Wednesday night and early Thursday morning, estimated that of the approximately 150 houses in Galilee, 125 were destroyed and perhaps two dozen were worth repairing. Docks and fishing boats were wrecked and about 75 pleasure craft in Salt Pond, several of them luxurious cabin cruisers, were ruined.

Walter Smith, a fisherman, said, "I was in a shack over near the wharf and the wind came up and blew the sand against the windows. I told my wife we'd better go, so we went to the house we live in on the road here. It wasn't any time before the water was coming up over the road. I went out with some others and we took people off the roofs of their houses in a skiff. We took John

Hamilton's wife and her two daughters off their roof, and several others. Later, I walked up towards the Coast Guard station and the water was up to my neck, right on the road."

Three youths from Narragansett, Harold Woodmansee, Peter Laurie, and Herbert Whitman, went down to Galilee to help and found a skiff with no oars, which they pushed and pulled along the road. "We found everybody gathered in two houses, Fred Gamache's and Charlie Champlin's and there were a few in the lunchroom, The Galilean," Woodmansee said. "There must have been about seventy all together, men, women, and children, some sick and some old. We had to carry some of them on tables for stretchers, and some of them in chairs. We carried them up the road. The tide had gone down a little by then. We had flashlights, but they weren't much use."

Mrs. Irving W. Smith was proprietor of a store at Galilee. William Whalen, Peace Dale war veteran and a charter member of Washington County Veterans of Foreign Wars, went to her store at Sand Hill Cove at least twice in an effort to get her to leave for a place of safety. The last time he went, she continued to refuse; within minutes, the building was swept to destruction and Whalen — who would not leave her alone, even to save himself — was drowned with her. No trace of the store remained afterward.

Thomas Mann founded the fishing village of Galilee when he built his shack — the picturesqueness of which had attracted the attention of several artists — near the post where the men of Point Judith Life Saving Station ended their beach patrol. He was known as the "mayor of Galilee," not only because he was a pioneer there, but because his fellow fishermen often came to him in time of trouble.

In poor health in the fall of 1938, Mann became exhausted trying to save what little he could of his gear and when it became apparent that the area would be flooded, an effort was made to leave Galilee in his car. Twelve men piled into and onto the vehicle but the water came up so rapidly that the engine stalled before they could get away. They returned to Mann's house, which was quickly flooded, driving them all to the roof. There they spent the afternoon and early part of the night; Mann became so chilled, increasingly ill from exposure and fatigue, that he said, "I would have given one thousand dollars for a fire to get warm by."

After the tide had turned and the water began to recede, Charlie McKenna, the head of his fishing gang, came along in a dory in which he had his mother and others and took Tom to higher ground, from which he was carried to South County Hospital. Mann's home was broken into two sections; half was demolished and swept away; all of his buildings also were destroyed except for the big shed in which he stored the largest stock of seines at Galilee.

At Jerusalem, the veteran fisherman was Ernest "Skip" Streeter. It was about 1:30 Wednesday afternoon when Streeter cast off in a fifteen-foot open skiff with a motor, accompanied by his seventeen-year-old helper, Norman Butler, to go "scalloping up Salt Pond." They were about two miles up the pond when it began to breeze so hard that Skip decided to forget about scallops for the day and return to the dock.

But he soon discovered that he could not return. "We turned toward Captain Knowles Point when we saw that it was going to be too tough to make, but although I drove that engine for all it had, we couldn't make any headway. The wind was kicking us around something awful and we were shipping a lot of water," Streeter said.

They turned for the lee of Great Island and made it, but then the wind shifted to the southwest and they had to move or get wrecked on the beach. Then the motor went bad; the intake of the cooling system was clogged and it was running hot. They ran it anyway and Skip said, "The sea was pouring into the pond so fast that we ran over one spot where there used to be an island fifteen feet high. I fought to make it to Beach Island; the wind was coming stronger all the time and it was picking up spray and dashing it against our faces. The air was full of it and at times, you couldn't see a thing."

Then they did see something, just off to the right — a man clinging to a piece of wreckage. "I think it was Hubert Higgins," Streeter recalled. "He was moving around to stay on the wreckage and seemed to be turning over as it went along with the wind and water at a terrific rate of speed. I tried to go to him, but every time I had to turn the nose of the boat; we were nearly swamped and I had to give it up and run with the wind."

(Mr. and Mrs. Hubert Higgins and their son, Hubert, Jr., driven from their home at East Matunuck by flooding, tried to start their car, parked in the dunes back of the cottage. The motor was wet and would not respond. A truck came by, driven by Charles Alford, and the three got into it. Within minutes, a wave hit the truck and overturned it. The three members of the Higgins family held onto a telephone pole until a storm wave, described by survivors as "mountains high" tore them loose. The younger Mr. Higgins lost consciousness. When he came to, he was lying on the shore of Salt Pond, two miles away. He remembered nothing of the interval between. After the storm, a neighbor said, "The son did not see his parents again. I was in their home, which was completely turned around. Furniture had been thrown about, but in the icebox, there was a small glass in which were two little asters the senior Mr. Higgins had been keeping fresh for his coat lapel. And Mrs. Higgins' knitting lay on one of the beds. . . .")

Aboard Streeter's little boat, the seas were slamming over them in a series of steady blows and he wondered if they were going to make it. "The boy stood up once to get his coat around him and as he did, the wind caught him and had him on the way over when I grabbed him," he said.

Finally, they made the island; Streeter jammed the bow of the skiff under a big oak tree that had fallen near the edge of the water. They tied a line around the tree and then settled down in the bottom of the boat, which was half full of water, to escape the wind. In the beginning, they could see boats blowing across the pond, but then darkness came and they just lay there, waiting for the morning.

They got the motor patched up and started for home about 9 o'clock Thursday morning. So the oldtimers were vindicated in their judgment of Skip's ability to survive in a hurricane. He and Butler came chugging down the pond in the skiff. Streeter tied the boat to a spile and looked across the clean-swept sands where a lifetime of effort had been obliterated — discovering that he was back where he started when he first went down to the breachway to wrestle with the sea that finally ruined him. It was forty-five years before that he went into Salt Pond to get a mess of scallops for supper, and that was the beginning. Before the storm, there were six buildings in the $12,000 plant known as Skip's Dock, and tied up nearby were twenty-five skiffs which he rented to fishermen, and two power boats. On Thursday morning, there wasn't a thing left.

But he was able to talk about building a new dock, about going up the pond for more scallops. "After all, you can't drown an old cuss like me in Salt Pond. I know it too well . . . ," Skip said.

This is Rhode Island's South County in the storm's aftermath:

Rigid and silent, the survivors stand just apart as they watch the digging that, sooner or later, will yield the bodies of the missing whom they seek. Blood-red crosses on muslin fields of pure white, the flags of the American Red Cross, are raised in the pastures back of the shoreline; simultaneously, they delineate the stations of succor, the margins of disaster.

An army of thousands — Civilian Conservation Corps, WPA, and volunteers — sweats, crawls, wades, scrambles through scrub, marsh, sand, and wreckage in search of the dead. The dead are elusive. Some are under tons of fine sand, in some places five feet deeper, mile after mile, than it was before. Some lie on the pond bottoms. Men wading in hip boots or dragging from skiffs seek them out in the still-roiled waters. The roar of the bulldozer and the big cat tractors rips the cemetery quiet as the machines chew into chunks of roofs, sides of houses, bellies of smashed boats, lifting and shoving to see what — or who — is underneath.

At Cross Mills, the little white building that once was the village school now houses the bodies awaiting identification or burial. The schoolyard is jammed with automobiles; their occupants stand, watch, and wait. They have abandoned hope and are here seeking only to recover their dead. Sometimes they look toward the beach, a mile away, and probably do not even see its utter desolation.

In the east section of Charlestown Pond, the tops of automobiles are visible. The fields far back from the beach are strewn with weed and broken lumber; over there, they are recovering the body of a woman — it is covered, carried away, and the search goes on. Here, sitting in an automobile, is George Holgate, keeping a vigil near the causeway, hoping that his wife will be found. On the afternoon of the hurricane, she had gone to Charlestown with Mrs. Mabel Reynolds, who also lost her life. The two women had arrived from Wakefield — where Mrs. Reynolds had paid the taxes on her beach property — just before the storm wave.

At the bridge near the beach stands an elderly woman; her head is bowed and her face is wet with tears, but you cannot hear her cry because a searching tractor thunders close by. It is almost beyond belief that only hours ago, in these places, there were dunes venerable enough to be familiar, houses old enough to have outlived their builders, and little girls spending whole mornings making sand castles.

Along the shore road back of Misquamicut, the remains of houses are scattered deep on the shore of Brightman's Pond. Gangs of men comb the coves and fields for bodies; hundreds more are expected to join the search tomorrow, for nearly thirty dead are still missing. Babies' cribs and high chairs are thrown up into the grass; somewhere, lie the babies. At the side of the road above

Misquamicut, a woman sits in a blue kitchen chair, surrounded by household goods, broken and strewn, waiting, waiting. . . .

Sometimes there are strange turns.

Here, six men slosh across the salt marshes of ruined Galilee. They move slowly and in step because they are bearing a heavy burden, half the side of a shed, upon which, as on a bier, they carry the body of old Charlie Keville.

There is a short, unshorn black man, a state policeman with the three scarlet stripes of a sergeant upon his arm, a fisherman in a blue sweater full of holes, a young fellow wearing a knitted cap, a man in a tan jacket, and a hatless chap in a brown shirt. The marsh sucks at their feet as they walk through the bright sunlight with the body of the old man.

When they found the body, it had a life jacket strapped about it. But that had not helped Charlie. The six men removed the life jacket and wrapped the body in a blue blanket and tied the blanket with a rope.

All the time they are sloshing to the edge of the marsh, where the medical examiner is waiting, the wind keeps up a kind of lonely, remorseful music. But the sun shines as cheerfully as on any other good September day and it is already hard to remember that the waves that rolled into Galilee on Wednesday were half-sand, half-water, and crowned with dirty white.

The six men put the body into a truck and drive away with it through a sunlit nightmare. Up through the barren sand, a pipe protrudes. It once had something to do with a house. You cannot find the house because the mills of the sea ground it to splinters and the storm blew the splinters away. Only the pipe remains. Here are two shotguns, some potatoes, and a birdcage, lying on a half-buried porch.

The truck carrying Charlie Keville inches down the road where he walked yesterday. Then, the road had been clear. Later, it had been covered with water up to his neck. He had stumbled along and drowned, despite his life jacket. Now, the ocean has gone back, leaving the road hidden under sand. Telephone poles, which yesterday paraded reassuringly, are drunken and askew; the few houses remaining kneel beaten in the new sand. Mostly, there are no houses now and no people.

Finally, there is a group of people from Galilee, with police and militiamen. The truck stops. A man lacking one finger on his right hand steps up on the rear tire, leans over, and lifts the blanket from the face. He looks closely. Then he steps down and says, "That's Charlie Keville. That's Charlie, all right." And the truck drives on.

So, on the Thursday night following the hurricane, Charles Keville was publicly declared dead. But as the Associated Press reported from Wakefield on the following day, "Charles Keville walked into a temporary morgue and looked at a body which had been identified as his. 'Nope,' he said, 'that ain't me,' and walked out again."

At Sand Hill Cove and the Breachway, there is nothing but sand and rock, no indication of a settlement of any kind. Lines of stretchers carry the aged and injured to hospitals on higher ground. The homeless struggle along the waterfront, uncertain of either destination or purpose. A German shepherd sits in an abandoned automobile. Rosary beads dangle from the steering wheel.

Captain Paul D. Higgison was master of the tug *May*, bound from New York for Buzzards Bay, Massachusetts, with a derrick barge and ten dredge pontoons in tow. His crew consisted of Joseph Rhoden, mate, and Al Niska. By the time they arrived off Point Judith about 6:30 on the morning of September 16, the wind was northeast, about 20 knots, and too rough for the pontoons. Rather than taking a chance on losing them on the long stretch across to Buzzards Bay, Higgison decided to put into the Harbor of Refuge at Point Judith and wait for the wind to drop.

They anchored the derrick with a 1,000-pound anchor on a 4½-inch manila line and tied the tug alongside the derrick. The wind continued fresh, gusting up to 25 knots, and the weather remained unfavorable for the tow for the next three days. They sat there and waited. On Wednesday, the twenty-first, the weather report called for "fresh to strong southeast winds, shifting to northwest tonight." The sea was building up outside the breakwater and some of the swell was coming in the south entrance. Tug and derrick were surging on the anchor, so they lengthened the rode until they were riding on about 500 feet of line. The wind was 25–30 knots from the southeast.

"About 11:50 A.M., I looked over toward the Point Judith Coast Guard station and saw that they had hoisted the hurricane warning flags," Higgison said. "That was the first I knew that there was a hurricane anywhere near. The wind was then 35–40 knots and too rough to try to move the tow to better shelter, so all we could do was put out more ground tackle.

"All we had beside the tug's 200-pound anchor was a new steel cutter head on the derrick that belonged to the dredge *Pittsburgh*. It weighed four or five tons, so we gathered up all the one-inch to 1¼-inch wire cable we could find, most of it in short lengths we shackled together, and put the cutter overboard with a buoy on it. It wasn't long before the anchor dragged enough for the cable on the cutter to come taut."

By 3:30 P.M., the tide had risen to the top of the breakwater and the seas were coming over. Tug, derrick, and tow were surging so hard on the anchor cables that Higgison was afraid they would part at any time; besides, it was getting too rough to lie alongside the derrick. So he decided to put wire bridles and a hawser on the derrick, get out ahead of the anchors, and try to hold the tow with the power of the tug's engine.

About 5 o'clock, Higgison felt the anchor cables part on the derrick, and the tow started to pull the tug backward. "We went by that anchor buoy like we were backing up," he said. "The wind I judged to be 85–90 knots at this time. When we had dragged back to where I thought we were getting close to the west jetty,

I told the boys we couldn't let the tow pull us over the rocks, so I went aft and took the axe we kept handy to the towing bitts for such an emergency and cut the hawser and let the tow go.

"With Joe and Al holding the wheel and me at the engine controls, we pulled up to near the beacon at the south entrance. The tide was up so that just the light on the top of the beacon was visible once in a while. The tide must have been at least 20 feet above normal. The wind was over 100 knots by this time and I thought of easing on out toward open water where we would have more room to maneuver but decided that the seas would be smaller where we were after they had broken over the jetty.

"At about 5:50 P.M. — that's when the pilothouse clock stopped, anyway — I saw a huge sea coming at us like a tidal wave, 50 feet high. It was breaking and had about 10 feet of foam on top of it. I yelled to Joe and Al, 'Get down on the floor; that sea is coming through the windows!'

"So we all three hit the deck, and sure enough, when that sea piled aboard, it took out all the pilothouse windows and filled the pilothouse with water. When the sea hit, as I was ducking down on the floor, I stopped the engine, and when the boat dropped down in the trough between swells, she broached and swung left.

"The next sea caught her and rolled her over one revolution.

"I was standing with my hands on the engine controls, which were near the port side of the pilothouse, when that second sea hit. It hit with such force that both Joe and Al came down on me and I pushed the two panels out of the pilothouse door and my big fat behind was stuck there. During the time the boat was rolling over, I thought she was going to the bottom and I was fighting to get out but could not get my rear end out of that door.

"Seemed like a long time that the water was swirling through that pilothouse, but I know that it took less than a minute for her to roll completely over and I could see daylight again. I pulled free of the door right quick then, grabbed the engine controls and started the engine ahead.

"I headed the boat up in the wind and sea again, but I could not hold her there. With no windows, and the wind, which I estimated at 120 knots, driving the rain and spray, it was like someone pelting you in the face with rocks. Watching the seas closely, I swung her around quickly, putting her stern to the wind.

"I suddenly felt that the boat was awful heavy and was positive that the engine room must be nearly flooded. Ordinarily, when underway, we kept the door in the after end of the engine room at least partially open, because that old two-cycle engine used so much air it would pull the ashes out of the furnace if the door wasn't partially open.

"What I did not know was that after I cut the hawser and let the tow go, I sent Al down through an escape hatch into the engine room and gave him orders not to go out on deck, but to reach out and take the remainder of the hawser loose from the towing bitt and coil it down in the engine room so that it would not get overboard and into the propeller. He did what I told him, but there was so much spray coming in the door that he closed it tight, thereby avoiding a tragedy. If he had not closed it, the *May* could have sunk or at least taken in enough water to disable the main engine so that we could not have gotten to safety.

"Not knowing the conditions in the engine room and not being able to hold the boat up in the wind, I decided to head for the beach. I told Joe and Al to get us each a life jacket and when we saw the beach, I would stop the engine and we would jump off the stern and swim to the side and try to keep clear of the boat so that we would land on the beach.

"Suddenly, I remembered the little channel leading into Galilee, so I just guessed at a compass course and hoped we would make it. It was raining so hard that the visibility was only about 200 feet. Nearing shore, I happened to look over the port side and down in the trough of the sea. I could see rocks. We were running parallel to the west jetty and not more than 10 feet off.

"With Joe and Al, one on each side of the wheel steering, I

screamed, 'Hard a-starboard!' They spun the wheel hard over, but the boat was running with a swell under her stern and it seemed like ages before she dropped down off that sea so that I could gun the engine and the rudder took a hold. We veered off to the right, and then I could see the high telegraph poles on each side of the inlet, so I headed in between them. When we passed the poles, I knew we had it made. I had anchored in the Harbor of Refuge two or three times previously but never attempted to enter this channel because there was only enough water to get through at high water.

"After we passed the poles, we groped our way along until we came to two boats — a small dragger and a sport fisherman. We dropped our anchor near the dragger. There was one man aboard her (the *Barbara G.*, a 35-footer). I will never forget him; Jimmy Gamache was his name; he owned the dragger and was a former mate on the Dollar Line ships.

"Just as soon as we were safely anchored, I went below to see how much water we had in the engine room. To my surprise, there was only 2 or 3 inches in the engine room bilges and about 8 inches in the crew's quarters, which had two 6-inch ventilators open down through the main deck. After surveying the damage in the engine room, I thanked the good Lord for bringing us into that safe harbor, because only He could have kept that engine running.

"The base of the engine was full of salt water, which only could have gotten in there through the two 8-inch-diameter exhaust pipes in the smokestack. The four large storage batteries had torn loose and smashed all over the engine room and broke the gauge glass out of the fuel day tank, draining all the fuel out on the deck. (The engine received all of its fuel by gravity from this tank.) The discharge pipe on the auxiliary fuel pump on the main engine that pumps the fuel from the main tanks to the day tank was completely broken off at the engine and the fuel was just spraying out into the engine room when the engine was running. The fuel injection pump reservoir on the engine only held enough fuel to run the engine about ten minutes at slow speed, so I have never figured out yet where the fuel came from to run that engine for the forty or forty-five minutes we ran it after we rolled over.

"On coming back out on deck after being down below, Jimmy Gamache called to me and said that he was tied up on the end of the State Pier; the pier, of course, was underwater. Then a man came out of the second-story window onto the roof of the porch of a two-story house that had washed all the way from the beach a half-mile away, to within a hundred feet of the State Pier. He hollered over to me and asked if I could come over and pick him up. I told him the wind was starting to die down and they would be safe there; besides, the docks were all underwater and the place was full of sunken boats. There had been twenty-one boats in the harbor before the storm hit and now there were only two afloat. The man on the porch insisted that we try to pick them up, so Jimmy Gamache said if we would help him put a dory overboard, we could pick them up in that.

"We shortened up our anchor line, started the engine and dragged the anchor over alongside Jimmy's boat, then put the dory overboard, so that we could pick up the two men and their wives, who were now out on the roof.

"On the way over, the wife of one of the men held a large envelope out the window and said, 'John, what should I do with this?' The envelope, I found out, contained all their insurance papers and $400 in cash.

"He said, 'Give the damned thing to the wind; it's got everything else anyway.' So she turned it loose.

"We took the four people aboard the tug *May* and started a fire in the galley stove to dry their clothes. I had all my winter clothes with me, so the women stripped off their wet clothes and put on some of my long-handled underwear and sat around drinking coffee until their clothes dried. Jimmy brought over a bottle and we all had a couple snorts, too. Jimmy told me that all during the storm he had not once thought of a life jacket until he saw us with them on. Then he rushed down below and put one on also."

"The day the tug *May* rolled over is the day I gave my soul to God and the rest of me to the crabs," Higgison said.

Some matters related to the hurricane took months to resolve; some memories proved unerasable. Months later, after lingering in South County Hospital in Wakefield, Tom Mann, the "mayor" of Galilee, died of the injuries received when he was forced to take refuge on the roof of his house. A man was fatally injured in a two-story fall to the ground because he forgot one night that the hurricane had ripped out a flight of stairs leading down from his back door. Older people who had ridden through the storm on roofs and mattresses died not long afterward of "heart attacks." A businessman who had lost several members of his family gradually fell into melancholy, became prematurely aged, and finally succumbed after a shock; the storm changed his personality and destroyed his life.

The official death list attributable to the storm might well be doubled if such loss of life as this were added to it.

Chapter 11

THEN THE HURRICANE ROARED UP Narragansett Bay, leaving its toll of death and destruction written in the shambles of the beaches at Warwick Cove, Oakland Beach, and Shawomet. There was one at Oakland Beach who was rescued and yet who was not. He shall remain nameless, but there are those still who know his name. He was not included in any list of the dead or missing; when the storm had passed, his home still stood and his possessions remained remarkably intact, but his life was over nevertheless and his worldly goods useless to him.

He had been a blacksmith for many years; he had a wife and one son. In 1932, the boy was accidentally drowned in nearby Brushneck Cove and the parents were inconsolable in their grief. Time did not heal the wound; the mother's health failed rapidly and she died three years after the loss of the son.

The man chose to remain where his memories were. He stayed in the house at Oakland Beach, living in solitude. When the hurricane ripped across the beach, his neighbors went to help him. They found him sitting there, oblivious to the seas that shook his home. All he said, over and over, was: "He's come for me. My boy has come back for me at last."

When that day ended at stricken Oakland Beach, many of its

refugees found shelter in the local schoolhouse and fire station. He was not among them. He had been admitted to the State Institution for the Insane.

However, as brutal as was the assault upon the outlying beaches of the bay, it was the city of Providence that suffered most dramatically from the storm's blow. For Providence lies at the bay's head, and there was no place for the high water to go but into the city.

At the climax, the Providence River was 17.60 feet above mean low water and the 100-mile-an-hour hurricane, coinciding with high tide, drove water 8 to 10 feet deep through the city's low-lying business section. Thousands starting home during the 5 o'clock rush hour stepped out into a storm that was at its worst between 5 and 5:15. Hundreds fled to the nearest shelter as soon as they discovered what was happening.

There were no trolley cars and few buses. The great glass skylight of the Providence Public Library crashed. Within minutes, scores of buildings were unroofed and heavy chimneys and cornices came thundering down into the streets. Ponderous signs were ripped from steel moorings and carried down. A power cable parted, and its dangling end spat fire in the faces of marooned pedestrians leaning against the wind or huddled in the lee of doorways.

As the city struggled with the hurricane, the storm wave struck, ripping hundreds of boats from moorings, battering ships and commercial craft, sinking many and smashing piers. A battering ram of water slammed against the underpinnings of Providence bridges, swirled through low-lying streets, inundated lower floors of business buildings and parked automobiles.

Power and lights failed almost completely at 5:15. Thousands were stranded in the high office buildings, stores, hotels, and theaters. For blocks along Fountain, Westminster, and Washington streets and in the cross streets, men and boys organized rescue

At Providence, Rhode Island, dockhouses are inundated;

a tug lies wrecked in the crib of the railroad bridge.

teams and helped women through the onrushing waters. Here were soda fountain girls in their white aprons; there, elderly women trapped in the bus stations, many of them confused by fright and fighting their rescuers. A boy waded along the sidewalk and carried a dog on his shoulders.

Some sought refuge in their automobiles and died. Clorinda Lupilo, nineteen, was fatally injured when the roof of a building fell on her car in Erickson Place. Hilda Pieczentkowski was killed on North Street when a chimney collapsed on the parked car in which she was sitting. Dorothy Atwood died when the roof and wall of a building at Friendship and Garnet streets fell on an automobile.

Chester Hayes, thirty, was drowned in the center of the city. Robert Whitaker, who was marooned four hours with fifty others in the Tribune Building, saw Hayes die. "He was clinging to a submerged automobile," Whitaker said. "Before a line could be thrown to him, a parked car floated down the street on the still-rising flood and lurched into the automobile to which he was clinging. He was swept into the swift current. A strong swimmer, appearing as if from nowhere, set out for Hayes as he was carried away, but was unable to reach him. The swimmer disappeared around the corner. Hayes was in water dotted with white caps. He drowned in Turks Head Square."

Between 5:05 and 5:10 P.M., the Weather Bureau instruments on the Turks Head Building recorded a velocity of 85 miles per hour. Then a skylight blown from the roof of the building demolished the recording instruments.

"The crowd marooned at Thompson's Restaurant stood on tables until the water crept up to the table tops," F. Arnold McDermott said. "Then they climbed out onto a fire escape and went to the bakery above, but it wasn't large enough and the water was still coming up. They climbed out onto the fire escape again and went into vacant rooms on the third floor. In the crowd was a

[200]

woman who had been blown against a brick wall in the alley outside the restaurant. They thought both her legs were broken and when they lifted her through the window, she screamed with pain.

"Another woman had been thrown through the big plate glass window of the restaurant. Her thumb was dangling off and blood was streaming all over her body. And there was a pretty blond woman, between 25 and 30; her front teeth had been knocked out and she was vomiting. Between her heaves, two men were trying to stop the flow of blood.

"Several men in white uniforms passed out slabs of hot apple pie which had just come out of the bakery ovens. About nine o'clock, firemen reached the alley between the Industrial Trust Building and Thompson's Restaurant. They got the stranded crowd down the fire escapes and took them in a lifeboat to the Post Office steps.

"In the restaurant at the foot of Waterman Street, across from the Baptist Church, the corpse of a middle-aged woman lay for four hours. She had been sitting in a car outside when the chimney of the building crashed down through the top of her car and crushed her skull.

"A dead woman was swept down the mall in the current of the flood. Rescuers from the Hotel Biltmore weren't able to buck the current to get to her. She went past."

Hundreds of workers and shoppers sought sanctuary in the churches. Grace Episcopal Church, immediately in the sweep of water up Westminster Street, provided refuge for more than two hundred, many of whom were forced to stay in the auditorium and parish house until Thursday morning. It was a bizarre scene within the church as the electric power failed and flickering altar candles in the chapel gave the only light. The shadowy figures, strangers to each other, brought together by common danger, crowded into the pews. Most were wet, some were hysterical, all were apprehensive. As the wind roared about the roof and tower and the flood poured into the basement several feet deep, they listened to the smashing of glass, the wrenching of wood and metal outside that could be heard even above the noise of the storm.

The inundated downtown stores, their windows smashed by the wind, yielded heterogeneous merchandise to the murky waters that flowed through the streets. Footballs, dolls, furniture, pillows, and automobile tires were washed along with the wreckage of buildings, pieces of smashed trees, and chunks of broken boats.

On the Rhode Island Hospital Trust Building, there was a bronze plate bearing this legend: "In the great gale of September 23, 1815, the wind-driven waters around the walls of this building rose to the level of this line — 11 feet, 9¼ inches above mean high water." On September 21, 1938, the water rose to the line on the plaque — and then went three feet above it.

A large gray rat rode a bobbing gasoline tin on Westminster Street, and down Weybosset floated a squadron of refrigerators. Four drugstore clerks and two policemen formed a human chain at Dorrance and Westminster and rescued twenty-four people from a shoe store. Among the rescued was a little boy who had just come from taking his violin lesson. He clung to his violin as long as he could, but it finally slipped from his grasp and went sailing down the street with the large gray rat and the gasoline tin. In one bar, the customers stood fast at the mahogany until the water reached their shoulders, at which point, they broke ranks and paddled out to the sidewalk. A man swam out of the Western Union office with a girl clerk clinging to him — it was surprising how many people could not swim — and struck out for the Industrial Trust Building, refuge for a score or more of other bedraggled people.

In the Tribune Building, Whitaker and others heard cries of alarm outside, across Exchange Street. He said, "The hundreds marooned there had discovered people in the doorway of a small sandwich shop on the Exchange Street side of our building. . . ."

The people in the doorway were Miss Emily S. Wickett, former secretary to the late Dr. William H. P. Faunce, president of Brown University and, at the time of the hurricane, stenographer for Superior Court Judge Patrick P. Curran; William Atkinson; George H. Foster; Earl T. Marceau, proprietor of the sandwich shop; and a fourth man, unidentified. They had fled to the restaurant for safety.

"We did not notice the water was rising so rapidly," Miss Wickett said. The first realization of their situation came when they tried to attract the attention of people in the Grosvenor Building to the predicament of a man — it was Hayes — seated atop an automobile, who apparently could not swim. At about this time, the four climbed onto the restaurant counters, but the water continued to rise and they knew they would have to leave or drown.

They had a desperate struggle getting the restaurant door open. "The restaurant man was on the outside trying to push the door open and I was on the inside trying to pull it open. The pressure of the water made it difficult, but finally the door opened," Miss Wickett related.

Outside, the water between the old newspaper plant in West Exchange Street and the Grosvenor Building was seven feet deep. Miss Wickett continued, "I swam out of the door and the current caught me. There were three automobiles on the other side of the street. I noticed the doors of one of the cars were open. Fearing that I might be drawn by the current into that car, I tried to swim away from it and finally managed to grasp a coping on the side of the Tribune Building." Her companions, weary from swimming, also gained the same sanctuary, and here they were helped by those in the Tribune Building who had been alerted by cries of the crowd outside.

Leo Scanlen and the Tribune Building janitor came down the fire escape, lowered a rope and hauled them to safety, one by one.

Van Wyck Mason, the author, was en route from Nantucket to New York to deliver a new manuscript to his publisher on the day of the hurricane. "It was beautiful sailing until our steamer, the

[203]

Vehicles in downtown Providence,

Rhode Island, were submerged.

New Bedford, passed Martha's Vineyard," he said. "From there on, it blew so hard that when we got to New Bedford, the steamer missed the slip and smashed into the next pier."

Discovering that no planes were flying out of New Bedford because of the deteriorating weather, novelist Mason left the city by bus, bound for Providence. "Experience No. 1 was a live wire falling on top of the bus, but luckily, the flaming end missed the roof," Mason later said. "Next, two trees fell directly in front of the bus. Then we got into water up to the running board. Still, we made Fall River safely and were going along fairly well just outside of Providence when, on a narrow, circuitous road, trees began crashing down like ninepins. I had with me this manuscript for a 700-page historical novel on which I had been working for a year and a half, and that was my chief concern."

As he alighted at Providence, a chimney fell nearby with a roar and shower of bricks, and he decided it would be prudent to use his suitcase as a helmet. He halted at one point to help extricate a woman from an overturned car and then hurried on to the railroad station. "Just as I got there," Mason said, "the roof of the station came off with a roar like a boiler factory." Standing in the remains of the station, he watched water rise "to a height of ten feet over the square. A woman seeking refuge on the top of her car was swept away before our eyes and drowned; there was nothing we could do. Another woman was wading to safety when she popped out of sight just like a jack-in-the-box; she evidently stepped into an open sewer.

"The lights of automobiles stayed on under the water, giving an eerie glow. Then the horns of automobiles all over the city short-circuited and kept up a deafening din all through the night."

Mason said it was impossible to sleep that night and he sat up by candlelight at the Hope Club. "For the first time in its history, women — refugees, of course — were admitted within its doors. The oldsters at the club didn't like it. They said no good would come of it," Mason added.

L. D. Lacy of Pelham Manor, New York, was among those standing in the main waiting room of the Union Station in Providence, waiting for trains that never came. "I was standing there," he recalled, "when the principal arch over the room began to give way under the pressure of rain and wind. As the first piece of glass broke away from the frames above, the crowd below scurried for shelter, but many were cut by flying fragments. In a few moments, the glass came down in a shower and as the arch started to crumble, it ripped metal roofing away, but fortunately, the roofing remained above."

Mr. Lacy ran from the station with others, hoping to find shelter in the nearby Biltmore Hotel. "The streets then were relatively clear of water, with the exception of a few inches left by the rain," he said. "As we reached the second-floor lobby of the hotel, it seemed as though we were comparatively safe. But we had not taken into consideration what amounted to an impending tidal wave from Narragansett Bay.

"Within an hour, the water in the street had risen as high as the second story, but did not quite reach the lobby. Stores, banks, and other places of business on the main level were flooded. Debris was floating by in great masses, and it seemed that the entire downtown was doomed. And then the water appeared to recede with the tide almost as swiftly as it had risen. The resulting damage was shocking . . ."

Although Providence was largely isolated by the storm, at least one outgoing telephone line remained. From his room on the second floor of the Crown Hotel, in the heart of Providence, Charles Toomey, a visiting businessman, described to a New Yorker what was happening:

"As I look out over Weybosset Street, one of the city's main thoroughfares, all I can see is desolation, submerged autos, abandoned streetcars hurled up onto the sidewalk. There's not even a rowboat in sight. Water high enough to cover a bus is rolling through the streets at the rate of six or seven miles an hour. A wind of about sixty miles an hour in velocity is still blowing.

"Across the street, clerks and customers of the Outlet Company, Providence's largest department store, are huddled on the second floor. I can barely discern their shapes from where I stand. The wind is so strong that it is blowing out windows and carrying glass fragments through the street in front of it. No one can venture out for fear of being cut down by flying glass.

"The water is still rising as I talk to you. It is pitch-dark and I have not yet seen a single light. No one is drinking water because it may already be contaminated.

"It started when a terrific gale and rainstorm hit the city shortly after three o'clock. The wind must have been traveling seventy miles an hour. At about five-thirty, the rivers began to back up into the city. Nothing like it has ever been seen by the local people. Within a few minutes, the wall of water was fully five feet high and in a half-hour, it was high enough to submerge automobiles."

In Dyer Street, a New England Transportation Company truck was floated from its parking space and grounded near the Wachusett Creamery, on the same street. The driver, who could not swim, yelled for help and employees at the creamery tied tableclothes together until they had sufficient length to reach him, when they hauled him up to the second floor of their building.

Solomon Brandt, a seventy-year-old printer, had a shop on the second floor in a building on Weybosset Street. "The first time I looked out," Brandt said, "I recall distinctly there was no unusual amount of water at that moment on Peckham Street or Weybosset, other than the regular rainwater. As I returned again from the presses to the stock table near the window, no more than five minutes from the previous time, I saw the most unusual sight I had ever seen in all my life.

"Water was rushing through Peckham Street toward Weybosset Street and I could see that the water was over the running boards of some of the parked automobiles. I stopped work and watched from then on. The water rose almost as fast as if you held a glass in front of a spigot. Within a very few moments, perhaps a minute, the water reached the tops of automobiles, and the first thing I saw moving toward me was an automobile floating down Peckham toward Weybosset, with a man on top of it.

"From windows in adjoining buildings and open doors, people were hollering to the man on top of the car. The automobile hit a street-sign post, with the man holding onto the post. The machine at the same time turned sideways and was being held against the post. The man was thrown into the whirling water.

"Suddenly, the lights went out. I stayed in the shop near the fire escape until past 10 o'clock."

Harrison McDonald of Lafayette, Indiana, still bound for Boston, had come from New London in a railroad-hired cab; he arrived in Providence at 11 Thursday night. "It was one of the weirdest sights I have ever seen. It was like a city in wartime," he said. "The entire business district was roped off and patrolled by armed soldiers. Huge antiaircraft lights pierced the night, shooting long slender pencils of bluish light into the darkness. You could pick out every cloud. And after you have seen about fifteen of those lights working at once, you can understand how they can pick out airplanes.

"There were no lights in the city and as you registered in the Hotel Biltmore, there was a sign reminding you to take a candle with you. You had to climb to your room as well, since the elevators were out of order. All the stores were guarded, food was rationed out as you put in your order; martial law existed, of course, and bars were closed."

In East Providence, Manuel Azevedo, once a horse dealer but now, in his old age, reduced to one horse, prepared to flee the rapidly rising water. He had to think of his horse, as well as of himself. That is why, at the worst of the storm, he was in the barn.

When the water came up to the barn door, he knew it was time for action. The old man led his horse across the railroad tracks to the higher ground of Boston Street, on the far side of the tracks from the river. But by now, even Boston Street was underwater; it surrounded both of them and it was coming up rapidly.

Mr. Azevedo, seeking a way to safety, led his horse northward, along Boston Street, parallel to the river. At the northern (or depot) end of Boston Street, there was a steep and high iron stairway, typical of such railroad station structures, that led up to Watchemoket Square. With all other exits cut off, the old man headed for the stairway and his trusting horse following him without a moment's hesitation — up they went, horse and master, up those thirty or forty iron steps, the animal never faltering or fearing, to the dry land and safety of the square above.

For six years, Ralph Rivers, his wife, Mary, and their family — nine children by 1938 — had been living in the cabin of an old barge at Sabins Point, Riverside; the craft was fast to a dock and a two-ton anchor buried six feet in the mud. It made them a good home, Mr. Rivers remarked, a better home than a lot of folks have, "and on washday, it always looked like a flagship flying signals in a fleet." On the day of the hurricane, Mary and six of the children, Ralph, thirteen; Elsie, eight; Raymond, seven; Frank, six; Joan, three, and Helen, one and a half, were aboard the barge.

"I was picking apples for Mrs. Charles Redding on Taunton Avenue [in Providence] about 3:30 o'clock Wednesday afternoon," Rivers said later. "I was up in the top of the tree when I heard a kind of moaning in the air. I've been to sea off and on all my life and I know the sound a hurricane makes when it's making up. I said to myself, 'This looks like something pretty bad; I'd better be getting home,' so I climbed down out of the tree and I got in my car.

"Mrs. Redding said to me, 'Ralph, won't you have a cup of tea before you start back?' but I told her, 'No, I want to get back to the barge.' If I'd taken that tea, I wouldn't have any family.

"I guess I was doing seventy in my old car when I passed Moore's Corner. By the time I got to Sabins Point, the gale was hitting ninety. There was the barge anchored at the end of the long wharf that jutted out from the beach. I crouched low and ran and got aboard. I said to Mary and the kids, 'We've got to abandon ship.'

"Just then, the boards of the wharf began to fly. I knew Mary and the kids couldn't make it across the stringers, so I said, 'Wait here.' I said, 'Well, here we are and it looks bad and we'll have to ride it out, and how about some supper?'

"Mary had supper about half-cooked, when the seas came piling up the bay. They hit the old barge with a smash like a battleship's broadside. Water came sloshing into the cabin and I forgot what we were going to have for supper; all I could think of was getting Mary and the kids into the pilothouse. There were six life preservers hanging on the outside of the cabin and I took them into the pilothouse, along with the children. I put five of them on the children and the other one on Mary.

"She wanted me to put hers on the baby but I said, 'No, what would be the use? She would only slip through it.' By this time, the old barge was taking the worst of it. The waves were slamming her over on her beam ends until the kids were almost standing on the walls of the pilothouse. It was dark and howling and all the downriver wreckage was hammering the barge with piledriver blows. I looked out of the pilothouse door and saw a big piece of spiling go straight through the cabin, in one side and out the other. Everything that came up the bay hit us.

"The worst was a great mess of wreckage; I guess it must have been part of the wharf at Crescent Park. It hit us with a slam and I was afraid the seas would pile it over on us and smash the pilothouse in, so I grabbed an iron bar and went out into the shrilling wind and the flying spume and somehow I pried the mass of timbers loose. Then I went back inside and it was about that time that Raymond said to me, 'Papa, we're going to die, ain't we?' I said to him, 'No, son, you're not gonna die. Look at those lights up the bay; that's a towboat coming to take us off.' I kept telling them that.

"I was pretty proud of those children. No whimpering, no cry-ing. A couple of the littlest were seasick and that was all. And Mary, there never was a woman like her. When it was getting bad, she said to me, 'Ralph, how about it, have we got a chance?' I said to her, 'Mary, we've got one chance in a million; if you haven't forgotten your prayers, you'd better say them.' She just closed her eyes a second and then she opened them and said, 'All right, Ralph.'

"I could hear the barge breaking up. When the deck went, up forward, I said to Mary, 'When you see me throw the first kid overboard, you jump!' They all had on life preservers. The seas would carry them right up the bay; they wouldn't land on the beach, but they'd be killed in the pilothouse anyway. Those kids never said a word. I said to the oldest boy, 'Come here, son,' and he came to me. . . .

"Just then the tide turned. I looked out and the shore was bright with lights. When the tide went out, it took every last bit of the wreckage that had piled up on the barge and left her high and dry — what was left of her — and what used to be the boatyard, but we could get off only amidships because the deck forward was gone and there was about four feet of water there. So I got a heaving line and lowered the children down and Mary and I got down the best way we could. . . .

"We don't have any home now, because nobody will ever live on the barge again, but I guess Mary and I and the children will make out all right."

In the Hanley Building in Providence, the studios of the Monday Morning Musical Club were located on an upper floor. Soon after the ground level of the building was flooded, the studio, well-supplied with candles, attracted an assortment of refugees — em-ployees of a first-floor restaurant, a pianist, a couple of music stu-dents, waitresses from a cafe nearby, an elevator operator, a janitor, and several others, including a hysterical woman who wandered in from the street seeking the comfort of light and companionship.

Anthony McCoy, a former boxer, who ran a gymnasium in the building, made short work of the hysteria. Facing the woman, he demanded, "Don't you go to church? Don't you believe in God? Don't you know that if you pray to Him, He'll take care of you?" Her sobbing gradually became controlled. McCoy disappeared, to reappear a few minutes later with sandwiches and coffee, saying only, "I happened to know where they kept them." The stranded people ate, and were quieted.

Then Royal Dadmun of Hartford, a concert baritone who had been teaching voice all day, went to the piano. He played and sang for an hour — spirituals, ballads, the light and humorous — and the anxious refugees became an appreciative audience. Girls trapped in another building across the street leaned out of the windows to listen, and applauded. And as the storm abated, one by one the refugees thanked the boxer and the baritone for the food, music, and comfort in an interlude of chaos, and went their separate ways.

In another studio, at 9 Penelope Place in Providence, artist Gino E. Conti did not mind that electric lights did not light, that the telephone did not ring, and that the radio did not play. Having neither electricity nor a telephone in his studio, he lit candles as usual, as he did on every other night. "With me," said Mr. Conti, smiling, "everything was just perfectly normal."

In the wake of it all, the Providence *Journal* published an editorial entitled "Faith in the Future," and commented, "Appalling as was the first shock of [the] disaster, the horror in those fearful hours now grows much greater as the full reach of the destruction spreads before the people of the state stricken by tragic loss of life and incalculable damage to property and the ruin of so much natural beauty beyond restoration for years to come.

[213]

"Calamity tests the stuff that men are made of. No tribute can reward fittingly the good people who have not been found wanting. They showed over and over again a generous measure of courage, tireless and unselfish labor. They realize that all must help in the task of comforting and caring for those bereft of dear ones, homes or means of livelihood. . . .

"Rehabilitation will be long and costly, demanding the best that is in every man and woman in the state, but it can be accomplished . . . so long as the people co-operate in earnestly considered efforts to preserve order, promote the general welfare, and return to Rhode Island all the lost treasures that can be brought back by working and faith in the future."

Chapter 12

RHODE ISLAND'S GOVERNOR, Robert E. Quinn, made an immediate post-hurricane survey of his state's sticken areas. This was the impression of Quinn's team, as they came into Bristol:

State highway workers using a snowplow to battle mud and debris. Signs on utility poles saying, "Boil all water before drinking" and "Warning: Start no fires under penalty of the law."

Under the arch of storm-ravaged trees that formed a threatening canopy above the street, a bathtub, overturned on a lawn. A rowboat, tied to a tree on the high school property. A fisherman's boat on the railroad tracks. An enormous fuel tank wedged between two houses.

Nothing but scattered concrete blocks where a building previously stood. A mill with a slice cut of its roof. In the rear of coal and lumber yards, a mess of boats, boards, hay, and mud.

The Prudence Island ferry jammed up against a wall. The state police boat buried beneath buoys. Off to the east, an automobile hanging from a dock by its rear wheels. The side of the armory blown out. An old upright piano in the gutter. Registration plate PA-123 just visible under a mass of tree limbs that covered the automobile; the driver ran out of gasoline and had just left his car when the tree blew down.

Birthplace of America's Cup defenders, the internationally known Herreshoff Manufacturing Company. A member of the governor's party recorded, "Approximately seventy-five craft of various types damaged; some reduced to kindling. Two huge storage sheds ripped open. *Resolute*, with one side gone, and the deck ripped out. *Vanitie*, tipped and ripped. *Ranger*, with her stern gone . . ."

The big sloops were not only damaged by the hurricane; they were, in fact, dead. For a moment, the storm thrust these graceful symbols of yesterday's dreams and elegance back onto the center stage to which they were accustomed, but even without the hurricane, the nation's changing economy and society were nudging them irreversibly toward oblivion.

Yet some remembered their great moments. All of Bristol turned out on April 25, 1914, for the launching of *Resolute* at the Herreshoff yard. On the launching stage were Miss Grace Vanderbilt, daughter of former Commodore Cornelius Vanderbilt of the New York Yacht Club, with her father, mother, and younger brother, and Charles Francis Adams II, who was to be skipper of the America's Cup defense candidate.

Precisely at 6:30 P.M., the appointed hour, Miss Vanderbilt was given a signal by Captain Nathanael G. Herreshoff. Raising her hammer, she struck the bottle of wine hanging over the craft's stem and, as the sound of hammers upon blocks and wedges rose from the ways, she cried, "I christen thee *Resolute!*"

On her deck were Robert W. "Bob" Emmons II of Harvard fame and former Vice Commodore Henry Walters of the New York Yacht Club, the only member of the syndicate to be on board. Captain Chris Christienson and several members of the crew were on deck and all hands were lying down as she went out of the north shop and started down the ways. All but Emmons; he was on his knees as she passed out through the big doors and as soon as he got a chance, he was up on his feet and when she dipped into the deep water, he threw both arms above his head and shouted.

That was the signal for the throngs gathered on both the north and south piers to cheer, and it was a mighty roar of jubilation.

The spectators liked what they saw. An eyewitness reported, "The craft is a tribute to the cunning of the Wizard of Bristol. She is by far the easiest lined boat of the three that have been built as candidates for the defense of the cup. She is a yacht that will be easy in a sea way and in a bobble of a sea will eat out to windward."

In the same spring, about three weeks later, *Vanitie*, the last of the new 75-foot sloops — the other two being *Resolute* and *Defiance* — was launched from Lawley's at Neponset. She was the only one of the three to be built at the expense of one individual, Alexander Smith Cochran of New York, and her lines were drawn by William Gardner. As with *Resolute*, she was built of manganese bronze, the plates of which were rolled in the mills of the New Bedford and Taunton Copper Company.

"At a few minutes before 3 o'clock, when the tide served its best," a Boston newspaperman reported, "the hull, polished till it took glint of gold under the sun's bright rays, was given to destiny." Aboard *Vanitie* when she took her maiden plunge were Mr. Cochran, Miss Eleanora Sears of Boston, and R. P. Perkins of New York. Miss Sears, then reappearing in the sporting world after a considerable period of retirement because of bereavement, was gowned in black.

Resolute won the trials that year, but World War I intervened and she was stored. In 1920, after another trial, she was again chosen cup defender and proved her merit. Off Sandy Hook on July 27 in that year, a yachting writer noted joyfully, "Defender *Resolute* gave the British challenger *Shamrock IV* the worst drubbing of this year's regatta in the final race for the series today, winning boat for boat by 13 minutes and 14 seconds, and the America's famous yachting cup remains American property.

"Overcoming a 40-second lead and the advantages of a windward berth which *Shamrock IV* had taken at the start, the fleet defender held a lead of four minutes and eight seconds at the halfway stake of the 30-mile course. In capturing the series and retaining the trophy, *Resolute* came from behind, after *Shamrock* had taken two races, and won by registering three straight wins. Sir Thomas Lipton, owner of the green British challenger, declared tonight, 'The best boat won.' "

Production of the all-steel, 87-foot J-boat *Ranger* was begun at Bath Iron Works in Maine in 1937. It was the first time in forty-four years that an America's Cup contender had not been built at the Herreshoff yards in Bristol. Nat Herreshoff scorned such devices as tank tests, which were used to select *Ranger*'s model, designed by W. Starling Burgess and Olin Stephens.

Ranger was described by experts as representing the most revolutionary advance in hull design in fifty years. She had a 165-foot duralumin mast and carried a parachute spinnaker with an area of 18,000 square feet, the largest sail ever seen on a yacht. Her cost was $500,000.

The spectator fleet that turned out off Newport for the July-August races between Harold S. Vanderbilt's *Ranger* and Tom Sopwith's *Endeavour* II in 1937 was so large as to suggest that the nation's economic depression was over. Light winds and the *Ranger*'s impressive sails, including a revolutionary quadrilateral jib of artificial silk, gave the American defender the first four races without a break. The *Endeavour* was beaten in the first race by the embarrassing time of 17 minutes, 5 seconds, one of the worst defeats in cup racing.

Although the loss of life at Newport was not heavy, mountainous seas engulfed the beach, crashed over the seawall, roared through buildings, and surged across the roadway into Easton's Pond, which, during the storm, resembled a white-capped ocean itself.

On the waterfront, damage to fish traps was estimated at more than a million dollars, the fleet of the Smith Meal Company took a pasting, and the 130-foot fishing vessel *Promised Land* was blown across the harbor and driven up onto City Wharf. Four hefty lines, each six inches in diameter, which held the New England Steamship Company's freighter *Pequonnock* at Long Wharf were sheared like shoestrings and the vessel was driven ashore.

The rescue of Pierrepoint Johnson, Jr., three-year-old son of Mr. and Mrs. Pierrepoint Johnson of New York and Newport, and the three adults who were with him involved both the Army and Navy. Miss Elsie Searles, a family employee who had been with the baby for two and a half years; Mary McManus, the household cook, and Andrew Healy, gardener, were stranded with the child in a seaside cottage when the storm tide inundated the first floor, demolished their automobile, and washed the garage out to sea.

Moments before the phone went out of commission, Healy phoned for help, reporting that they could not leave unaided and that the house was in danger of being demolished. His message was passed to Lieutenant Commander E. H. Kincaid, U.S.N., of the Naval Training Station. Kincaid discovered that communication with the local Coast Guard was impossible and that proceeding to the scene by boat was out of the question because of heavy seas. He then contacted Fort Adams, which dispatched Captain Harold S. Ruth and Lieutenant William F. Meany and a detachment of enlisted personnel to the scene.

By this time, waves were thundering against the foundation of the house, which was showing signs of collapsing. Healy tied bed sheets together and lowered the nurse and child, then the cook, and finally himself, from the second story to a nearby rock. He guided his party through shallow water to a house close by which appeared more substantial.

Commander Kincaid and Captain Ruth and his rescue group arrived; Healy signaled to them, so they would know that his party had moved to another house. The rescuers ran lifelines to three houses, and along these lines, Lieutenant Meany and three enlisted men waded and swam several hundred yards, risking death all the way. They reached the stranded group and, with Healy's help, started back. A heavy sea broke over all of them, and Miss Searles, who had handed the baby to Healy, cried, "Don't let water get in the baby's mouth!" as she was swept away. Meany, an excellent swimmer, immediately detached himself from the lifeline and tried to reach her, but could not. Her body was recovered later at Viking Beach.

One of the bitterest tragedies of the hurricane occurred at Jamestown on Conanicut Island.

Norman Caswell, driver of the school bus, had aboard eight pupils from the Thomas H. Clark elementary school and was taking them home. At Mackerel Cove, it was necessary to cross a low causeway; several vehicles were already stalled on this road and the tide was exceptionally high and still coming.

On the bus were Marion Chellis, seven; her brother, Clayton, twelve; Constantine Gianitis, five and a half, and her brother, John, four, both of whom had moved from Newport only two weeks before, and four children of Mr. and Mrs. Joseph Matoes — Joseph, Jr., thirteen; Teresa, twelve; Dorothy, eleven; and Eunice, seven.

A storm wave thundered up the cove, wiped out a beach pavilion and bathhouses, and swept the bus overboard, off the causeway. Joseph Matoes, Sr., was an eyewitness. "In the afternoon, I got to listening on the radio about a storm coming. So I started for the schoolhouse. For my kids," Matoes said. "They had already left on the bus, so I started to come back and when I hit the beach, the water was about four feet high. At Mackerel Cove, the waves were getting worse and worse, the wind was getting stronger, and pretty soon the pavilion went just like that, and the water was so high that my car and two others were swept into the water. I jumped overboard; my car was in a deep spot right near the cemetery, and I got ashore alongside a stonewall, all soaking wet.

"There was a woman and a boy in a car [Mrs. William Ordner and her son, William] and she drove down the hill and they were

*Seven children were drowned at Jamestown, Rhode Island,
when this school bus was washed overboard.*

washed overboard too, and both drowned. I was still by the wall; I
saw Norman Caswell coming around the bend with the bus and I
waved him back. I don't know whether he saw me or not. I saw the
school bus go over — with the kids. Caswell opened the doors, let
the kids out. Well, I had two daughters on top of the roof of the
bus, screaming their heads off. I saw them get swept off."

A huge sea struck all of them. It was impossible to reach them
immediately or even to see clearly what was happening; the wind
still blew hard. "I saw something coming through the water,"
Matoes said, "something moving and stretched out, so I took a
chance and went down from the wall to the water. I got knocked
down twice because the wind was so strong, but when I got there,
it was Norman Caswell.

"He was laying on his stomach. So I took my boot and kicked

him, you know, in the ribs. He grunted. 'Well,' I said, 'he's still alive.' He says, 'Please let me die. I lost a whole bunch of the kids I had in the school bus. Everything's gone. Please don't move me. Let me die.'

"I picked him up and threw him on my shoulder and I walked up the road where there was a wall to divide the roads. I said, 'You stay there until I get onto the other side and I'll take you into my house.' I put him down on the wall and he just turned over and rolled off and I had to pick him up again. Then I took him to my house. He said, 'Where's my bus?' I said, 'Down there in the pond.' I gave him some dry clothes and I changed myself; he stayed until nine o'clock. Then the tide went down and we went down and looked at the bus."

Caswell said later, "I saw that we would have to leave the bus or be drowned like rats. I told the children to grab each other tightly. I had hold of several when the huge wave came over us. I went down twice. When I came up, I saw Clayton Chellis swimming around. He was the only one who was saved besides me. Joe Matoes [Jr.] could have saved himself but he was drowned trying to rescue his younger sister."

While Caswell and Matoes stood there beside the pond looking at the bus, Mr. and Mrs. Chellis came up. Matoes recalled, "Caswell said to him, 'I got your boy, but your daughter's dead — gone' and Chellis got mad and he went down to the road and he took some rocks and he just crashed them windows out of that bus until he bust them all. He was really mad."

Matoes, in his early eighties when I talked with him at Jamestown — a strong, handsome native of the Azores and a fatalistic man of the soil — said, "We never did find one of my children — all but one. Four or five days later, Mrs. Chellis called to her husband and she said, 'Carl, what's that going down the bay there, half white and half red?' Well, she didn't know at the time; she didn't ask my wife, but she thought it might be a lobster buoy.

"But there was a kid who asked my wife, 'What kind of clothes was Dotty wearing?' and my wife told her, a white blouse and a red skirt. She went out to sea.

"Well, so that's the way it went. Took me three years to get over it, took a lot, go through a lot of hard labor — there's a lot of stuff, you know. Ah, ahhh!" Here, his voice broke, he paused to regain his composure, and I ended the interview.

There were equally tragic footnotes to the school bus incident. Edward Donahue lived next door to the Chellis family. He recalled, "The boy who survived said that when the bus driver let them out of the bus, he was holding his little sister's hand; she was only seven, and the last thing he remembered was that she told him, 'Clayton, don't let the water get in your eyes.' "

A Jamestown resident of many years commented, "Norman Caswell was descended from old, old Jamestown settlers. When they got to Mackerel Cove on that day, nobody knew what a hurricane was or that this storm was anything of the kind. They got to the east side of the [Beaver] Neck and the seas were so high that Caswell stopped the bus. By this time, they couldn't get back. He told the children to hold hands, in a line. He put the Chellis boy at one end of the line, because he was the biggest of the children, and he put himself at the front end.

"When the great wave came, it washed over them and the littler children couldn't hold on. The line broke in the middle.

"What happened left Norman Caswell in very bad emotional shape and actually, he died from the shock of this thing.

"The Gianitis family, they were a young couple. They simply disappeared after the accident. They left as soon as you could cross the Neck, after the water went down. They left everything in their house just the way it was. They didn't take anything with them and when we went down to the house afterwards, here were all their things, including some stamps they were collecting and all the little things of a household.

"The Chellis boy who had helped Caswell came out in good shape. The Lord had saved him from this, you see, and he wasn't drowned. When he got to the proper age, he joined the Navy and he was out on the West Coast and went swimming in somebody's pool and he drowned for no reason at all in that pool. Now if that isn't a story. It makes you cry, but God was after him, somehow or other, right?"

There is a minor official aspect to the tragedy. Carl Chellis, who was keeper of the light station at Beavertail and whose seven-year-old daughter, Marion, was among the children drowned, received a routine request from the Superintendent of Lighthouses to submit to the government a list of what he had lost in the storm, including age of items and estimated value, with the idea that Washington might reimburse him.

In the National Archives in Washington, there is filed this response: "As requested in your letter of October 4, 1938, I am forwarding a list of personal effects lost in the hurricane of September 21st: Two bicycles, five years, $15; two pairs boys overshoes, one year, $3; one set stove grates, five years, $6; one sled, two years, $2; one ice cream freezer, four years, $4. (Signed) Chellis."

The loss of Chellis' child was not included, because it was not officially includable.

On September 23, the Newport *News* reported, "The bodies of sixteen persons drowned in the hurricane were dug from the wreckage that was Island Park and from the ruins of submerged automobiles in Hathaway's peach orchard Thursday. Many cars washed across the road by the high tide into the swamp on the north side of Anthony's Road have not been reached by WPA rescue workers. It is feared that they contain more bodies. Martial law has been declared and the entire population has been ordered to evacuate what houses remain standing. Only three houses were left on the water side of the road, with the various amusement places being among those swept away.

"When Island Park was at its deepest, it was estimated that sixteen feet of water covered Cedar Avenue, near the Hathaway peach orchard. One eyewitness saw a house floating by with a man in it shouting frantically for help, which could not be given, and he drowned in view of many."

The John W. Reynolds, Jr., family lived in a cottage on the north side of Park Avenue, Island Park. Their children were Ann, ten, and John, eight. "My brother and I returned from school about 3 o'clock in the afternoon and found nobody home," Ann said. When the storm began to get worse, Mrs. [Joseph] Jackson, our neighbor, came to our home and asked us to come over to her house. We entered Mrs. Jackson's cottage just as the water began flooding the cellar.

"At this time, two women and a baby who said they came from Common Fence Point asked to come into the house to get out of the storm. Mrs. Jackson told them to come in.

"When the water continued to rise above the first floor, Mr. Jackson ordered us all upstairs to the second floor. About 5 o'clock, when the water was still coming up and the waves were crashing against the house, Mr. Jackson said that we ought to leave the cottage. With the help of Mr. Jackson and his twenty-two-year-old son, Earl, we were taken out and placed upon an improvised raft.

"The two women with the baby refused to leave the house, believing they were safer in the building than outside. Just as we floated off, we saw the house swept away by the tidal wave, with the women and the baby still in it.

"Mr. Jackson had Johnny on his back, but when his weight took him under water several times, he passed my brother to Earl. Earl and my brother floated away in another direction and we lost sight of them. Just before we reached high land, Mr. Jackson slipped off the board which we used for a raft, leaving me on high land, where the water reached only to my knees. Mr. Jackson rushed back and caught Mrs. Jackson just as she was going down for the third time."

[225]

The Reynolds family lost all of their possessions. The Jackson house was demolished. John Reynolds and Earl Jackson, found the next morning by Mr. Reynolds, landed safely two miles away.

Sarkis Kayarian of Woonsocket operated a wholesale tailor supply business and on September 21, he was on a business trip. "I was alone in my car and I left Newport about 3:30 P.M., headed for Fall River. The wind got so strong that I stopped my car near a house. There were about ten other cars stopped in this section of the road at Island Park," Kayarian said later.

"About a quarter past four, the water came right up to the road from the bay near the Stone Bridge, where I was parked. I saw two other fellows, one in a Chevrolet and another in a Ford, who were parked near me, jump out of their cars and try to open the door of a house. The wind was so strong it pushed the front of my car around. The water was getting higher and was up to the seat when I tried to get out of the car.

"The waves were so strong that I could not get the door on the driver's side open. I managed to open the door on the other side and waded up to the house, holding onto a pole and the steps. The other men smashed in a window and got into the house. I followed them in. Six men left their cars and came into the house. There was a Packard car in the road with three women and two men in it. When the next wave struck, it must have washed the Packard away, for after the wave had passed, I was unable to see the Packard or the people who were in it.

"The water kept getting higher and higher, so the six of us went up to the second floor. By this time, the seawater completely covered our automobiles on the road. The waves then ripped the porch away from the front of the house. Next, the house was washed off the foundations and started to float away. The house was nicely furnished, and when the waves started to break in the upstairs window in the room where we were, we pushed the furniture against the windows and put a mattress and the bed slats up to keep the water out. Then the entire wall on that side of the house was blown away. We went into another room and shut the door. The windows were blown out, and I moved a cedar chest over so that the other fellows could put up a bedspread over the window to keep the wind out. We all decided to lie on the bed, expecting that it would float when the house broke up.

"One man took out a package of cigarettes and said, 'Let's have a smoke; it looks like we are all done.' We all had a smoke. Then the wall on the right side of us was blown out and the floor and bed started to sink. One of the fellows had found two flashlights in the room. He tried to signal outside. The wind was blowing the house in a northeasterly direction and people saw our signals. They signaled back to us, but could not come to our rescue. One fellow found a life preserver and he left us, and disappeared.

"Another fellow saw a roof floating by. He grabbed it and disappeared. At this time, so much was going on that I did not notice how the other fellows left. But when I looked around, I was all alone and I felt that this was a hell of a way to die. I reached out and grabbed a piece of the roof joint just as the rest of the house crumbled beneath me. I managed to keep afloat by holding onto this roof joint.

"I drank plenty of water and I can still taste it. It tasted terrible, but I cared for nothing as long as I could keep afloat. I managed to get to the outer edge of the roof, and I found four of the fellows up there. I yelled for one of them to help me up and one of them who had a life preserver came down and took my left hand to help me up the side of the roof. I lost his grip and fell back into the water, but the second time he tried, he was able to pull me to the top of the roof.

"We stayed there and called for help. Sergeant Keenan from the Portsmouth Barracks of the State Police heard us. He stopped a mail truck and, with others, came to our aid. The roof was caught in the top of some trees and had swung around toward high ground. The men put a long plank from the high ground to the roof, and we were able to walk ashore. We had rode on this roof more than three-quarters of a mile and the time we spent on it seemed like several hours.

"The next day, I went back to see if I could get my car. It was about 150 feet away from where I left it. It was still under water and all I could see was the top of it."

At Sakonnet Point, the storm wave flooded the land to a height of twenty feet. It swept away fifty of the seventy-five cottages and shanties that made up the Sakonnet fishing colony. Nine men and a woman sought refuge in a two-story garage on the F. F. Grinnell estate; four died. Allen Kimpel, one of the survivors, still bearing scars on his face from being crushed between the garage and a boat that saved his life, was mending fishing net with a twine needle — sitting in the middle of a great net spread in a sunny field — when he talked about what happened.

"The water was washing out the bricks from under the garage," Kimpel said, "and finally a big sea that broke just before it hit the building knocked it off its foundation.

"The wave ripped off our part of the building and flung us and it into the river. As we floated up the river, I kicked out a window in the peak and some of us climbed out. The garage was starting to break up and we thought the end had come, but we kept a weather eye open for something we could jump to.

"As we floated along, the *Wahoo*, owned by Edward Brayton of Fall River, loomed up and as the building was passing it, I jumped and caught onto the mooring head fast. I was thrown between the building and the boat and squeezed there until they separated; my face was badly cut. I got into the boat and started the motor. Bill Lewis of Tiverton Four Corners, Maynard Blades of Nova Scotia (Blades went to the hospital with broken ribs and head injuries), and Ernest Vanasse got into the boat with me. Frankie Henriques grabbed a piece of wreckage and hours later floated up on the shore with all his clothes ripped off and bruised and cut all over.

"The four who drowned — Al Sabins, Ebenezer Keith, and Mr. and Mrs. Vasco F. Souza of New Bedford — hung onto a piece of the broken building. When they were last seen, only two of them were still holding onto it.

"It's a good thing the *Wahoo* was a staunch craft or it never would have weathered the awful seas. We had all we could do to stay in the boat and we were using both hands to hold on. In the worse part of the storm, the lines broke, and she parted from her mooring, but we were ready and with the order from Bill Lewis, who was the engineer, I gave it full speed ahead and I don't mean maybe.

"Boy, did we come in. People on the Point who were watching the sea from a safe elevation saw the *Wahoo* come in and they said it looked like an airplane. We thought of the ledge and avoided that, although we ran into some submerged wreckage, but that didn't slow us up. We put her into the lee side of the wharf and climbed up on the dock; the *Wahoo* drifted onto the beach and was one of the few craft to survive the blow.

"If there's another hurricane," said Kimpel, "I want to be up where the hills are high."

That was the manner of the hurricane in Rhode Island. One thinks, at last, of the two men at Newport Beach who gathered from the sand two cans of pennies, these being all that was left of their investment in an amusement arcade. One sees the red brick base of Whale Rock Lighthouse, where Walter B. Eberley, father of six, died alone when thundering seas destroyed the beacon. And recalls the story of the Coast Guard cutter *Taboe*, reaching Prudence Island after the storm. One of her officers called out on the loud hailer, "Where are the dead?" A voice from the shore replied, "All washed to sea."

Book V

Massachusetts

Chapter 13

Now, THE HURRICANE was coming to us.

The New Bedford *Standard-Times* city desk tried to place a long-distance call and the operator was vague about whatever the difficulties were, but it wasn't placeable.

In the wire room, the teletype machines still clacked, and occasionally their bells rang with the urgency of the message, but the stories were little more than bulletins. Increasingly, one sensed that the stories were hours behind the events. Eventually, the last bell rang and the machines quit all together. The ties with the world were being cut and we were coming to face our ordeal alone, as Westhampton had faced it alone, as Westerly had faced it alone.

Outside, the hot wind was wild; the weather lay lower upon the land, as if to smother it.

Even as late as this, the outlying sections beyond New Bedford knew what was happening before the city did.

Reporter Joseph Slight of the *Standard-Times* covered the suburbs. He was making his afternoon police checks on September 21, sometime between 2:15 and 3 P.M. It had been a run-of-the-mill day; children back in school, workers returned to their jobs (those who had jobs), and vacations over.

The wind was freshening. He phoned Dartmouth Police Chief Clarence H. Brownell: "Anything doing, Chief?"

"You better get here quick! Three or four big yachts have broken loose from their moorings in Padanaram Harbor and are smashing up against the Padanaram bridge!" Brownell replied.

Slight said later, "The wind buffeted the light sedan I was driving. At first, there were only broken branches in the streets, but by the time I had gone a mile, great elms were crashing to earth. Wires were coming down; trees began to block the roads.

"When I got to the bridge, men in oilskins and sou'westers were struggling to save three large sailing craft that were smashing against the concrete and steel span. I bucked the wind to a point about one-third of the way across, salt water drenching me, held onto a post with one hand and with the other tried to take a picture of a big sloop that was hitting the bridge with sickening crunches. The water was coming up rapidly; it was up to my ankles. I called the office to give them a bulletin and went back to the waterfront.

"I got there just in time to see a big restaurant that featured a roof with a huge lobster designed in the shingles float out into the harbor and break up. It was virtually raining shingles torn from roofs and walls. Trees and utility poles were coming down and the waters of the harbor were churned into a white froth dotted with overturned and sinking pleasure boats and the mastheads of sunken craft. It was about 3:30. That was the beginning. . . ."

Beyond Dartmouth, there was Westport — Westport Harbor and Horseneck Beach — where twenty-three died and dozens of substantial dwellings were demolished; the West Beach was left a jumble of wrecked cottages and the East Beach, swept clean of its summer settlement.

Ann Mills, twelve, daughter of Mr. and Mrs. Everett B. Mills of Fall River, was standing at the window of their Westport Harbor home when the storm wave struck; beside her was the maid, Miss Mary Frances Black. Ann dove out a window, grabbed a piece of floating wreckage. Miss Black, who had a fear of the water, called

Empty posts in foreground once supported houses wrecked and jumbled at Westport, Massachusetts.

to her, "Good-bye, Ann!" The youngster eventually abandoned the wood to which she was clinging because it was not taking her in the direction of safety. She swam a considerable distance and finally reached higher ground and was assisted from the water. The maid, last seen holding on to a pole, as the sea dislodged the house, was drowned. On September 23, the Mills house was found on the sixth fairway of the Acoaxet Golf Club in Westport. The Millses' dog was discovered alive in an upstairs cupboard of the house.

Dr. Andrew F. Hall of New Bedford was one of the early colonists at Horseneck; he had had extensive property holdings at Allen's Point for years. When two small cottages near his home were washed away, he became concerned for the safety of Mrs. Mark Sullivan of New Bedford and Mrs. John de Nadal of Fall River and her baby, who were in Mrs. Sullivan's house about 100 feet down the beach.

Ali Aberdeen, proprietor of the Point Breeze Restaurant at the intersection of East and West Beach roads, came to help him. Hall tied a line to a steel stanchion of his house and Aberdeen struggled through the surf and fastened it to a post on the Sullivan home. The post lasted less time than it took to tie the knot; the next sea carried it away and slung it onto the main highway, but the iron stanchion held. Hall and Aberdeen worked their way across the open stretch of water to the Sullivan house, got Mrs. de Nadal and her baby, and made the trip back safely by holding onto the rope.

Aberdeen went back for Mrs. Sullivan; the water was well above his waist. He got her partway to the Hall house when the sea tore her away. He recovered her and tried again. A wave knocked them both down; the seas were getting heavier, Aberdeen gave up temporarily, after getting Mrs. Sullivan back to her home. He made his way alone to the Hall house.

Meanwhile, the ice cream concession on Town Landing was swept away, crashing into the front of Aberdeen's restaurant. The force of the blow drove the restaurant from its foundation and once afloat, it destroyed the De Nadal cottage. Where the restaurant had been, there stood a pole, bearing a vertical white sign reading "Clambakes." A white board, about the width of the sign, borne by the wind, struck the pole in a horizontal position about three-quarters of the way up the sign, forming an almost perfect white cross. As if it had been nailed there, the board remained against the post and did not drop until the wind let go.

After an hour had passed, Mrs. Hall glanced out the window at the storm and saw Mrs. Sullivan holding onto a telephone pole which was directly in front of her home on the West Beach road. She was waist-deep in water and apparently had been washed off her porch. Using the pole as a shield against the debris-filled waters, she was moving from one side to the other, dodging planks and timbers. Even as they watched from the Hall home, the flood waters became nearly shoulder-deep, rampaging across the land with equal force from both the southwest and southeast.

Mrs. Sullivan, whose survival hung on a miracle a moment, as wreckage that could have killed her — tons of it — shot by her on the crests of the muddy seas, was no more than 150 feet away from those who were helpless to aid her, yet she was frequently out of sight behind solid water and stinging spray that clouded the air. Again and again, they were certain that she had lost her grip and been carried away, yet each time that they could see across the troughs and the air cleared momentarily, there she remained. Until finally, they could not see her at all.

Minutes passed; she was not at the pole any more. Then suddenly, they saw her on hands and knees, moving along the edge of a wall on the north side of the Hall property. In a moment, she was reachable; Aberdeen and Hall crawled across the intervening stretch — surrounded by cement walls that acted as a breakwater — and dragged her back to the house. She said later she had no idea how she got from the pole to the wall, a move that undoubtedly meant for her the difference between life and death.

"About 12 o'clock that night, the police came," Hall said. "We went with them through the water to John Reed Road and climbed aboard a truck that had been caught on the Horseneck side of the Westport Point bridge when the storm broke. The trip to the Point was impossible to describe; darkness, except for flashlights; trees had fallen and it was necessary to crawl over or under them. In the truck, there were four or five refugees; one man had a broken leg."

Walter Blackmer and his wife, in a West Beach cottage, decided to leave about 4 o'clock, when wind and rain made such a roar that, "we could not hear each other, even when we shouted.

"We walked out of the building, which already gave signs of weakening and waded to the highest sand dunes. From there, we watched an awful sight. Cottage after cottage was torn from its foundation and carried off. Everywhere, there was the screech of wind, the crack of smashing timber, and the thunder of the great waves. Even far from the sea, we were not safe; the water reached almost to our feet. We walked five hours through water, woods, and dunes. Never will we forget. . . ."

Elzear Plante of Fall River was the proprietor of a West Beach pavilion. "Right under my eyes," he said, "my whole business was swept down. When the sea and wind began to wreck my pavilion, I went like crazy. I was trying to keep windows and doors closed as the waves smashed them open. My son, Henry, and his wife and baby waded out and made for the road to Westport Point.

"Water was knee-high inside the building and furniture, fixtures, and stock were floating. I saw it was useless to stay and I left, too. From a distance up the road, I saw the pavilion's roof and cement block walls crash to earth. Houses along the West Beach were carried a thousand feet from their foundations. It was awful. . . ."

Mr. and Mrs. James A. Blakney had a cottage on the East Beach; they had spent twenty summers at Horseneck. "On Tuesday," he said, "we thought everything would be all right and decided to stay at the cottage. I put my car in a nearby garage."

For a while on Wednesday afternoon, as the sea came higher on the beach, bringing with it flotsam of all kinds, he tried to dig away the cultch from around his house so that the water could flow beneath it, rather than sweeping through it. He abandoned the effort; it was futile, and in a matter of moments, the water had increased to a dangerous flood. Blakney decided he and his wife should cross the road to a larger cottage with a stone foundation.

At that point, however, he said later, "I was asked by a Providence man to assist him in getting his mother and his son across the road from his car, to the stronger cottage. The water was sweeping along with such force that it almost ripped the woman away from us. In trying to hold her, the man's son was torn from my grasp. I tried to hang onto the woman and to a nearby post, but was unable to and I never saw any of the three again.

"I then tried to get my wife across to the house. After a hard struggle, I finally got her across. I had a screwdriver in my pocket and pried open a rear door. But that house was soon knocked off its foundation and we got down into about three feet of water in the lee of another cottage. I noticed that its chimney was beginning to buckle and tried to get up the steps of another house nearby. The heavy tide swept in and almost broke my hold on my wife. We finally got up the steps of the house across the roadway in time to see the cottage of Dr. Holt swept away."

By 4:15, the Blakneys were afloat in a house; they described the waves on the East Beach as thirty feet high. "The cottage we were in was swept along for a distance of about a mile and swung around," Blakney said. "I grabbed a piece of three-by-four, using it for a pole, hanging onto it, until the house started to break up.

"I looked around and saw the roof of my own cottage coming toward us. We crossed it and the roof of another house. I found a board and we used that to cross to a third roof. The cottages were in about ten feet of water. All of the time, we could see houses being swept by us. We noticed one couple making a raft of beds inside their home, piling one on top of another until they nearly reached the ceiling."

The Blakneys drifted a mile north of the beach before the building they were on was grounded.

James Gill was an employee on William Almy's Quonsett Farm. When the storm began to assume major proportions, he left the farm in his automobile and drove along flooded East Beach Road, headed for his Reed Road cottage to assist his wife and baby.

"While driving along the beach — there was no road, the water had washed it away — my car was blown over several times, with me in it. I got out somehow," Gill said.

"Houses were floating across the road. I started to walk and saw people on the porch of an East Beach house. They called me to come with them. I was exhausted and glad to be with someone. These people were from New York. There were three couples. I didn't know their names.

"I had only been there fifteen minutes when there were three huge waves and the third was the tidal wave, which crushed the house like a paper bag. All the people were drowned. I was the only one left.

"As the house fell in, I got on part of the roof of the porch; it broke loose from the house. As soon as I got on it, away it went, up the river. I was going so fast I could hardly hang on.

"I saw a boat and I swam to it and said, 'My Lord, if anything would stay on top of water, it would be a boat.' It was getting dark and I crawled in and stayed all night. I was so cold. Half of my clothes were torn from my body.

"The next morning, I got out of the boat and looked around; at first, I didn't know where I was. Then I recognized some places and walked back to Mr. Almy's farm."

Although Mr. Gill did not know until the morning after the hurricane how his wife and infant son — whom he had started out to help — had fared, Mrs. Mary E. Hart did; she lived on John Reed Road. "A young woman who had a bathing suit on came to the door and said that water was coming down the road," Mrs. Hart related. "I had just started getting supper for my children; one was eight months and the other, 1½ years. I was nervous because it was windy, the screening had blown in on the porch, my husband wasn't home, and we had no phone.

"When I went out to look, the water was up to the house next door. John Pettey's house was across the street; it was on a rise. I went over there; he was lying down, and I told him and he got right up and said he would go help the people in Mosher's Lane. Henry Gidley went with him. [The Gills lived in Mosher's Lane.] They told me afterward they had trouble because so many people wanted to get in the boat.

"They picked up Mrs. Gill and her baby, Fred White, and Kate Rogers, who had a broken arm, and they took them to a cottage on higher ground, about three-quarters of a mile back from East Beach. They had no milk for the Gill baby, so they gave it strips of cloth wet in sugar to suck on.

"When I got out of my house, I didn't think of myself; I thought of my children. The water was swirling around the backyard. The house did move some, but it stayed there. I wanted to get back into the house and get some food but the water was flowing across and I couldn't get to it. Through the efforts of John, I and my children got into a car. We went to the Midway Road. Another car came along in the water with the spray flying over it. It was my husband.

"His car got stuck west of the Midway Road. We stayed there and the men put markers out so they were able to tell when the water stopped rising and started to recede. I was worried about my baby when the water was coming up; I was afraid it couldn't live if we had to get out and leave the car because the wind took your breath away.

"I had two quarts of milk in the car and as soon as the water went down, my husband, Roger, and John Pettey — they had to hold onto each other because they kept falling into potholes made by the storm — took a quart to the Gill baby.

"And when the water went down, all those people came out from the dunes to Midway Road. We didn't realize even then how bad it had been. It was 5 P.M. when the woman came to the door to tell me about the water. It was 8:30 P.M. when all the people began coming out of the dunes and when I had a chance to look at East Beach, I didn't believe it, I couldn't believe it. . . ."

As a footnote, the substantial house where James Gill and the six others had sought refuge was owned by James Sinclair of Fall River. When the storm was over, the bases for its fireplaces remained, although overturned; there were one or two stone posts, and smashed sections of the lower story of the house, which also was built of stone. Nothing more remained of the dwelling.

Slight went to Horseneck on September 22 to write the storm story for the *Standard-Times*; he had driven that way on the day before the hurricane and this was his reaction to the change that had occurred in forty-eight hours:

"As I passed the Almy estate in a bright sun and turned toward East Beach, my breath was taken away and my heart virtually stopped. This couldn't be Horseneck!

"What I saw was a wasteland of sand and stone, with not one stick left of the scores and scores of buildings that lined the shore. Even the paved road was gone. I could see that the hurricane-whipped seas had swept away everything, mingling with the marshland until all was one angry expanse of water.

"Over in the marshes, I could see debris — the peak of a house, part of a sidewall, a smashed chimney. The only evidence that there had been buildings along the shore of East Beach was a piece of cement foundation tipped over and half buried in the sand here, part of the stone posts of Charette's hotel there, the base of a fireplace in another spot.

"The scene was repeated at West Beach. Miles of summer places — from small cottages to large residences of seasonal visitors — smashed from their foundations and the debris was carried by mountainous waves into salt marshlands and sand dunes.

"Most of the dead were elderly people who had stayed on at summer homes after grandchildren had gone back to school, their vacations over, and the parents had returned to the city, coming back to the beach weekends.

"There was no warning. After all, no hurricane had hit this area in the memory of those who lingered on at the seashore for the warm and beautiful days of September and Indian summer. So when they felt the wind increase and the sea rise, they thought it was just an ordinary storm and they could batten down the hatches and ride it out.

"Some of those who died there had boots on. It is believed they were building sand barricades to save the places they loved so much. Some were boarding windows to keep out the rising surf. Never again will they return to their beloved Horseneck — the place of sun, sand, surf, beautiful sunsets, and sparkling sea. No more will they hear the laughter of children discovering the joys of nature in one of her most beautiful settings.

"Thomas and Margaret Logan of Fall River survived that terrible day. They had a nice cottage at West Beach; we were good friends and my wife and I had often visited them there. A sign on the front of the cottage labeled it aptly, 'Uncle Tom's Cabin.'

"Mr. Logan's brother died two days before the hurricane hit. Tom and Margaret were at the funeral in Fall River on September 21. They thought about going back to Horseneck and their quiet shore retreat after the funeral, but decided to stay at home in the city another day.

"On the twenty-second. I walked to the spot where the Logan cottage had stood at Horseneck. Nothing was left but the cement foundation and the porch of the two-story house. To the eastward, in what remained of the sand dunes, was a jumble of wreckage that included parts of their home, identifiable because of the sign that said, 'Uncle Tom's Cabin.' "

And then there was Cammie, a non-pedigreed cat, who for more than a decade had seasonally shuttled back and forth between the West Beach summer home of Chauncey R. Mosher, Dartmouth highway surveyor, and their winter residence in town. Mr. and Mrs. Mosher's cat was probably better known in the West Beach summer colony than any other household pet.

When the household was forced to flee, Mrs. Mosher carried Cammie in her arms. Water was rushing over the highway, and Cammie, frightened, broke away from Mrs. Mosher's grasp and was carried off by the sea. At dawn, there was no sign of her.

A week passed. The family had searched all the wreckage in the area and concluded the cat had drowned.

On October 2, Mrs. Roy Hawes, a sister of Mr. Mosher, was at the beach. She passed a pile of wreckage on which rested the roof of one of the family's outbuildings, which had been swept several hundred feet into the dunes. As she did so, she heard the cries of a cat, beneath the roof. She called Cammie by name and the cat came out from under the pile, twelve days after the hurricane, and unharmed.

Captain Ernest Woodcock was skipper of Clarence Warden's 42-foot sloop *Tar Baby*, which was moored in Padanaram Harbor. On the twenty-first, he and his brother, Harold, drove to Padanaram about noontime; high wind had been predicted, storm warnings were posted, and Woodcock wanted to check lines and gear. When they walked down the wharf toward their dinghy, the heavy stillness of the atmosphere, the sharp slashes of wind across the harbor made Woodcock uneasy, although nobody ashore was apprehensive at that time.

Once aboard the *Tar Baby*, he decided immediately that the single mooring line, fast to a 120-pound anchor, was not enough. He started the engine, ran up ahead of the mooring and dropped the boat's large anchor as well. The sea in the harbor was running about 6 feet high; it was cresting, but not breaking and the wind was taking the tops off the waves, as it does with an offshore sea. The sloop's bow was rising higher with each oncoming wave, sawing up and down, and when it dipped, water came pouring aft, filling the scuppers and slopping the deck with white foam. The rain began to fall heavily, driving in slanting torrents; footing on deck became precarious.

They decided to try to pick up two additional moorings that had been vacated at the season's end, one on each side of the bow. With the engine still able to make headway against the wind, they ran ahead first to starboard, then to port, succeeded in snaring the floats on the mooring pennants and finally were able to tie into the bridled moorings. The engine was now running red hot because there was sediment in the intake. But they were fast to three moorings and two anchors, weighing an estimated total of 700 to 800 pounds; they had scope and weight enough to hold a 100-foot vessel and *Jar Baby* was less than half that. They felt a measure of confidence.

The wind was now straight out, and the brothers, in oilskins and sneakers, squatted in the cockpit, watching the weather, constantly checking *Jar Baby*'s position. A huge wave crested under their dinghy, tied astern, raised it high in the air, and the wind whirled it bottom up. The dinghy sank in that position in the trough of the following sea.

A Herreshoff Fish-boat class sloop broke from her mooring abreast of them and bore down swiftly upon *Jar Baby*. The Herreshoff fortunately passed just astern, but her mooring line wrapped around their propeller shaft. Now they were engineless and without a dinghy.

The harbor was being emptied of boats. Craft of every description were lunging crazily in all directions, headed for lawns, rocks, and pastures, as they parted their lines or dragged their moorings. Wind and heavy sheets of rain lowered visibility to a couple of hundred feet.

Captain Woodcock related, "Strangely, I noticed an unusual triangle of calm nearby, off our port beam, throughout the entire storm. For some reason, this narrow area of still water prevailed against all the turbulence; the two or three boats in this area, including the sloops *Kotick*, owned by Dr. Prescott, and *Amantha*, forerunner of the famous Crocker-designed, Scott-built charter boats, and owned by C. Gardner Akin and Arthur F. Spare, remained easily at anchor in the inexplicable vacuum."

Gradually, the position of these sloops in the calm water began to change relative to *Jar Baby*, and Woodcock knew then that his craft was moving, dragging down the harbor toward the bridge. She had started to drag when the harbor bottom began to let go under the strain upon it; ordinarily, the gear that held her would have resettled on the bottom and the fact that it did not indicates the force of the wind.

Woodcock felt "an increasing awareness of impending catas-

[245]

trophe and a feeling of helplessness. I was damned scared. Movement on deck was no longer possible and the storm was now furious beyond my experience. I don't think we consciously admitted it, but we thought it was the end. We saw other boats going and we thought we were going the same way. There was nothing for us to do then.

"My brother, now a doctor, was then involved in college entrance examinations, and I remember that he said, 'I'll never worry about another exam if I get out of this.' "

The stone bridge, where Slight tried to take his news picture "of a big sloop that was hitting with sickening crunches," was much nearer as *Tar Baby* sagged steadily to leeward. It was deadly slow dragging, but the ground tackle kept the sloop's head into the wind. The Woodcocks could now see clearly the jumbled mass of boats and buildings, the flotsam of all sorts that surged against the bridge's foundations and littered the shore at the east end of the Padanaram bridge.

Captain Woodcock said later, "Among the many large boats in the harbor was a rugged seagoing Norwegian cutter named *Escape*, owned by Llewellyn Howland. She was a pilot ship, formerly from either Norway's coastal areas or the North Sea. She appeared so heavily built as to be indestructible. But now — with one tremendous thrust full broadside against the bridge's heavy stone base — she hit once, bounced back, promptly split cleanly down the middle and, while we watched, sank immediately.

"It was as if we were in a bad dream. Our spirits were low and hope was almost gone. The bridge was close now, yet it seemed to be disappearing slowly into the water, each new tremendous wave covering more of it. We had held out longer than most, but like the other boats already destroyed, we seemed certain to follow. We were virtually upon the end of the bridge now; the backwash slewed *Tar Baby* and for the first time during the storm, she was broadside to the full force of the wind."

That was one factor that saved them and the sloop. Broadside, the wind knocked her down and she drew four to five feet of water, rather than her full seven. At the same moment, there was a surge of high water that flooded over the bridge at almost the time they got there. *Tar Baby* hit a couple of times, but carried her draft bouncily over the bridge. When she was over, the Woodcocks felt her bow jerk into the wind's eye, and the sloop came to an abrupt halt. They now had the biggest mooring in the harbor — their assortment of lines and anchors had become hooked to the bridge stanchions as they slid over.

About 5 o'clock, it was over. The wind subsided; it was calm and mild, almost tropical. Fortunately for *Tar Baby*, the wind did not veer into the northwest and blow hard as it often does in the area after a southeaster; had it done so, it would have driven the sloop upon the bridge again.

"Our luck held. We lay down, mentally and physically drained," Captain Woodcock said.

Chapter 14

THEN THERE WAS THE MATTER of the three islands.

Offshore, south of Padanaram, lies Cuttyhunk, westernmost of the Elizabeth Islands chain. There, houses and vessels were shattered; especially for a small community in modest circumstances, it was a disaster. I talked to John Cornell, Cuttyhunk fisherman, when he finally brought his vessel, *Marie* — her port side battered by the island's breakwater — across Buzzards Bay. "The fishing village is wiped out," Cornell said. "I lost everything except for what I stand in. My brother Tom is over there with a wife and four children — no clothes, no food, no house." His brother Howard's two-story house was swept from its foundation and the open cellar filled with huge boulders blown from nearby stone walls.

At high water, the entire beach between the village and the Coast Guard station was boiling surf. The water supply for the island, owned by Mrs. Elizabeth M. Allen, barely escaped the ocean, which at one time came within sixty feet of the wellhouse. Boathouses, bathhouses, buildings, and planking from the town wharf were swept away, and the steel weather tower at the Coast Guard station was bent to the ground. Walter Loveridge's new house, completed the day before the hurricane, after being two years under construction, was demolished even before it was furnished.

Charles H. Cahoon of Fall River was supervising construction on Cuttyhunk of a new Coast Guard boathouse, on rocks midway between the island and the Coast Guard station. "At 3 P.M., the biggest waves I ever saw ripped out the reef of rocks and washed away the lighters and equipment," he said. This left Cahoon and ten construction men adrift on a pile driver. They narrowly escaped drowning; in the full smother of the storm, Coast Guard Chief Boatswain's Mate Alfred Volton and his boat's crew performed a remarkable feat of seamanship in getting them off without loss of life or injury; the pile driver grounded and broke up.

"After they got us off and while they were taking us into the lee of the harbor, the Coast Guard's boat crew hauled seven fishermen out of the harbor with boat hooks. Houses were being swept into the sea and hens and chickens were picked up in yards and carried considerable distances by the wind," Cahoon related.

"I would say that waves were dashing up forty feet on the lighthouse. The Coast Guard station's pet Airedale was sleeping in a little shack beside the station when the storm broke, and dog and shack were carried into the water by the first giant wave. The shack was never seen again, but that animal came swimming in from the open sea the next morning practically exhausted, with nobody knowing how far out he had been swept."

Cahoon kept the tattered American flag that flew over the Cuttyhunk Coast Guard station on the day of the storm as a souvenir; it was not only torn, it was knotted many times, as if by hand, and so ripped that it never could be flown again. The station flag, flown daily, ordinarily lasted six months. That one was hoisted, brand new, on the morning of the hurricane.

Chief Volton and his crew, Norman P. Cupples, Allan L. Potter, and James A. Yates, were credited with saving at least twenty lives, including those of the eleven men stranded on the pile driver, and they were awarded Coast Guard Silver Medals for Heroism.

Of September 21, Volton, who entered the Coast Guard in 1926, observed, "It was the worst experience I have had during my service. . . ."

Southeast of Cuttyhunk, there is the island of No Mans Land, where a man alone struggled for his life.

Cameron E. Wood, sixty-seven, was the caretaker of the Crane estate on No Mans Land. His wife, Nellie, had gone to the mainland on September 12 for her annual vacation. There were no other people on No Mans Land on September 21.

To understand what happened, it is essential to visualize an ingenious contrivance of Mr. Wood's making, which saved his life even though that was not its purpose.

"At a short distance from our house was a stone breakwater, which used to form a little sheltered anchorage," Wood said. "Unfortunately, this was silted in with sand and beach stone, so that no boat could lie there. Therefore, the only boats I could keep were a 16-foot dory and a 10-foot skiff, which I had to haul out on the beach.

"In order to do this alone, I placed two masts set in the ground, each about 25 feet high, one 50 feet above normal high-water mark and one at low-water mark; they were about 100 feet apart. At the top of these masts and fastened between them was a heavy wire cable. From the top of each mast was a guy wire or backstay. The one on the inshore mast was anchored about fifty feet inshore; the other was moored to the breakwater. Turnbuckles were used to keep the wire taut.

"On the horizontal cable were two trolleys, to which were fastened two 4-ply tackle blocks, with which I could hoist my boat and run it on the trolley for launching and to haul it up.

"On Wednesday morning, September 21, I heard over the radio that a gale was coming up the coast, so I went down and pulled my dory and skiff way up to the inshore mast and tied them. At about 4 P.M., I saw that the water was up to my boats, so I put on rubber boots and went down and waded out to the boats and hoisted the skiff a little higher above the ground to a point where I thought the invading waters would never reach, it never having done so before that I knew of.

"After I hoisted the skiff, a heavy sea came in and filled it. I bailed it out and hoisted it still higher, to find that the waters were rising so fast and had got so deep that I could not touch bottom under me. The seas were running so strong that I did not dare to try to wade ashore, for fear that I would be swept off my feet by the undertow."

Mr. Wood said he felt certain the water would soon recede from the unusually high point to which it had come crashing in on his little domain of 860 acres. Confident of this, he climbed into the skiff to sit out the storm. "But the sea got higher and higher," he added, "and I was forced time and again to hoist the skiff and myself higher on the mast, until I was about 20 feet above the ground. In the meantime, the wind had increased to a hurricane and was blowing 100 miles an hour.

"The skiff was swaying on the cable at a frightful rate; the great seas were coming in 20 feet high and you could not see the breakwater or the tops of the spiles in the basin. The waves would strike the mast and fly into the air and drench me to the skin. After every three or four seas, I had to bail out the skiff, as I was afraid that the extra weight would break the ropes and drop me and the boat into the surging seas."

Perched high, buffeted by the terrific wind, finding it increasingly difficult to keep his craft above the sea and wondering every minute if his masts and gear could stand the battering, Mr. Wood still was poised enough to survey the island and observe the damage being done. "The seas began to rush between and under the buildings on the shore and they started to go . . . whirling by me and out to sea." From his perch, he philosophized on what would happen to him if he should be plunged into the water. The answer was obvious, he concluded, but he derived a kind of grim comfort from looking at his predicament in the worst possible light and saying to himself, "We all have to die sometime."

He related, "I found the thought that my body might never be recovered or trace of me ever found made me feel more low than the imminence of death. After all the buildings along the shore were gone, I looked at our house, which was about 200 yards away, and I could see the waves go by it." Looking at the house, he thought of his wife and how she would feel when she returned to find it gone.

"After what seemed an interminable period, I felt myself getting weak," Wood said later, "but I knew that I had only myself to look to for rescue, so I tried to climb to the top of the mast, thinking that possibly from there, I could slide down the backstay and then when the sea ran down, make the shore before the next wave caught me.

"I got out of the boat, but I was too weak. I tried to hold onto the mast, but the first big sea caught me and snatched me away as if I were a straw and rolled me under water."

With thoughts of making peace with his God still strong in his mind, he was abruptly surprised to find solid earth beneath him. Even though the seas were pounding about him and thundering over him, he was nevertheless able to inch his way to a rock large enough to have withstood the barrage of waves, and he clung to it. As soon as he was able, he covered the short stretch to grass and safety with great and painful effort. "I do not know how long I lay on the ground," Wood said. "I did manage after a time to crawl to my house, which was then about 100 yards away. I found the job of getting my rubber boots and clothes off almost as hard as that of reaching safety.

"When I succeeded, I crawled into my bed and lay there all night, trembling and unable to sleep. The next morning, I was sore all over, so much so that I could hardly get out of bed, do my chores, and cook my breakfast. The cows and hens did not get fed or milked the night before, so I had an extra lot of milk to carry to the house.

"Thursday, the twenty-second, I slept all day and all night.

Friday morning, I felt good, but still lame. I walked around the island that day to survey the damage, and found my dory gone, all of the year's wood, which had been stored in one of the buildings, and many other things.

"The whole shoreline was changed. In some places, the cliffs had been washed away almost twenty-five feet inland at a point where they were thirty feet above the waterline."

On September 24, the master of the Coast Guard cutter *Pont-chartrain* dispatched the following message to headquarters: "Stood out at daylight, communicated by radio with Gay Head Coast Guard station, it being understood that this station often communicated with No Mans Land, using a special code of signals. At 0610, Gay Head reported that no signals had been received from the island, but that the house looked all right through binoculars.

"Anchored off north side of No Mans Land 0750, and sent Lieutenant (jg) Craik in motor surf boat to investigate. He found that five small houses on No Mans Land had been destroyed, the only occupant, caretaker Cameron Wood, was well, despite being in water for 2½ hours during the storm in a successful effort to save his boat, and needed nothing except radio batteries.

"While Lieutenant Craik was there, a private plane circled the island and dropped a message from Mrs. Wood, who had been in Providence."

Wood added, "The plane came over and dropped a letter, newspapers, and food. My wife was aboard the plane, but I did not know it until later. The plane could not land, as the field was all water and mud.

"On Thursday, September 29, my wife came home on the *Emily H.* of Newport. Then everything was once more all right."

To the northeast lay Martha's Vineyard.

In Edgartown, the tide rose until it flooded summer homes along the harbor front. Piers were under water, fences went adrift, and so did boathouses and boats. Captain Fred Vidler, keeper of the harbor light, said that at least twenty and probably more boats of various sizes went out past the lighthouse in the tide. Seven or eight were battered against the lighthouse bridge, a number sank, with only their masts visible, and the Chappaquiddick ferry lay shattered. Water rose halfway to the eaves of the Edgartown Yacht Club; within, the piano was afloat.

Thomas P. F. Hoving, now director of the New York Metropolitan Museum of Art, summered in Edgartown; his family had a house on Pease's Point Way. "I remember the smell of the eye of the hurricane," Hoving said. "It smelled like six billion air-conditioning sets dispensing ozone."

He was seven years old, small enough to fit under a card table. "That was where my mother put us while the hurricane was going on. To keep us children calm, she put two or three card tables together and laid blankets over them, and my sister was instructed to tell us all the ghost stories she knew. She stretched the one about the screaming skull over about three hours. We were so scared of her ghost stories we forgot about being scared of the storm till it was all over.

"When the smell went away and the storm had subsided, we went out to see what damage it had done. Where Vincent's drugstore is was the waterline. The 125-foot, steel-hulled *Manxman* had been torn loose from her mooring and had knocked down the top of the coal dock."

In Vineyard Haven, water was knee-deep over the steamboat wharf. The lower streets of the town were flooded to a depth of two or three feet and the harbor-front lawns were strewn with boats and wreckage. Antone Silvia was marooned at the Tashmoo home of Katharine Cornell, where he was at work, and he became concerned for the safety of Miss Cornell and her guests, Miss Caroline Pratt and Miss Helen Marot, Menemsha summer residents.

Waves were washing through the Cornell house when Silvia went out to attempt to cross the nearby Herring Creek, which lay between them and the road to the village. Breakers were rolling through the creek; he could neither wade through it nor jump it, so he attempted to swim. The floor immediately swept him before it; half-drowned, he managed to clutch a clump of tall beach grass on top of the bank and haul himself to safety. When Vineyard Haven police officer Simeon Pinkham arrived shortly afterward, checking the shore danger areas and assisting in evacuation, he suggested to Miss Cornell that the situation might easily have become dangerous. She replied, "Oh well, I guess I could have grabbed hold of something and held on."

It was "up-island" where the greatest damage was suffered and the Vineyard's only loss of life occurred.

My father, Joseph Chase Allen, wrote his story for the Vineyard *Gazette* immediately after the storm with his automobile headlamps for light.

"The ruin at Menemsha Creek constitutes something unbelievable, with virtually everything along the waterfront except the grocery store wiped out completely . . . the inrushing tide was so strong that it cut the sand away from pilings, while huge breakers reared above the jetties, foaming and racing clear across the anchorage basin and sweeping everything before them. Boats, buildings and docks, together with tangled masses of fishing gear, went swirling up into Menemsha Pond, some of the men sticking to their boats and going with them. . . ."

Benjamin C. Mayhew, Sr., was one of them. "I would have been all right and perhaps mightn't have gone ashore at all if it hadn't been for the masses of pond grass and weeds that clogged the intake of my water system and the engine got hot. I could only run for the beach and lay her ashore," he said.

The town pier was swept away, together with several rods of the surfaced highway that led to it. The fish market of Ernest Mayhew and the store of David Butler both went, as well as the land they occupied. The water rose so quickly around the Butler store and the building collapsed so rapidly that Mrs. Bessie Frances, Butler's daughter, and her aunt, Mrs. Welcome Tilton, had to be removed in a boat. "When the water reached the porch of the store, I began to ask the fishermen as they passed, whether they thought it could continue to come higher," Mrs. Frances said. "None of them believed it would. But it was finally over the porch and lapping at the threshold. Then the men outside called to us to leave the store. In the next five minutes, the water had risen two feet deep on the floor. . . ."

The narrow point of land extending between creek and basin was about wiped off the map. It stood some twenty feet above the regular level of the tide but the water came up until, with the washing of the sea, it was submerged and boats of considerable size were washed across it.

George Dolby, the only Vineyarder whom the storm caught out fishing, was in Vineyard Sound. He started to run for Vineyard Haven, but arriving at West Chop about 2 o'clock, found the sea too heavy to buck with his small boat. Swinging about, he headed westerly for Menemsha, keeping in under the land and fighting wind and sea. Three hours later, he entered the creek, only to be swept ashore, boat and all, shortly after. He was grateful, nevertheless. "If the engine had ever stopped in the Sound, it would have been the end of everything and I wouldn't be here now," he said.

At Menemsha Pond, boats torn from their moorings in the creek were stranded high up in the fields, in many cases, hundreds of yards from water. My father concluded, "The scene of destruction goes beyond anything recalled by the oldest inhabitants. Indeed, there were some who doubted if there would ever again be a harbor at Menemsha, but within twenty-four hours, the indomitable fishermen were planning the salvage of their boats and restoration of the waterfront."

Donald LeMar Poole, Menemsha fisherman, wrote an account of the storm "in the back of one of Uncle Chester's diaries." The parenthetical inserts are by his wife, Dorothy Cottle Poole, who made this account available to me.

"On the 21st, we were struck by a hurricane from the SE with a tremendous sea from the N. In less than two hours, it ruined the waterfront. Blew quite hard all day and picked up fast after dinner. At three P.M. was called out of the clubhouse [Ernest Mayhew's boathouse, where the men played cards on stormy days] to help Father [Everett Poole] tie up his boat. That done, a good gale blowing, we went down to my boat and found the dock had washed away and I was unable to get aboard. About this time, the tide rose rapidly and we found our retreat over the footbridge across the brook was gone. In less than ten minutes, the sandbanks behind my boathouse began to go under, and my boathouse, too. (Mrs. Everett Poole, our not-quite-eight-year-old son, Everett, and I were on the hill above the basin and saw all this happen. A huge wall of water swept over the breakwater and engulfed everything.)

"When we got back to the hill above the harbor, not a boathouse was left and every boat was adrift. Some went up the pond and went ashore there. From Lobsterville to Kathleen Knight's house, all was ocean, clear to the hills behind the harbor. All the boats and buildings on the Old Creek — and even the State Road — all gone, clear to Carl Reed's store. The tide rose eight feet above normal high water.

"At seven, the tide ebbed and the wind moderated. My boat, Rasmus Klimm's, the *John and Billy* of New Bedford, the *Lena Avila* of New Bedford, William Hand [the well-known yacht designer and naval architect] in the *Gossoon*, all went ashore on what used to be the sandbank behind my boathouse. These boats took a terrific pounding and are badly damaged. Father's catboat went adrift up the pond, with my little boat in tow. His boat ran into his own boathouse and went right through it like paper. When the tide turned, she came down again, went ashore on Gardiner's dock, where she lays now, with a stake up through her garboard.

"My little boat went over the breakwater, out to sea and came back in the night onto the beach outside. . . . The launches belonging to Frank and Walter Manning and to Reginald Norton are a total loss, one outside the harbor and one in. Ernest Dean lost his trap boat. . . . My big boat is badly damaged. . . . The beaches around the pond and outside are six feet high with all kinds of wreckage: parts of buildings, boats, old and new lobster pots, buoys, barrels, tubs, stakes, net and twine — in fact, everything but bodies.

"The same storm struck sooner on the backside of the town, overwhelming Stone Wall Beach and took every house away, drowning the cook in one house, the only loss of life hereabouts.

"Out of our fleet, every boat broke away but one and every dock and boathouse went and none were found in anything larger than pieces six by eight feet. We lost two large boats outright, seventeen went ashore, and at least a dozen small boats, skiffs and dories, were lost."

At Menemsha, as hard-hit as it was, no lives were lost, and, as Captain Everett Poole concluded, "It's bad, mighty bad, but when you go out to probe in the rubbish to see what can be saved, you don't have to dread uncovering the body of your brother."

Yet there was a death on Martha's Vineyard because of the hurricane, as Donald Poole had noted in his diary.

At about 4:15, Benedict Thielen, summer resident of Chilmark, left his shack on the beach and went to his house. The sea was high, but the wind was nothing extraordinary. He stood at the window with his wife and they both looked out at the sea. Bits of foam were blowing over the top of the dunes and, after a while there was a little trickle of water. This trickle increased and later, there were two streams, one on each side of the house, but the water was not more than an inch deep.

Mr. and Mrs. Thielen had tea and, as time passed, they continued to watch the storm, and still there was nothing of a frightening nature. As the water increased, however, they decided to leave the house and walk to dry land. They put on boots, sweaters, and oilers and prepared for a walk in the storm. Their maid, Mrs. Josephine Clarke, thirty-eight, of Jamaica, went with them, wearing a raincoat. As they left the back door of the house, the water was about eighteen inches deep. Then, when they had walked perhaps a half-dozen steps, a wave came, overwhelming the land, and the water was up to their necks. In another half-minute, the next great wave broke, and the water was over their heads. There was nothing for it but to swim. Mrs. Thielen reached a sort of knoll and managed to get her boots off. Mr. Thielen was struggling in the sea with great difficulty, because of his boots and heavy clothing.

Both Mr. and Mrs. Thielen were good swimmers, but the blowing spray was blinding and choking and the drag of Mr. Thielen's clothing was a great handicap. He was giving support to Mrs. Clarke, who could not swim, and trying to guide her toward land, but in a desperate effort to free himself of his boots, he had to let go momentarily and she was swept away. Mr. Thielen managed to swim again, and finally made his way through wind and water to safety, but Mrs. Clarke was gone.

This is how Mr. Thielen remembered it. "We watched the hesitant, then rapid, then pausing, then flying-forward, yellow flecks of foam. It looked like the vomit foam of a sick animal. Finally, the water for which we had been waiting, came. A little trickle, as if someone had emptied a glass, flowed gently over the crest of the dune and was quickly soaked up by the sand. A moment later, there was a second one, but this was a little longer and a little wider than the one before. Presently, a dozen narrow threads of water were running across the sand on all sides of the house. Then a small stream was flowing down a hollow on one side, and then another, until on both sides of the house, there was water flowing. But it was only an inch or two deep, and we knew that, since the house was built high, even a few feet of water passing beneath it would do no harm. We kept watching the slowly increasing flow of water.

"And it is the slowness that stands out. There was no sudden crash of overwhelming waves but only a gradual drop-by-drop addition to the volume of the waters. But now the tops of the waves sent up spray from the dunes, and all over our land the water was flowing to the pond behind. It was no more than ankle deep, and there were many higher places that were still dry. But in the swishing sound of the flowing water there was now something different. There was a thin clicking of pebbles being carried along by the sea. This sound soon deepened until it became a dull rumbling as the stones which were beneath the sand were also uncovered and borne away. The heaviness and deepness of the sound increased, and now, from time to time, there were hard thuds against the foundation of the house as boulders struck it.

"The water still was deepening only slowly, but there was a sense of increasing strength, and the sound of it was different from any we had ever heard before. It was then that we decided to leave — reluctantly, because we felt it was like deserting a ship in distress. As we were putting on sweaters, boots, and oilers unhurriedly, there was a crash of glass somewhere in the house. There was something incredible about it, as though a new and perfect machine should suddenly, for no reason, develop a flaw, crack, and begin to disintegrate.

"We stepped off the back porch into a foot of water and began to wade towards the high ground beyond the shore. Virginia went ahead, and I followed more slowly, holding our cook by the hand. It was not difficult, although by now the water was flowing fast and you had to brace yourself against the wind. We took five or six steps in the shallow water. But now the tempo of the sea and tide changed. There was no slow, gradual increase of the water. There was a swirl and a noise of rocks and splintering wood, and the water was up to our waists. There was a second wave and it was up to our necks. Josephine could not swim. I held on to her. Something huge rushed from the beach, and the water rose above our heads.

"Up to a point you can describe things consecutively, but beyond that there is no sequence of events. The things that happen have their reality only in the manner in which they exist in or momentarily impinge on the mind of the person caught up in their midst. The mind of that person does not see consecutively: it is impressed by a series of images which in themselves have no logical connection but exist only as isolated, unrelated phenomena. The mind, in art and in life, feels a basic need for some kind of arrangement of these unrelated phenomena. Suddenly deprived of this, it finds itself facing a horror and a loss that is far deeper than any mere physical distress of the moment. There is a kind of eerie surrealist dream quality about it. It is like this:

"The poor frightened black face rises, then disappears in the gray whirling water. Above it is a blue felt hat with a green feather pointing upward. An immense surge of current sweeps in from the sea. But I am a very good swimmer. I was brought up by the sea, and I have always felt that water was my natural home. I still have her wrist tightly in one hand, but my boots are filled with water and I can't kick to swim. My sweater is like lead on my arms, and my oilers are stiff and heavy with the cold. Also, I am looking for my wife. I see her sitting on the last bit of dry land, a hummock covered with the pale gray-green of dusty miller. I call to her to swim towards the pond shore, and I see her take off her coat and boots and start.

"There is a screaming in my ears of this sinking woman and the wind blowing at ninety miles an hour — across this water where there was once land. I know about lifesaving and try to swim backwards holding her with one arm on my chest. I cannot move my legs with their water-filled boots. To get them off, I must submerge completely, lean down, and pull at each one with both hands. I must let go my hold on this dark reaching hand. A bathhouse drifts by, half over on its side. I see the dark face sink in the water, then rise again. I dive under twice, once for each boot, then undo the buttons of my oiler and then go under again to pull off the trousers and their tangled braces around my shoulders. I see my wife swimming slowly ahead of me. The other face is gone. A woman's hat with a green feather is floating, spinning slowly around in the water.

"In the filthy water — the water is yellow, filled with slowly turning clumps of bushes with muddy roots. The clear water that we knew is the color of stale weak coffee and soured milk. My wife turns about, and her face, her mouth, is smeared with black mud. I lean back for a moment to float and rest before swimming to the pond shore, but when you lean your head back the wind drives the spray with the force of a vaporizing gun down into your throat and lungs. The small house behind ours, which my wife used as a studio, is floating ahead of us. I had not seen it go past. It is floating neatly, on an even keel, like a houseboat. Each time I lift my arm to swim, the water-soaked sweater pulls it back. I don't want to submerge again if I can avoid it. But I find I must, to get the sweater over my head. Timbers and parts of houses are floating past, but not near us. After every few strokes I turn my head towards the ocean, into the wind, to see if any are coming towards us. I come up to Virginia, and we swim slowly along together.

"Out in the pond the waves are smaller than they were back there on the beach. It is not hard swimming. It feels almost quiet now except for the driving spray. We swim towards the nearest point of land, but the current carries us past it. Suddenly I have a strange and unbelievable sensation: I wonder if we shall get to the shore beyond. It is something that never occurred to me before, because we are both good swimmers.

"The filthy yellow water streams by, and a big clump of bushes in which my arms get entangled for a moment. The only color anywhere — in the water and in the sky — is this smear of dirty yellow. Everything else is in shades of gray and white, like a movie. It reminds me then of all the silly movies that I've ever seen, of all the broken dams, floods, storms, and charming young women (with neat hair and perfectly made-up faces) and stalwart young men battling for life. 'I'm struggling for my life. Yes, that's what I'm really doing. I —' The words go over and over in my mind, and I feel embarrassed, as though I had been cast in some fatuous part in amateur theatricals. But it is true. I feel utterly exhausted, and it is still far to the tossing bushes on the shore. There is a sense of wondering unbelief at the sight of the high and solid land and the green of the swelling fields. But slowly, like a small limp worm, I crawl nearer.

"Some cows stand shivering in the spray — looking strangely firm and secure on the ground. Moving slowly in the heavy water, I know what the bushes at the water's edge will feel like in my hands. They are wild rosebushes and briars and bayberries, hard and coarse and thorny. They are just beyond the deep slime and tangle of mud and grass and broken roots. Then I feel them, the hard thorns, the gnarled stems, strong and tough against the hands, like rope by which you can pull yourself up from a deep place.

"Then, to get warm, you can drink all the rum they hand out to you and you can get drunk on it, but it won't make you sleep. The wind cries all night long around the house, and every time you close your eyes you see the immense slavering arch of the oncoming wave, the yellow spittle dripping down, and a dead face in the sullied waters."

Raymond R. Cook of Squibnocket Farm was standing by the Herring Creek on the Hornblower property — near the southwest corner of Martha's Vineyard — when he saw the great storm wave coming. He said it was gray; from trough to top, it had a 25-foot front, with spray and foam reaching 10 feet above the actual wave. It picked up a fish house, weighted down with sand and rocks washed in by the sea, lifted it 10 feet above the ground and set it down on the creek.

The wave seemed to come broadside, sweeping down along the shore, and it was followed by a second and a third, neither reaching the height of the first. They worked up a "tremendous sea," which lasted about an hour; the fish house was demolished, water broke over the beach and filled the road with rocks the size of a barrel, and the Squibnocket cliffs, one of the beauty spots of the island, were cut back an average of 30 feet. Spray broke over

[263]

the top of Cook's house, which was about 150 feet back from the shore; Zack's Cliff, two miles from Gay Head, was "cut way back; although the rocks are left, the landmark is unrecognizable," he said, and the shoreline was "smashed." From what he saw, he believed that only the upper end of the island was struck by the great wave.

Others corroborated this. Carl Reed, at Menemsha, said he was looking out over the water as the storm came and he saw three huge waves sweep across the creek, carrying everything before them. On the other hand, Frank Osborn, who stayed aboard his boat in Edgartown Harbor throughout the storm, said there was no sign of a tidal wave there but that the sea was accounted for by a rather fast rise in the tide that took about an hour to reach its peak. It was generally concluded that the storm waves struck the upper end of the island, splitting and rolling down both the south and Sound shores with force diminished by the time they reached the lower end.

Chapter 15

ACROSS VINEYARD AND NANTUCKET SOUNDS, the storm belted Cape Cod and, although deaths occurred and damage was extensive, one of the most important, and largely untold, aspects of the Cape's hurricane experience concerns the deaths that did not occur and why they did not.

Cape Codders, wise in local weather lore, sensed the approach of a natural catastrophe, and the forethought and quick action of such authorities as Chief Ray D. Wells of the Falmouth Fire Department, Police Chief Harold L. Baker of Falmouth, and Police Chief William R. Crump of Bourne were credited with preventing at least 100 deaths.

At 1:30 Wednesday afternoon, Chief Wells made a tour of the shore, noted the conditions of the sea at low tide and anticipated what was to happen six hours later at high water. He telephoned State Police, Troop D headquarters in West Bridgewater, informed them that the Cape shore would be inundated and asked that boats, equipment, and volunteers be sent without fail immediately.

The alarming message, so incredible at that hour, prompted the State Police to verify its authenticity. Five minutes later, they telephoned Chief Wells at Falmouth to make certain that he had called. Wells impressed upon them the danger that he foresaw, and the West Bridgewater headquarters relayed the appeal by teletype to Cape stations.

At 3:45, the storm wave thundered in, and all communication with the Cape was cut off at the Cape Cod Canal. But the call for help had brought response and already, volunteers with dories, rope, floodlights, and trucks were rolling over the highways, bound for the stricken area just as the emergency commenced.

The Falmouth police log recorded: 6:35, bridge at West Falmouth to Old Silver Beach out. Call from Woods Hole. Family on roof, house flooded. 6:36, Henry W. Maurer reports Alice H. Maurer in car on Beach Road. Car washed off road into pond. Doesn't know if she went in or not. 6:45, call State Police, help from anywhere, SOS. . . . 7:11, call Massachusetts Department of Public Safety, no connection. 7:13, Barnstable radio off until further notice. 7:13, sergeant called radio station, Chatham, for weather. Nothing. . . ."

But help was on the way.

Barnstable sent a crew with trucks and dories which arrived first and aided Chiefs Wells's and Baker's forces in rescuing 38 people who undoubtedly would have lost their lives otherwise. The Chatham Naval Reserve unit which went to Bourne arrived in time to assist Chief Crump in rescuing approximately 50 people in danger of drowning, who spent the night in hastily arranged quarters in the town hall. At Woods Hole, 15 people were rescued from an inundated house on Gardiner Road. At Maravista, firemen and volunteers found a man and woman marooned in an automobile and took them to safety; the couple then revealed that they had placed their three children in a cottage that they thought would be safer. The water was making up so rapidly that on the return trip the firemen had to take a skiff to get to the house and after rescuing the children had to row inland nearly a mile before landing.

Chief Wells commandeered every available boat and man for rescue work, while Chief Baker called out reserve policemen and civilians to aid his department. Trucks loaded with men and boats came from as far away as Provincetown; scores of town employees and civilians joined in an extraordinary effort to open streets to relief workers and to mark points of danger along highways. Firemen, Coast Guardsmen, police, and civilians made rescues from North Falmouth to Menauhant; crews worked at West Falmouth, removing families from Chappaquoit and Pine Islands, both of which were cut off from the mainland, and boatmen labored for hours getting families out of Woods Hole's Millfield Street, with heavy ropes tied between poles and trees to prevent the small craft from being pitched into Eel Pond by the turmoil of water emptying into the pond.

In at least one instance, hurricane tragedy required the courts to determine which is the weaker sex.

Mr. and Mrs. Andrew F. Jones of Dorchester were pioneer colonists at Silver Beach, North Falmouth; they had been going there for thirty-seven years — there were only two cottages there during their first summer, and they were instrumental in the organization of the Silver Beach Association. When they observed their golden wedding anniversary in the summer of 1937, invitations were sent to more than 250 Cape friends, and about 400 were served in the recreation room of their Silver Beach cottage, which stood on the waterfront. It was called "The House That Jack Built." It was directly in the path of the storm.

Both Mr. and Mrs. Jones were seventy-one; he had not been in good health since he broke a leg during the previous winter. When the waves inundated his yard, at 6 P.M., he tried without success to start his car. The sea continued to rise; Mr. and Mrs. Jones went to the second floor of their home and finally managed to climb to the roof.

When the house went to pieces, the roof floated off with them on it. Neighbors in a nearby tearoom saw the Joneses' roof sweeping past their building and tied blankets together, in an effort to throw a lifeline to the elderly couple, but the wind swept away the frail effort. The roof, driven inland, finally was smashed as it struck another house; husband and wife were thrown into the water.

Both bodies were recovered, that of Mrs. Jones bearing thousands of dollars' worth of diamonds and other jewelry she had put on immediately before fleeing to the roof, in the hope of saving her life and some of her valuables. On September 27, the wills of Mr. and Mrs. Jones were filed in Suffolk Probate Court.

Mr. Jones's will had been written March 11, 1915; it left all his belongings, including the cottage at Silver Beach, to his wife. The will of Mrs. Jones was drawn on February 9, 1933, and left all her money and possessions to her husband. Jones asked that his wife be named executrix and Mrs. Jones asked that her husband be named executor. The question arose as to who was next of kin, as there was no mention of any children in either will.

At the time of filing of the wills, an attorney commented, "There is a natural presumption in law that the man, being the stronger of the two, probably survived the storm longer than his wife. Unless this can be rebutted, it is reasonable that the heirs of Mr. Jones would obtain possession of the property. . . ."

Miss Alice H. Maurer, forty-two, a retired private nurse, was a summer resident of The Fells, Falmouth; she had been going there seasonally with her family for fourteen years and planned to return to her winter home in Rochester, New York, on the Monday following the hurricane.

Early on the afternoon of the storm, she and her nephew, Henry W. Maurer III, went to Falmouth and did some shopping. Mr. Maurer mentioned that the car might need gasoline but Miss Maurer, in a hurry to reach home, thought there was sufficient for the short drive. The car ran out of gasoline when they reached the road by Oyster Pond.

Shortly afterward, E. Gunnar Peterson of Falmouth came driving by. He offered to take Mr. Maurer for gasoline and urged Miss

Maurer to go with them, but she said she preferred to wait in her car and watch the surf. When they returned, the Maurer car was in the pond and Miss Maurer could not be found, either in the car or in the water nearby.

A group of sightseers who also went to the Falmouth shore to watch the surf were only a few yards away, near the Moors Pavilion, but were horrified and helpless witnesses to Miss Maurer's tragic end.

The sea was sweeping across the shore in waves of muddy water; a huge comber smashed through the pavilion, the seas broke over its roof, showering the nearby road with thick spray. Watchers on the beach suddenly found the water well above their knees and moved hurriedly toward the higher section of the road. Somebody directed attention to two cars stalled near the bathhouses and expressed the hope that their occupants had left in time.

"Suddenly, we realized there was a figure moving slowly, pulling itself along the highway fence — it was made of cement posts and steel cables — that bordered the beach road," said Miss Eleanor Brooks, one of the group. "I ran to a car that had just driven up and sent its driver back to the fire station for help."

The figure — they could not tell whether it was a man or woman — remained by the fence, not moving one way or another. Higher surf was rolling in across the road. Intermittently, the rain and spume blotted the person in the water from the view of those who watched. The pavilion was breaking up under the sea's pounding.

Two boys drove up and the beach watchers ran to tell them that someone was caught in the surf. One of them removed his shoes, rolled up his trousers and waded into the water; it rose to his armpits and a sea knocked him off his feet. He tried once more, although because the rolling seas were much higher now and the spray thicker, it was impossible to tell whether either the fence or the figure was still there. Overwhelmed by the water again, the boy gave up and had all he could do to swim back to safety.

Firemen arrived, and two of them tied themselves together with a rope, but the stretch of surf was now so wide and the breakers so high that although they went into the water up to their shoulders, being able neither to make headway nor retain their footing beyond that point, it was obviously futile and dangerous to make further effort.

Chief Baker's men made extensive search after the storm, and at 2 o'clock on the following Sunday, Miss Maurer's body was found near the center of Salt Pond, off the Moors. When it was towed ashore, a warm sun was shining; the pond and sound were a gently rippled blue. Sunday strollers gathered to watch the arrival of Chief Baker and the undertaker. Some turned away as the body was brought to shore; others took photographs.

Woods Hole caught the full force of the storm. At 4 o'clock on Wednesday, the first rush of water came. As it neared the top of the steamship wharf, station agent Robert C. Neal grew uneasy; he had never seen it that high other than at exceptional flood tide. He phoned the Falmouth *Enterprise* office, learned that high tide was not due for at least three hours, and gave orders to have all tickets and money removed from the office, which was located near the end of the pier. In the relatively short time that it took to clear the office, the water rose three feet and Ronald Densmore, ticket seller, had to be helped from the swaying building.

Swiftly the water came up. Books and valuables were taken out of Samuel T. Cahoon's fish market when water reached the floor. Fishermen whose vessels were lying nearby fought to keep their boats from floating onto the steamboat dock as the sea lifted them. By 5:45, Woods Hole's entire Main Street, as well as Millfield Street, Spencer Baird Road, and Penzance Road, were flooded. Firemen waited until water reached the fenders of their engine before moving the apparatus up the hill to the post office. Still the water rose.

On Dyer's dock, the second largest wharf in Great Harbor,

struggling men gave up their effort to pull automobiles clear; they retreated slowly, to higher ground, with the rush of water pouring behind. Automobiles parked on the dock were thrown into the water; other vehicles parked near the harbor were submerged, and the dock itself was beaten to pieces; a large gasoline tank that had been used to provide yachts with fuel spun in a great whirlpool over the place where the dock had stood.

At the Woods Hole Oceanographic Institution, the crew of the big ketch *Atlantis* ran out additional hawsers to nearby buildings as she rose above the wharf spiles. Small boats were being destroyed all about the ketch; a party boat was sunk under her stern, and nearby, a yawl was pounding a sloop that was being wrecked against a seawall. From the roof of Community Hall, Eel Pond and Woods Hole harbor looked one and the same — a flood of turbulent water.

At 6:15, the cry went up from those gathered at the drawbridge that it was being washed away. As one side of the bridge started to lift, Sidney Peck, the draw tender, yelled, "Look out for the planks! Those who can manage better come across now." Women in light housedresses were carried across to the high ground past Rowe's Drug Store. Sheets of rain made it impossible to see across the street in the gathering dusk. The Naushon landing, Crane's pier, the Bureau of Fisheries dock all were reported smashed by the heavy seas that continued to roll in. Near the Oceanographic building, the water turned black when the coal in the rear of the Penzance garage washed to the surface. Somebody passing hollered that Penzance Point was cut off in two places. "It's an island now, but if the water keeps coming, it won't even be there!" one man shouted, his voice hardly audible above the wind.

On Penzance Point, P. Milton Neal and his father, Albert W. Neal, caretaker for many years of the Hector J. Hughes summer estate there, were attempting to board up doors and windows. The wind and tide changed, sweeping water from Buzzards Bay back through Great Harbor. Realizing that the foundation of the house had begun to sag and that the building offered no sanctuary, the son aided his sixty-year-old father in getting to a nearby utility pole, to which he clung. The son made his way to another pole a few yards away and they hung on, while storm and sea battered them, for about two hours. At the end of that time, a large wave swept over them, and the older man, weakened by long exposure, lost his grip; he was swept away and drowned while his son watched. Milton clung to the pole for nearly two hours more until a rescuer, tied to a rope held by others, was able to reach him.

Also on the point, William Briggs, caretaker at the F. A. Park estate, left his home to check damage at the Park boathouse shortly before the water rushed back into Great Harbor. The sea had already created a deep gully between the boathouse and his residence. On the way back, the water came up fast and Mr. Briggs took off his shoes and stockings to wade, when he lost his balance and fell into the swift current. His son, Edward, tried to throw him a rope, but without success.

In the November, 1938, issue of the U.S. Coast Guard magazine, on page 21, there is an "In Memoriam" notice, edged in black. It reads: "Machinist (T) Frederick T. Lilja, Hayward T. Webster, motor machinist, 1st class; John A. Steadman, radioman, 3d class. Killed in action. Hurricane Rescue Operations, Woods Hole, Mass., Sept. 21, 1938; U.S.S. *General Greene*, C.G."

A party of five volunteers from the patrol boat *General Greene*, including these three men (Steadman had been assigned to Woods Hole only three weeks before), responded to a call for help from residents of flooded areas on Penzance Point. With civilian volunteers, they worked heroically to evacuate residents. Of the rescue party, two Coast Guardsmen and two civilians survived.

Albert G. Borden, Jr., Penzance Point summer resident, related what happened to Webster and Lilja; with Ned Harvey and the

[272]

Coast Guardsmen, he had been engaged in rescue work on the point during the late afternoon and evening: "About 5 P.M., we all started from Penzance Point to Woods Hole, after having helped make boats fast and carrying people from flooded houses. As we neared the Frank J. Frost house, the rushing tide that had already crossed from the harbor to the bay came rushing back. We tried to run through the water across the broken road, but any speed was impossible.

"Suddenly, what appeared to be a solid wall of water tore out of Buzzards Bay and picked us up as it rolled toward the Hole. Before I knew it, I was abreast of the George Clowes yacht, about thirty yards from shore. I grabbed the anchor chain and was hauled on deck by members of the crew.

"Later, I learned that Ned Harvey had been swept clear to the Bureau of Fisheries dock, where he held onto the pilings and made his way to shore.

"We were the last to see the two Coast Guard fellows. All I can remember is hearing one of them shout that he couldn't swim and then I went under myself."

Steadman, who had already carried at least one child out of the danger zone, returned to make sure that everyone had been assisted who wanted to leave the area. In doing so, he had to recross a low area and was caught by the same backwash that carried the other four into the sea. The remaining two members of the Coast Guard party were able to reach a house, where they remained on the second floor until the sea went down.

The federal buoy station at Juniper Point was reduced to confusion by the flooding water. Dozens of buoys, some of them weighing tons, were lifted from the dock — light buoys, gas buoys, bell buoys, and spar buoys — and scattered along the shore. Mrs. George Robinson, who lived nearby, said, "When the water rushed up to its greatest height, those big red buoys, row on row, suddenly appeared near our home. The flood picked them up and sent them piling against the side of the house. Doors were smashed and the garage bashed in. The buoys banged and rang until the water went down and they were left practically in our front room."

Dr. Columbus O. Iselin, director of the Woods Hole Oceanographic Institution, informed the Falmouth *Enterprise* Wednesday morning that a hurricane might strike the area before evening, although he added after the storm that he had no idea it would be as severe as it was. He concluded that a tide seven feet higher than normal high on the Nantucket South side at Woods Hole and a corresponding abnormal tide on the Buzzards Bay side, two or three feet higher still, combined to produce the Woods Hole flooding. "I am convinced the water rose here because it was caught in a bottleneck," Iselin said. "It had no other place to go. High tide was at 7 P.M. If the high tide had been at any other time of day, there would have been no flood. The tide was rising just as the wind was rising. The high point of the tide and the height of the effect of the storm coincided. At 7 P.M., the water was rushing like a millrace through the Eel Pond channel into the harbor. It almost immediately began to recede."

Hurricane news from the Cape was transmitted circuitously. Charles R. Knight was in New York the night of the hurricane. Mrs. Knight and her sister, Miss Ella Hardcastle, were at Woods Hole, where the Knights had summered for many years. There was no communication from New York to Cape Cod, and the artist was worried about his family, so he cabled to Orleans, Massachusetts, by way of the French Cable Company. His message went across the Atlantic to Brest, and back to Orleans. From Orleans, it was possible to telephone to Falmouth. Dr. Roland O. Parris, a friend of the Knights, drove to Woods Hole, found the family safe, and telephoned a reassuring cable to Orleans. Back it went, twice across the ocean, to New York, and Mr. Knight received it at 9 P.M.

News of the Cape's experience reached Richfield, New Jersey, by way of London. A Richfield friend wrote the author George Harmon Coxe of Pin Oak Way, Falmouth. Mr. Coxe received first a telegram, then a special delivery letter after the storm, asking for details of the hurricane, news of which was heard in New Jersey by shortwave radio from the British Broadcasting Company.

Mostly, the lower Cape escaped; the heaviest damage was to its fish traps — after the hurricane, only 19 out of 58 were operable. The lowest tides in the recollection of the oldest inhabitants saved the area; before the storm broke, the tide had retreated far from shore, leaving sandbars and shallows where normally water would have been several feet deep.

On a hilltop in Truro, a late-staying summer resident was writing to his wife when the storm came. He said, "As I wrote, the wind became a moan, as if great quantities of air were sucked up and suddenly let go. A neighbor described it as being like a dog worrying the end of her house like a bone. Presently, I looked at the water below me. It had become a whirlwind of flying spume; piled lumber was being flung about. . . ."

"I opened the door a crack, but flying sand cut my face like ground glass and I slammed it shut. I knew that safety lay in the event that none of that furious wind found its way inside. Once it did, the house would go like seaweed. Through the floor of the sun porch, the wind came up like knife thrusts. I looked at the fireplace and wondered when the bricks would begin to fly.

"I found myself changing that letter from badinage to seriousness and ending it finally with a message that if I were not alive when she found it, the note would be self-explanatory."

The writer lived to mail his note.

Agony in a natural disaster such as this is not necessarily measured by the number of dead or dollars' worth of damage. At Race Point, an Orleans quahog dragger and its crew were saved from destruction by the Race Point Coast Guardsmen and the patrol boat *Argo*. The vessel, with owner Harry Hunt and Bernie Taylor aboard, was trying to make the shelter of Provincetown Harbor, when heavy seas smashed in the pilothouse. Ashore, Hunt's wife, Gertrude, followed the dragger down the Cape along the back shore and arrived at the Race Point station to learn that her husband and his crewman had not made their destination and were trying to ride out the storm, in a 70-mile-an-hour wind.

Without hesitating, she kicked off her shoes, disappeared in the swirling sand and gale, and found her way to the spot, more than a mile down the beach, where her husband was battling for his life. Race Point Coast Guardsmen rigged lines from the dragger to the station's tractor on the beach, and held the vessel into the wind until the *Argo* arrived at the scene, got a line aboard the fishing vessel, and towed her to a secure anchorage.

At the "gateway" to the Cape, in Wareham, the water rose on lower Main Street to a level twelve feet above ordinary tide levels; it crippled the town's business section, caused damage of more than one million dollars and took nine lives in the outlying beach areas. Both the Narrows highway bridge and the railroad bridge were swept away. A floating gas stove out of the Wareham Coffee Shop was used as a raft by two exhausted men trying to swim to safety in Main Street. David Wilcox, who had carried the mail from the post office to the railroad station, became stranded there on top of a baggage truck and was rescued by two men in a canoe.

William L. Ross, Jr., was manager of the Warr Theater. "Charlie Hatch was crippled and operating a tiny eatery," Ross said. "He was hollering, sitting on top of the counter, with water all around him, pots and pans, etc. Two doors down, the Chinese man was also screaming, in the same condition. My projectionist and I rescued these people with a boat we found floating near the railroad tracks. Water peaked at about 9 feet in this area on Main Street."

In the Onset Fire District, more than $1 million in property dam-

Wrecked boats, autos, and bridges at Wareham, Massachusetts

age was reported, including $300,000 for pleasure craft, together with the loss of 325 houses, rendering 400 homeless.

Because of the rapidity with which the storm wave charged up the Wareham River (within moments placing upon the railroad bridge a burden it could not bear), a major tragedy might have resulted there had it not been for the alertness of a New York, New Haven and Hartford Railroad engineer.

William Reed was proceeding on his regular Hyannis-to-Boston run with sixty passengers aboard and he was within a few hundred yards of the Wareham bridge when he saw a boat float over its rails. Until that moment, he had not realized the force of the grow-ing storm. Even as he watched, water surged over the bridge and started flowing toward the train. Reed reacted instantly, recognizing the quickly growing danger. (The flood ripped up whole sections of ties, twisting and bending the steel rails attached to them.) He backed the train a distance of two miles to the Onset station. He was unable to go farther because tracks to the rear had been washed away.

Train crew, passengers, mail, and baggage were taken to Boston over the highway the next day, but the trackless train remained marooned at the Onset station for about three weeks.

Donald G. Trayser, Boston *Globe* correspondent in Hyannis, had to drive all the way to Middleboro before he could find a telephone that worked, in order to call his newspaper on the night of the storm. He had to go through Onset back roads to get around Wareham. Returning after midnight, he saw the lighted train, with steam up, on the track at Onset. "Where are you going?" he called to Reed. The engineer replied, "Buddy, I can go back two miles or forward a mile, and that's all."

At Swift's Beach, where three died, approximately ten acres of waterfront was swept clear and the wreckage left in heaps so that it was impossible to tell one house from another. At 6 P.M. on the twenty-first, just before the hurricane obliterated the colony, a deed to one of the cottages was delivered to its new owner by an attorney. The latter said, "It's all yours now, and here are the keys." Shortly afterward, the new owner watched the sea smash the building to pieces.

Publisher Lemuel C. Hall of the Wareham *Courier* interviewed one of the rescuers at Swift's Beach; without their efforts, the death toll there unquestionably would have been higher. "Black and blue and cold from five hours of immersion in the tidal wave that swept [the colony] into oblivion, 18-year-old Northfield [Massachusetts] Seminary graduate Miss Marguerite Bryant of Worcester is the heroine of this beach community," he reported.

Miss Bryant's father was an invalid. At about 5 o'clock, when she saw the ocean "suddenly appear to rise up and come towards the shore in a wall-like mass of water," she ran from the house for help. A Wareham police ambulance responded; its crew, up to their waists in water, carried her father out of the house on blankets, and led other members of the household to high ground.

After Miss Bryant had gotten her own family to safety, she learned that the postmistress and her two children [Mrs. Victor Brown, her son, Richard. eleven, and a seven-month-old infant] were not out of the flooded area. She attempted to wade and swim through the wreckage-filled waters, found she could not, got a boat, and finally made her way to the post office, where she took aboard the mother and two children, as well as a second woman, all of whom were on top of the building, which soon after was destroyed.

At Hamilton Beach, Miss Elizabeth I. Holliday and Mrs. Fanny Butler were occupying a beach cottage with Mrs. Clarence Willard. Miss Holliday said, "There was no warning of the storm in the way of rain. We were in an exposed section and the wind blew increasingly. Finally, the tidal wave came at us, it seemed, from three directions. At first, we tried to save the steps of the cottage, which were whirled this way and that with the force of the wind and the current.

"Mrs. Willard went for help with her car. Then, it became clear that we could save nothing. By this time, the water pouring into the cottage was waist-high. With things we found at hand, we forced up a screen on a rear window. As we climbed over the window ledge, the house tipped, like an unbalanced boat.

"Outside, Mrs. Willard, who had been forced to abandon her car because of the water and trees strewn everywhere, was calling to us. She had become afraid we were lost and was upset and crying. We made our way on foot for over a mile until a car took us to the little settlement and post office that served the beach. The owner of a little rooming house invited all the wet and frightened people into his kitchen to dry themselves. Everyone was splendid; they were confused and fear-struck, but it was a revelation to see the unselfishness and consideration everyone displayed. I put on another woman's shoes and she put on mine and we never noticed. . . .

"Then people came to check among the survivors, looking for missing members of their families. One old man was looking for his wife and daughter. He found their bodies, one under the steps of his cottage, the other beneath the porch, both drowned. . . ."

Wareham Police Chief Chester A. Churchill phoned his wife from Police Department headquarters on Main Street, shortly before communications failed. He said, "The water's up to my waistline." She replied, "You'd better get out of there." Afterward, she recalled, "I didn't see him for the next three days."

Churchill said, "We lost the people on the beaches because the water came in behind them, cutting them off from the mainland. We couldn't get to them and they couldn't get out. One husband and wife had planned to leave for Ohio the day before, but they postponed leaving because the weather was bad. They were both drowned."

Leroy P. Ellis lived on Onset's East Central Avenue. "I looked out toward the lowland flats and the firemen were taking people out of the second-story windows," he said.

"East of the pier, there was a big black schooner anchored; she was about 60 feet and belonged to Hamilton Garland. She was all provisioned for a long cruise. She started to drag and somebody came to me and said Garland was offering $1,000 to anybody who would get hold of her and keep her from going ashore. If I'd had my boat, I'd have given a try but she was in a good safe place and I didn't want to move her. That schooner must have drawn 6 feet, but the water came in so fast it floated her over a wall and left her in the middle of a paved road east of the Point Independence bridge. I'm sure it cost him more than $1,000 to get her floated again; house movers had to cradle her and roll her over the wall.

"Every house on Onset Island broke up and floated; there was eight feet of water over the island and one woman and son saved themselves by staying up a tree until the water went down. Captain Harold Hatch was on the motor sailer *Goosander*, off the yacht club; a house floated down on him from Onset Island, driven by the southeasterly wind, struck his boat, and it split on his bow, half of it drifting by on the port side and the other half on the starboard.

"There must have been at least twenty big boats ashore after it was over and I believe it would have been a lot worse if it hadn't been for the Cape Cod Canal, which took a lot of the high water — water went through the canal at a speed of at least 15 knots.

"There was a man and some other people drowned in a house in the canal when it smashed up against the Bourne bridge. The man had a small cabin cruiser, 25–30 feet, tied out in front of his house at Gray Gables. It was in a sheltered place and it didn't take any harm. Two or three days after the hurricane, I got a call asking if I would tow the boat to a boatyard. His widow didn't want to have to look out the window and see the boat anymore. . . ."

The drowning of the people in the house in the Cape Cod Canal was one of the most crushing single tragedies which the storm inflicted.

The home of Mrs. Elizabeth Lane, seventy-four, on Jefferson Road, Gray Gables, was a two-story frame building located a couple of hundred feet east of Buzzards Bay and about fifteen feet south of the canal. The house rested on a foundation of concrete blocks, but was not attached to the foundation; the south bank of the canal at this point rose approximately nine feet. In the house with Mrs. Lane were Mabel V. Wells, sixty-one, of Mount Vernon, New York; Emily Needham, sixty-two, of Vineland, New Jersey; and Joseph Needham, eleven, a schoolboy, who was Emily Needham's adopted son. None of them could swim.

Hayward Wilson, fifty-four, a boatman and a good swimmer, lived on high ground nearly 300 feet southeast of the Lane home.

*Five died in this house, afloat in the Cape Cod Canal;
it grounded at Bourne, Massachusetts.*

The canal in this area was 540 feet wide, with a normal depth in midstream of 35 feet at high tide; the Lane house was 30 feet high.

About 3:30 P.M., the tide was rising and was already unusually high; the wind was more than 50 miles an hour, and increasing; in the canal, there was a strong current to the northeast, and wind-blown spray reduced the visibility greatly. Wilson, observing the storm conditions, visited a house east of the Lane residence to make certain that two elderly people there were all right. He then went to a nearby cove, pulled several rowboats up onto the bank for greater security, and checked the lines on his own boat at a landing. Because of the wind, he had difficulty maintaining his footing and part of the time lay flat and clung to the landing.

Conditions became worse, and about 4:20 P.M., Wilson noticed that water 3 to 4 feet deep was moving northeast in waves, nearly 300 feet east of the normal shore of the bay and south of the Lane home. He knew the normal tide would be high at 5:45 and expected still higher water. The occupants of the Lane home were new residents. He thought there was at least one woman in the home besides Mrs. Lane and he told his wife that he would visit the women to make sure of their safety.

Wilson could swim 250 feet; he could tread water and float. He was familiar with local wind and tide conditions. He did not indicate to his wife that he thought the Lane house was in danger of being washed away.

He walked rapidly northwest from his home to the north side of a house that was east of the Lane house and then for about 40 feet more, he was observed walking west downgrade, and holding onto trees and bushes. At that time, he was on dry ground, but the water may even then have been about a foot deep in front of the Lane house. So far as is known, Wilson was not again observed outside the Lane house.

Fifteen minutes later, he telephoned to his wife from the Lane house and told her he was safe, but that he would be unable to leave until about 7 P.M., when the high tide would have receded somewhat. He told his wife to telephone for a man to bring a rowboat to the Lane house to get the women out. He also instructed her to telephone people in Boston and Brockton to send someone to save their launches, which were in the cove. Wilson spoke calmly and firmly, and Mrs. Wilson felt relieved. He did not say anything about conditions at the Lane house, but he did say, "I'm going to wait here until the water goes down. It's impossible to get back."

Mrs. Wilson telephoned to a family three miles away for aid; the message was relayed to a man who started toward Gray Gables. Blocked roads and high water prevented him from reaching there. Meanwhile, the storm increased in violence. Mrs. Wilson wanted to telephone to her husband but was unable to get the number of the telephone at the Lane house.

Shortly before 6 P.M., the tide rose to 10 feet above normal and the water extended to within 10 feet of the Wilson house. Very soon afterward, the Lane house drifted northeast into the canal, submerged to within a few feet of the top of the roof. No one was observed on or in the house. After drifting 2 miles, the house lodged against a pier of the Bourne bridge. It was sighted there at 11 P.M. by Katherine Keene, a Buzzards Bay telephone operator, as it lay grounded against the abutment.

A work force led by Bourne Police Chief William R. Crump, Fire Chief Thomas Wallace, and Naval Reservists headed by Lieutenant Samuel Freedman of Chatham risked their lives to break through the roof to get to the occupants. At midnight, they found five bodies on the second floor; all had drowned. A bloody bruise was on Wilson's forehead and his hands were badly bruised and lacerated; he had made a last desperate effort to break through the roof to get the women and little boy out of their water-filled prison. Wilson was awarded the Carnegie Medal for Heroism, the reverse side of which reads: "Greater love hath no man than this, that a man lay down his life for his friends."

The Town of Marion's eighty-sixth *Annual Report*, for the year ending December 31, 1938, states: "Never before in the history of the town has it been necessary to put our town under control of town and state police and only by the act of God in His wisdom and beyond our control did the Almighty see fit to cause the tidal wave to come upon us, which was of short duration, lasting but a few hours in the late afternoon, but causing heavy damage."

[284]

There were 89 buildings in the community declared a total loss and 187 partly destroyed. The replacement figure was set at $2,304,800; Tabor Academy alone sustained a loss estimated at $100,000. As for the town's fleet, the Marion correspondent of the Wareham *Courier* reported, "The many boats of all kinds and sizes which filled Marion Harbor before the hurricane are now resting in either a complete state of wreckage or partially so on the marshes of the upper harbor or high and dry on the once-green lawns of an estate." Charles A. Ellis said later, "One of the clearest recollections I have is of boats ashore — big boats. Coming along Route 6, the swamp at the head of the harbor, north of the highway — they had been blown over the highway — was jam-packed full of boats."

Edwin L. Newdick was a student at Tabor Academy on that day and he wrote: "One of the great disasters in the history of New England struck Tabor from four to eight o'clock on September 21. Only four hours, but this comparatively brief stay cost the school approximately $100,000. The most destructive element was not the wind, but the accompanying tidal wave that filled the main living room to a depth of six feet.

"Proceedings began in earnest at four o'clock. At this time, the wind had almost reached its full force, but its effects were just beginning to be noticeable. Boats, large and small, were swept down the harbor by the force of the wind and the inrushing tide.

"The anchorage at the southern end of the harbor, formerly crowded with large yachts, was swept bare. Tall masts were barely visible through the spray-filled air down the harbor.

"With increasing rapidity, the second element of the storm attacked the school — the 'tidal wave.' At five o'clock, massive waves were breaking over the seawall. At a quarter of six, they were at the doors of Lillard Hall, and at six-thirty, boys were swimming in the Oval [the horseshoe-shaped drive at the entrance to Lillard Hall, with a green in the center] with the water over their heads. . . .

"During the flood, every effort was made to save as much as

possible. Tabor boys were engaged in pushing cars from the flooded areas, moving furniture in stranded homes and even rescuing people from their flooded homes. It was practically impossible to save any boats, for the force of the wind was so great that no boat could navigate the harbor. . . .

"When morning finally came, it revealed a scene of terrible destruction. Bits of wreckage were strewn all over the grounds, a Herreshoff lay near the north entrance of Lillard Hall and both piers were wrecked. The most serious damage was to the gym floor, where the water, 8½ feet deep, had caused the surface to buckle. The three best [rowing] shells had been saved, but the fours and one eight were lost. . . ."

Arthur M. Brown, also a student at the academy, won the Tabor *Log*'s $20 prize for the best story of the storm. From his window, he observed: ". . . Nature has rebelled against man. There is water all about; yes, water and waves. The beautiful lawn with the paths and bushes has disappeared. Instead, there are large breakers bounding across the campus. The groaning trees are bent low by the howling wind . . . the water is rising higher and higher.

"The sea stretches out its destructive arms and tears apart windows and doors, which are soon swallowed by the oncoming water. The breakers charge against the gymnasium. Spray shoots high into the air. A boat comes staggering into view, bouncing from tree to tree. Pieces fly here and there.

"The incessant whining of the wind and the splintering crash of destruction grow louder and louder. People are trying to swim from the boathouse across campus. Desperately, they fight against the waves and soon disappear behind the dormitory. Furniture and planking are bobbing about. The small field house comes charging down among the trees. Branches are torn from their limbs.

"All the time, it is getting darker and darker. . . . I am frightened. I can hear people shouting back and forth. . . . The water comes on and on. There are no fences, no boundaries, for the water has covered all. There are no lights — it is dark. The water pounds against the house. I hear the whistling and howling of the wind, the creaking of the loose boards and the swishing, rushing water.

"I see no grass through the window now. . . . A battered post lies here and an old chair there. Swollen books are scattered about the rotted grass which once was a lawn. The large green doors of the gymnasium are jagged holes in the wall. The battered nose of a racing shell pokes out . . . The limbs of the wide-spreading evergreens hang helpless from their lifeless trunks. The poplars are bent like a bow. . . ."

Raymond A. Dennehy, professional at the Kittansett Golf Club in Marion, had a golf date at 1 p.m., September 21, with Charles Peirson, the club treasurer, and John MacDonald, a member. "It was only blowing and cloudy to begin with, but pretty soon, it got serious. We hit some of the longest damned shots with the wind," Dennehy said, when I talked with him.

Undoubtedly, the most extraordinary shot of the afternoon was made by Peirson, who, with a surprisingly strong southeast wind at his back, decided to chance carrying the trees that guard the corner of the dogleg at the fourth hole. This is a shot that requires tremendous carry to reach the fairway beyond the thick woods. The distance from tee to green is 350 yards; the trees on the corner are 250 yards out and about 40 feet high. Peirson hit the ball perfectly; it was high and well-carried, and all three of them saw it clear the woods on the corner and head for the green. It bounced once in the fairway and disappeared into the woods on the far side. Few golfers in the club's history had ever successfully reached the fairway on that shot. Peirson had carried the woods beyond. "We never found the ball," Dennehy said, "but there is no doubt that it carried the corner, went over the green and into the woods."

But hitting against the wind was impossible. (Golfers in Dartmouth, a few miles to the west, who were playing at about this time on the twenty-first, told of hitting balls that went straight up in the air.) The three Marion players decided to quit and walk in; they soon discovered when they got to the clubhouse that they were cut off from the mainland because the ocean had poured across the point.

MacDonald had a brand-new Chrysler. When the water came in over the road, he was still showering and had no chance to drive it to higher ground. All its windows were closed, making it tight, and the waves picked up the car and floated it right out into the bay. He was in time to see that and remarked, "Damn, there go my golf clubs."

"I got into my car on the 18th green and parked it there," Dennehy said. "That's the highest land on the point. MacDonald waded through shoulder-high water to the club. I thought I would be better off in the car because buildings were beginning to go. Also, I had a German shepherd with me and I didn't want to risk letting him get loose in the storm.

"At Bird Island Light, just offshore, there was a two-story house. I could see that being smashed up. Water was at least two-thirds of the way up the lighthouse itself. Pretty soon, I saw the wreckage of the building on Bird Island came floating by. My whole golf shop started to disintegrate.

"The [Beverly] yacht club was a substantial two-story building, on cement posts. The water rose around it and bit by bit, it just caved in and broke up, and three of the club cottages, too. It wasn't too long after that before I saw the wreckage of the yacht club come by. The clubhouse was demolished in much less than an hour.

"My car was sitting in four feet of water. It was over the floorboards. I was one scared guy. I don't like water much.

"With all the buildings going down, I thought the clubhouse would be next. Its first floor was flooded and everybody in it went to the second floor, except that there were a couple of women and they grew so nervous, feeling the building wouldn't last, that they persuaded somebody to put them into an oak tree, an old-timer, next to the building. They didn't know it, but the tree was covered with poison ivy; they got a terrible case of it.

"I think I was probably in the car about four hours. Finally, the tide went out, awfully fast, and the water was full of wreckage. Everywhere, there were boulders, sand, and debris. There was a bathtub on the fairway; it came out of one of the cottages.

"That was Wednesday. We were supposed to have our big four-ball tournament for 150 golfers on Friday. I called my boss in Andover (Golf Committee chairman Rodney W. Brown) and told him we couldn't have it because everything was ruined. They hadn't gotten much storm there and he didn't believe me. He said, 'Have you been drinking?' and I said, 'No, but I wish to hell I had.' He spent all the next morning getting down to Marion to see for himself, because there were trees and everything in the roads. We didn't have the tournament."

Actually, there were more than two people in the oak tree. Mrs. Wiley Wakeman, the woman manager of the club dining room, and three caddies were in the Kittansett clubhouse. When the water rose to their waists, they went out the window into the tree and stayed there for about three hours.

All the boats at Marion did not go ashore. Jakob M. Svendsen was aboard Otto Braitmayer's 65-foot yacht *Fearless* II, which was lying in Planting Island Cove. As the wind increased in intensity, various small craft, power and sail, broke loose and drifted down toward him. Fending these craft off kept him busy for some time, at which point he realized that the painter on his skiff had parted and the boat had drifted down the cove.

The cove is very shallow; its narrow channel is only 7 feet deep at low tide. Water safe for *Fearless* was sharply limited, and the cove by this time was extremely rough. Suddenly, the swivel below the mooring buoy let go. It was imperative to get rid of the mooring line to prevent the buoy from punching a hole in the hull.

"I immediately started the engines to hold her up," Svendsen said. "I eased up as close as I dared to Planting Island. The water was now on the causeway and you could not see Meadow Island at all. When I reached a point as close as I dared to go, I disengaged the clutches and prepared to get the buoy away. Since there was only a low single wire rail on the foredeck, I stripped down to pants only in the event I went overboard. I then went forward and discarded the mooring line, allowing the buoy to drift away.

"By this time, we had drifted back to a dangerous position and I again proceeded to work my way back to Planting Island under power. I realized I would have to get the anchors out as soon as possible. We carried one small mud hook in one hawsepipe and two 135-pound anchors on deck. One was attached to the chain in the port side hawsepipe and the other was a spare. In order to use the spare, I had to retrieve a long cotton line which was stowed in the lazaret in the afterdeck.

"I then proceeded to move up close to the island, disengage the clutches, rush aft to obtain the anchor line I required, watch my position as I drifted back and rush forward to the pilothouse to move up again. I continued this — moving up under power, then drifting back, time after time after time. I was, of course, completely soaked and extremely cold by now. By the time I retrieved the anchor line for the spare anchor, attached one end to the anchor and the other to the capstan, placed the stocks in both anchors and put the port side one in the davit ready to drop, I probably made 25 to 30 trips to the island.

"When all was ready, I had to use the sounding lead to determine where I wanted to end up, not knowing how far the tide might drop going out. There were no more landmarks visible for me to use. After deciding where I hoped to end up, I eased forward to where I believed the anchors ought to be. I then made my way to the bow again and threw the spare anchor over the bow and released the two anchors attached to the chain in the hawsepipes. I allowed all of the cotton line to play out to get as much scope as possible and then adjusted the remaining two with the winch.

"I now had three anchors and I was still using the engines to ease the strain, but kept an eye on the temperature gauge since the water was extremely dirty with all the stirring up from the storm. When the engines started to heat up, I immediately shut them down to prevent overheating and possibly freezing them up tight. At this point, the anchors appeared to be holding, with waves breaking over the bow.

"I then went to the engine room and proceeded to turn the engines over by hand to prevent them from binding up from excess heat. The warmth of the engine room was a blessing, since I was very cold from my activity on deck in the wind and waves.

"My wife and son were constantly at the water's edge with a light that enabled me to get some bearing on my location. As soon as the storm subsided, I pulled in the anchors and made my way into Marion Harbor and deeper water, where I anchored. Some sections of the anchor chain were literally tied in knots and the anchor stocks were all bent."

Dr. Raymond H. Baxter was the medical examiner of Marion. "My street was blocked by downed trees so an ambulance could not get in," he recalled. "A man put his arm through a broken window and severed the radial artery. This is an operating room job, but it was up to me to do something in the light of flashlights and candles. My twelve-year-old son was watching the breakers coming up my street and at the height of my sweating, he announced, 'The water's only a little way from our house, Daddy.' By the grace of God, I got a clamp on the artery practically in the dark and got a suture around it. My office looked like an abattoir the next morning from the bloody spurts. . . ."

Mrs. Parker Converse was on Converse Point, Marion, which has been owned by the family since 1898. Although the sea had begun to pile over the seawall and dock (which was eventually under eight feet of water), she prepared to drive to meet her husband's train at Wareham. She wrote in her diary, "Took son (he was six) and general maid across the road to caretaker's house, which was on higher ground. As I turned back to the house, Tony Cruz, the caretaker, and I were appalled to see a tidal wave lift the

35-foot motor sailer that was tied to the dock, carry it over the pond, and deposit it in the woods."

Finding the Wareham road underwater, she drove back to Converse Point and wrote later, "Met by breakers, abandoned car. Told that it was impossible to get to the Moorings, as the end of point [where her home was] was underwater. Managed to get to garage. The caretaker took his two small girls and I, my small son. We ran with them until we got to low land, put them on our backs and struggled through the breakers, with furniture sweeping and tumbling by us. Reached dry land just as our strength was giving out."

Mrs. Converse added a footnote to her letter to me in which she reported the entry in her diary: "Recollection of this proved to be more frightening than the experience. Am shaking all over."

I asked Benjamin D. Dexter of Marion, who described himself as an "old-timer," what he remembered about the storm.

"I had a thirty-foot boat pulled up in a field about six feet above mean high water," Dexter said. "Soon, the water was up to her and I was concerned that she would float and smash into a stone wall nearby. So I got an anchor and line and proceeded out into the field to secure the anchor in the ground. I was wearing hip boots, a long raincoat and a sou'wester. As I bent over to hook the anchor in the ground, the thought came to me that I must be dreaming. 'Here I am anchoring a boat in the middle of a vegetable garden,' I said to myself. Just then, a wave broke over my head, but I had hooked the anchor, so I held on and the wave passed.

"A Mr. Fernandes living off Route 6 [the waters of Marion Harbor rose over Route 6] had his barn floated away. Later, he found the barn intact and his cow in its stall chewing hay.

"At Great Hill, Arthur Griffin, then superintendent of the Stone estate, had a new boat in a boathouse. As he watched, the boat came up through the roof and took off for Wareham, where he later found it, with barely a scratch. As for the height of the water, I saw a story and a half house sitting on Dummy Bridge in Onset.

That bridge is some 10 to 12 feet above mean high and that house must have floated at the eaves, making about 20 feet of water there.

"Steven Watts was caught outside in his power boat. He sought refuge behind Ram Island, but so much refuse began to come off the island as the water rose, he decided to make a run for the shore. He ran his boat ashore at the Marion campgrounds in Hammett's Cove. There, he learned that his boat shop was burning; some live wires had ignited the shop, and the Fire Department had responded but with several feet of water, the firemen had to take to boats. One boat capsized with a fireman holding a nozzle. He went under holding the hose and the force of the nozzle sent him zagging about in all directions. He said that only the hose kept him from being jetted out into the harbor. This man must have been the first, and probably the last, jet-propelled fireman."

In late September, this advertisement appeared in the *Standard-Times:* "$5 reward. Lost in Marion Harbor, a narrow board, part of a mantelpiece bearing the carved legend, 'Give me a good wife, a good boat, and ready money.' Finder deliver to Barden's store, Marion, or to Lorraine's, New Bedford, and receive $5."

Chapter 16

At MATTAPOISETT, Dr. Austen Fox Riggs, internationally famous psychiatrist and head of the well-known Stockbridge, Massachusetts, foundation bearing his name, was in his seashore cottage in the Hollywood Beach area. Including his chauffeur, secretary, and household help, he had with him a staff of six.

By 4:30 in the afternoon, the tide was 3 feet higher than Dr. Riggs had ever seen it there; he knew that high tide was not until two hours later. Within ten minutes, he told the household they would have to leave, and his chauffeur had discovered Riggs's station wagon was in the water and useless.

"I got all the help to hold hands. The water was up to our armpits. Only a few of the party could swim. Miss Leary [Susan Leary, sixty, the cook], a woman about 5 feet tall, was so short that we had to carry her. The water was about 6 feet high on the tennis courts," Riggs said in an interview.

"I got to the garage and backed out a larger car. My portable office had been swept away and I saw another portable house smashed to pieces. I packed everyone into the car, only to find the drive flooded. The car stalled and a large swell came in. Mrs. LaFarge [Mrs. Warden LaFarge, his literary secretary] and I managed to get out and open the door. My chauffeur [Harry Bell], Mrs.

LaFarge and the others clung to pine trees. I lifted Miss Leary to the top of the car. As the water continued to rise, I got her to swim on her back and got her to the gate post and to the wall. We left her there.

"I swam 150 yards to get help. By this time, the water was 8 feet deep. I reached the home of William Corey, a neighbor."

Corey and Raymond Winslow found oars in a nearby house and set out in what Captain Walter E. Bowman, a licensed Buzzards Bay pilot for a half-century and an eyewitness, described as "breaking surf" to rescue the stranded members of the Riggs household. All survived but one. Riggs said, "When I got back, I discovered Miss Leary had been washed from the wall. She got back to the top of the automobile and Bell clung to her arms for more than an hour before a wave swept across them and he lost his grip. Two days later, they found Miss Leary's body under a lilac bush near the gate, 100 yards from the house."

Mattapoisett Constable Frank P. LeBaron estimated immediately after the storm that 170 cottages were destroyed at Crescent Beach and 15 more at adjoining Pico Beach. Revised figures ranged from 125 to 160. But whatever the exact total was, it meant that the Crescent Beach settlement was no more.

Dating from somewhere between 1910 and 1913, when "Grandpa" Hiller, who initially owned the whole beach, began to sell house lots there, Crescent Beach became a substantial summer colony. William H. Raymond ran the area's only general store prior to 1938, and one of the colonists whose growing-up summers were spent at this beach recalled that the store was "a heavenly place, where they had penny candy and a wind-up telephone. . . ."

Mrs. Ruth Taylor, Mr. Raymond's daughter, recorded in her diary the events of September 21 and the days that followed:

"Day started out hot and quiet, but more or less normal for this time of year. The Putnams were getting ready to leave for Florida and did, before noon. We saw them off and it was very sultry and still and sort of yellowish sky.

"At 5 P.M., the shingles began to blow off our house. Dad went to the cellar door and opened it; the oil barrel was floating at the top of the stairs. When our floors began to buckle, I told the girls [her daughters, Barbara, thirteen; Jane, eleven; and Elizabeth, seven] to get their coats, as we were leaving.

"I went into the store to go out the door to get the rowboat over by Burns' house. The front step was gone and I went into water to my hips and boots filled up. I found there were two rowboats upside down and tied together. Called to Dad and he brought over the banana knife.

"I caught my foot in the rope and went down under the water, which was waist-deep by then, and thought to myself, 'Oh, how easy things would be to just stay here and drown, then there wouldn't be any problems.' But then thought of my three girls and all the others in the house waiting and I came up in a hurry. We cut the rope, flipped the boat over and went to the window that was just above the water. Dad and I took the folks out the store window.

"We all went up to the Hiller homestead and there were about sixty of us there. We felt some better, until we heard of the others missing. Mrs. [Fred L.] Heyes [Mr. Heyes was former agent of cotton mills in New Bedford and the South] came in exhausted. She had to swim from her house to the main road through tons of debris. Mr. Heyes [who had recently been hospitalized] wouldn't try to come with her, so he died in the wreckage.

"Mrs. [Albert] Norlander and her son-in-law [John R. Pyne] and his six-week-old baby [Richard] and Mrs. [Harry P.] Mc-Allister lost their lives on this beach and Mr. and Mrs. [Paul J.] Ewald [handyman and cook] at the John Duffs, did, too. By daylight, the beach was a shambles. Not a house left standing south of Silver Shell Avenue but Aunt Nellie's stone house and the lower floor was wrecked. Eight of Dad's houses ruined.

"Mrs. [Jennie] Brown [seventy-five years old] also was lying

under a pile of wreckage for about three or four hours until someone accidentally walked over the pile that was over her. She went
to the hospital with three broken ribs, but is expected to recover.

"September 25: Mr. Pyne and the baby and Mrs. Ewald were
found the first day [after the storm]. We are under military rule
and state troopers are here. Around midnight the day of the storm,
the men from Mattapoisett cut through the road and Billy and
George brought us some water. Things from here on were so mud-
dled that I can't tell one thing from the next. I found my thimble
in the sand by raking. Dad had cellar pumped out and got his safe.
Found the cash register. Found Mother's pocket book, but someone
stole mine.

"September 26: Found Mr. Ewald in Wareham.

"September 27: Our houses are spread from Waterman Street,
near the Heyes', way up to the Crescent House. We found a piece
of Myra's green bedstead up side of Sherman's store. Of course, we
lost nearly all of our clothes. We have found glass dishes with
bricks in them, electric light bulbs in lamps, not even cracked; one
of Mother's large vases was still whole, with half a house sitting on
it. Dad lost his car because he put it in King's garage and it was
over in Web Wilde's yard, bottom side up. We spend most every
day down by the houses, picking up dishes and valuables and
bedding. The state cops are all very nice and help us as much as
they are allowed. No one is permitted to leave the beach with anything they don't report. Mr. McAllister came in to see Mother and
broke down. He has lost his only family, his wife. They found Mrs.
Norlander and Mrs. McAllister tonight; they were both under one
small house.

"September 30: Helen has been down with lots of water and we
finally got town water. There are too many things to remember and
try to write them down, so guess this will have to do as an account
of the storm.

"October 13: Henry and I uncovered a lot of Aunt Nellie's silver,
buried deep."

The Norlander-Pyne-McAllister deaths shocked not only residents of the Crescent Beach colony but many in New Bedford and Worcester as well. The Norlanders lived in New Bedford; Mr. Norlander was well known in the textile industry. Mrs. McAllister, a Worcester resident, was widely regarded as a church and concert singer. Mr. Pyne, who had been the husband of the former Elizabeth Norlander only since June of the year before (their son was born July 27, 1938), was one of the youngest members of the Worcester City Council. The McAllister and Norlander cottages were close together; there was a warm friendship between the two families.

Miss Anna M. Norlander, nineteen, a Radcliffe College sophomore, was the daughter of the Albert Norlanders and a younger sister of Mrs. Pyne; she was an excellent sailor and swimmer. "My sister and I left the cottage late Wednesday afternoon to go to New Bedford on an errand for my mother," she said. "While we were gone, Bill Crampton of Mattapoisett drove out to the cottage to visit me. When he found we were gone, he started toward the city to meet us. When he did, both cars headed for the beach."

Mr. and Mrs. Pyne and their infant son were staying at the Norlander cottage, where John Pyne first met Elizabeth Norlander three years before. Mrs. McAllister was visiting Mrs. Norlander. The Norlander daughters had been gone about a half-hour when the sea began its persistent rise. The cottage group gathered on the front porch, about ten yards from the normal high-tide mark. Mrs. Norlander called a general store on the main beach road, asking the owner to head off her daughters on their return from New Bedford, as the water was still coming up. The storekeeper warned that in that case they had better vacate the cottage. Apparently they attempted to do so, but there was not sufficient time left.

"When we got to the bridge over the creek [about a half-mile from the cottage], the water was beginning to come up. Bill's car got over the little bridge, but mine stalled. Bill pushed me back and my sister turned the car around and drove off, after we told her we'd got to the cottage. Bill and I left the car and began to walk; then we ran; the water was up to our knees and then to our waists," Miss Norlander said.

"Pretty soon, we couldn't walk at all and when we were about twenty yards from the cottage, we had to swim. As we tried to get to the cottage, we could see Jack [Mr. Pyne] trying to force the back door open against the push of the water. He got it open a little and saw us swimming. He shouted, 'What will I do with the baby?' He was a poor swimmer, but, with the baby, he was trying to get out.

"The waves pushed us back. I yelled that we'd go for help. We turned in the water and began to swim as fast as we could. Then we saw an empty rowboat that had been washed about two hundred yards inland. We pulled ourselves into it. We tried to row but after we had gone a short distance, the tidal wave came in and cottages, and parts of cottages, and furniture began to bump us so we couldn't make it."

The storm wave at Crescent Beach was described as a fourteen-foot wall of water that drove inland a quarter of a mile. When it retreated, the search for the dead began. In the following days, hundreds of WPA workers, townspeople, twenty-eight members of the First Baptist Church of New Bedford (which Mrs. Norlander attended) and twenty-seven Worcester men, including thirteen members of the city government, searched through the heaps of timbers, planks, and pieces of houses strewn five and six feet thick over a mile-long strip of waterfront.

Of the total settlement, only five cottages remained. Along the shore and even back into the woods were strewn the details of disaster: smashed crockery, plumbing, broken toys, soaked furniture spewing its stuffing, curled books, their pages puffed and stiff from salt water. In one cottage standing on end, there was a letterhead bearing an address written in a masculine hand. Below it was written, "Dear Al:" The remainder of the page was blank.

The evidence suggests that John Pyne gave his life in attempting to save his six-week-old son; their bodies were separated by only a few feet. The bodies of Mrs. Norlander and Mrs. McAllister were recovered under tons of wreckage on September 29 by National Guardsmen; they were about three hundred yards from the site of the Norlander cottage.

Carl B. Forman, who lived at Crescent Beach, was recovering from two recent operations. Despite this, he rescued Joseph B. Ellis of Attleboro, who was partly paralyzed, and whose home was swept away, and Mrs. Walter Pratt, whose leg was in a cast. "The screams were terrible. You could hear people in all directions calling for help. I tried to get in to Mr. Heyes but I couldn't reach him because of the water and wreckage," Forman said.

Later, volunteer workers found a belt on a heap of debris; it bore Mr. Heyes' initials. They also found his crutch.

The newspaper account concerning Mrs. Jennie Brown was brief; it said, "Reported among the missing, [she] was first discovered beneath the roof of a collapsed cottage at Crescent Beach, Mattapoisett, when her voice was heard by searchers. Pinioned beneath the housetop, Mrs. Brown was released when poles were used to pry the boards from her body. It was feared that she had suffered broken legs and body bruises, and contusions were numerous. Her clothing was cut from her body. She was wrapped in coats and carried more than a half-mile through remnants of cottages to a waiting Army truck. She remains at the hospital, where she is under treatment for chest injuries."

The man who found this seventy-five-year-old woman under the wreckage and undoubtedly saved her life was Edwin L. Perkins of Mattapoisett. Of the night of September 21, he recalled, "That evening was a bright moonlight night. I guess it was a near full moon. I was in the plumbing and heating business and the superintendent of the town Water Department contacted me to see if I would go to Crescent Beach and shut off as many water services as I could find, so that we wouldn't lose so much water.

"I drove down as far as the Cedars, right at the curve to go to the beach, in my truck. I could go no farther because the debris was in sheets. I remember I got out and started toward Crescent Beach. There was no road to see, just pieces of houses, roofs, doors; they covered the roadway.

"I crawled over what I could and headed toward the middle of the beach. That night was so bright that all I could see was a stone house across from Bill Raymond's store. The store was demolished. I walked over tops of houses, furniture; there didn't seem to be a bare spot of ground. I had to go on everything, from houses to furniture.

"By the time I got to the middle of the development, I heard a voice. I did not know at first whether it was a woman or a man. The wind was blowing a little and it was hard to tell, but it said, 'Get me out, get me out.' I started to go toward where I heard the voice. Then I didn't hear it. Then I recognized that it was a woman's voice, saying, 'Please get me out.'

"I traveled sort of a circle, bigger and bigger. I found out after why she didn't say anything all the time. She was in and out of consciousness. Then she said, "I am Mother Brown. Please get me out." I was five, maybe ten, feet from the voice. There was debris everywhere, four to five feet thick, halves of roofs, chairs, doors, everything. She heard me walking over the debris; that's how she knew I was there.

"I said, 'Are you all right, Mrs. Brown?' and she didn't answer. For a couple of minutes, there wasn't a word. That was an awful feeling. Then she said again, 'I am Mother Brown; get me out.'

"I said, 'I am Mr. Perkins, the plumber. I know you.' I reached down with my right arm between the debris until I touched the top of this woman's head. I could just feel her hair. She said, 'Mr. Perkins, please get me out.'

"I suppose it sounds funny now, but I said, 'Mother Brown,

[301]

don't move; I'll get help.' She couldn't have moved if she had tried.

"So I said to her, 'I'll go get help,' and I said to myself, 'How will I ever find her again?'

"I had on a black and white plaid shirt from L. L. Bean in Maine, and I found an oar and I put the oar handle down the sleeve of the shirt, then I stuck the oar in a loose place in the debris to mark the spot. I walked way up to where the road was clear; they were allowing only the State Guard and police there. I told one of the State Guard men and he said, 'We'll get a crew and follow you.'

"Eight or ten National Guardsmen then came along. We found her again, we spoke to her and there was no answer. I was afraid she was dead. The men started hauling away the debris.

"When we got to her, she was on a slant, sort of huddled down there. The only thing she had on was a piece of cloth around her left arm and shoulder. Everything else had been ripped off her body. She came to then, but she couldn't move. Two of the National Guardsmen found a door ripped off something and they used that as a stretcher and took her from there way up to the cars, where the road was clear. They got her to the hospital.

"She was very bruised; no bones broken, but shocked. They took sixty-eight pieces of wood out of Mrs. Brown's body — they weren't ordinary splinters — and we figured the water must have pushed and pulled her, back and forth, because it not only ripped off all her clothing, but some of those splinters were in as if she had gone against them going down and some as if she had gone with them, in the same direction. She was in the hospital for some time and had to go back in again. I went to see her.

"As we found out later, Mrs. Brown had started from her cottage to Angelica Avenue after the water came up to her piazza. 'I think I better go to dry ground,' she said. She got partway and she said, 'I left all my jewelry, watch, and diamonds in the cottage.' So she went back. By the time she got the jewelry and had started for high ground again, the big wave came. She couldn't go anywhere.

Houses were going to pieces. How that woman ever lived through it, I don't know. That big wave, with debris, must have overwhelmed her. She must have been washed back and forth. And her jewelry was never found.

"The hurricane hit at about 4 P.M. I found her about 10 P.M., so she must have been in there five or six hours."

When I interviewed Mr. Perkins in 1974, he showed me a gold wristwatch inscribed, "J. M. B. to E. Perkins, 9–21–38." He said, "About a year after the storm, James Stowell, a friend who knew her well, brought this watch and a letter, and gave them to me."

The letter was as follows:

September 19, 1939

My dear Mr. Perkins:

"In appreciation of your effort in locating me after hearing my voice and then your continued effort in my behalf by bringing aid who made possible my rescue. I present you this token of my sincere appreciation.

With kindest regards and sincere best wishes, I am,

Most sincerely,

JENNIE M. BROWN

The storm of September 21, 1938.

Many of the beaches that were swept clean by the hurricane had been summer sanctuaries for a sufficient number of generations to acquire an atmosphere of permanence. On September 21, this atmosphere of peaceful certainty with all of its symbols, large and small, was swept away, and into the raw vacuum flooded alien feelings of fear and caution, on a tide of inevitable change. Crescent Beach was an outstanding example of this, and a woman whose family bought some of the first lots that "Grandpa" Hiller sold there wrote poignantly of those things washed away that could not be rebuilt: "I went alone to Crescent Beach soon after sunrise on

September 22. It was, as everyone who experienced it knows, a brilliant and benign morning. [Some fourteen years later, Hemingway was to comment, in *Old Man and the Sea*, 'There is no more beautiful weather than in hurricane season when you're not having a hurricane.']

"My most vivid memory is of the clarity of the air after the tropical oppressiveness of the day before, and of the terrible cleanness of the sweep. From one point of the crescent [for which the beach was named] to the other, the sand was empty. All that marked the fifty by one hundred–foot lot where our two-story cottage had stood was the foot pedal of a sunken garbage pail.

"Dozens of big shingled cottages like ours were swept into a giant pile on the north side of Angelica Avenue [a paved street running immediately behind the beach], rather as if in readiness for a Gog and Magog bonfire. All that my mother found of our nine-room place, in that heap, was part of a rocking chair which had been used for some twenty-five summers on our broad front porch — part of the Victorian ambience which vanished so swiftly after the storm.

"The only other aspect of that morning which I remember clearly is the way in which the brown and cheerful creek, which flows down into the bay from springs far up in Rochester, had swollen, deepened, and stretched east and west across the flat, wet sand as it raced toward the sea. Later, we were to learn that its changed course had swept away the land on which the big cottage of Dr. Charles E. P. Thompson, for many years school physician in Fairhaven, had stood — surely one of the strangest losses of property in beach history. Before the storm, the brook had made a little copper-colored arc behind his house, on its way to the bay; a narrow, wooden bridge crossed it at that curve, and was used by all of us on our thousands (I suppose) of trips to William Raymond's general store. Among my happiest childhood memories are those of seining on the banks of that creek for tiny, black, eel-like fish, which my brother and I would put into sand pails, attempt to count, admire for a suitable period of time, and then dump back into the water.

"On the morning of September 22, someone had thrown a stout plank, balanced gingerly on stones on each side, across the creek. I remember teetering to the center of the thing, falling in, soaking a red plaid suit, sloshing back up onto the sand, and realizing the insignificance of such minor damage.

"During the following summer, buildings went up again here and there, timidly, but no one paid much attention to the symmetry of the former crescent — that solid symbol of order and, because it had allowed all beachfront dwellers maximum views of the water, of courtesy. The new cottages were small, cheap, obviously temporary and unsure of themselves. My own family put up a frame garage toward the back of our lot; it served as bath and storage house and a sort of squatters' headquarters on sunny days in summer. Strange contrast to the environment of the chauffeur-driven tenants my parents had had from July 1 through Labor Day for the preceding decade.

"Some of the affluent families did not rebuild. One lot, still empty, is marked by fieldstone steps on which is etched, 'R. M. Kuechler, 1926'; the steps lead from the beach now only into a field of wild coreopsis, once-cultivated rambler roses, and an occasional beer can.

"Today, a few of the 'back cottages' have scraps of lawn and little gardens again, but the large lawns and gardens which had been so important a part of the scheme of the pre-1938 beachfront properties, in our midsection of the shoreline, have never returned. My mother's was more or less typical, perhaps: a fenced square of carefully tended grass behind and to the west of the cottage; borders of petunias and larkspur, rambler roses, and here and there, an edging of white stones which she had picked up on our beach. . . .

"It is provocative to remember that the things which survived the 1938 hurricane were fragile. Under the sand, as months went on, we found a set of Sandwich glass berry dishes, one by one, which I still have and use. Also, assorted pieces of porcelain and blue china, most of which were intact. . . ."

Reportedly the only home owner in the town who had hurricane insurance was Mrs. Charles S. Hamlin. Not so much as a pane of glass was broken in her home by the hurricane, while uninsured houses on both sides were blown to bits.

To the west, in Fairhaven, the entire stretch of Sconticut Neck suffered; whole neighborhoods of cottages on the peninsula were wiped out, and more than 40 police, former servicemen, and other volunteers rescued at least 200 people from the remains of houses and from trees, utility poles, and boats. First reports, after the Acushnet River had risen to 11.53 feet above mean high water, indicated that the Greater New Bedford area had 69 known dead, 40 still missing, and damage of at least $5 million.

Fifteen-year-old Edward Minnock was at the family cottage at Pope Beach, with his five-year-old brother, Thomas. Their father was at work; Mrs. Minnock had gone to New Bedford to arrange to have the cottage's gas and lights turned off, since they were moving back to their winter home the next day.

"Tommy and I were getting quite a kick out of the high tide when we felt the house move," Edward said. "Then I noticed Mr. Flanagan's house next to ours was right up to our windows. And before I could move, the tidal wave came roaring in through the house.

"I grabbed Tommy and we were pushed by the water to the back door and I noticed our steps breaking away. I put Tommy on my back and jumped. The water was up to my neck. I managed to get over a pile of rocks. The water was getting higher and higher and there was no one around but us. We jumped in the water and I swam as good as I could, with Tommy on my back. Tommy wasn't scared; he was getting a lot of fun out of it.

"We had a good 200 yards to go and the water was getting

deeper and very rough. I was terribly scared and I didn't think we could make it. I was swimming toward the store at the corner and I was losing my strength fast.

"We got to the store and I was just going to grab it when it let go and floated down the street. That was when I gave up hope and I was praying for my brother and myself when a big log came floating right up to me. I grabbed that and we went right on to Hathaway Street, where the water was only knee-deep. Then we were noticed by people at the head of the street and they came running to help us.

"The police were trying to locate us; Dad and Mom were trying to find us. It was 10:30 when we were reunited and we were all crying. I can still hear that water roaring."

At Shore Acres, Sconticut Neck, John Rimmer, seventy-nine, realized that his cottage was about to be swept out to sea and that he could not save himself. He opened a window, leaned out, and fired his rifle as a signal for help. The shot was heard by seventeen-year-old Eugene Barboza, who waded and swam to Rimmer's house, got him out through a window and carried him to safety. The Rimmer house broke up and was washed away.

Lena K. Arden, my friend of many years, was a New Bedford schoolteacher, a serious musician. As a child, she had played juvenile roles on the English stage in plays with her mother, Kate, who was known professionally for nearly two decades as Katie Peerless. At the time of the hurricane, Miss Arden was engaged to marry Charles A. Fernandes, a prominent New Bedford pharmacist. On the afternoon of the twenty-first, they went to her cottage at Winsegansett Heights, Sconticut Neck, to make sure that everything was in place and locked up.

"I began to gather a few things to take back to the city. I looked out the front window. The waves were over the top step; the sea struck my 15-foot rowboat and smashed it against the wall. I ran out to tell Charlie and he said, 'We're getting out of here,' " Miss Arden related.

They had driven no more than a few feet in his car when the water was over the hood. There was a stone wall back of the house and they thought they could walk along it to higher ground, where they could see other people standing. "We began walking, one behind the other," Miss Arden said, "and holding on tightly. We were doing quite well when a tremendous wave came right over the top of the house we were passing and crashed into us.

"I came to in the water and began to scream for Charlie. I couldn't see him. A piece of fencing came floating by. I climbed on it. The fencing bumped into a garage. I climbed on the roof. I lay down on my stomach and held on tightly. I saw a little bantam hen sitting calmly on a nest which rose with the water. I sometimes wonder what became of her.

"A young man came swimming and he said, 'Put your hand on my shoulder and don't fight.' I said, 'I won't fight,' and he took me to land. There were two priests there who had come for the fishing and I said to one of them, 'I want to see Charlie.' The priest said, 'Be calm and grateful for what has happened to you. You will see Charlie someday.' I looked into his eyes and knew what he meant. . . .

"After that, I saw my cottage go floating on the swamp water, north out of sight. Charlie's body was found three days later. It was carried into a small hollow near a clambake pavilion. The doctor said that when the wave threw us into the air, he had evidently landed headfirst on his car and that was the cause of his death."

There were occasional small miracles.

At Knollmere Beach, Mahlon Faunce, Sr., of New Bedford went to the assistance of a Mr. and Mrs. Logan and their dog. Mrs. Logan was partly paralyzed; she was lying on her bed with the water lapping over her. Faunce, though husky, knew that swimming with them was impossible and wished that he had a boat.

A small sailboat, with mast gone, and full of water, raced by. He caught it and wondered how he could bail it out. Then some buckets he had left at his own back door about two hundred yards away bobbed by; he grabbed one and bailed out the boat. And at that time, his garage went to pieces, releasing his oars; he caught two when they floated past him, and paddled the Logans and their dog to safety in the boat.

And there were lighter touches.

Elia Gubellini, the post office janitor, was at his home on Middle Street, which is close to the waterfront. He fell asleep in a chair, with his feet on another chair. His cat kept jumping up on his lap; mildly annoyed, Gubellini brushed the animal off each time. The cat persisted, Gubellini was finally aroused and stood up impatiently, to discover that he was standing in a foot of water. A short time later, Mr. Gubellini and his cat were rescued from the second floor.

Book VI

New Bedford and Thereafter

Chapter 17

THE LATE EDITION of the *Standard-Times* on the twenty-first had a page 1 bulletin of several paragraphs, reporting that "the city was struck late today by a 45-mile-an-hour windstorm. A driving rain hit New Bedford for a few minutes after 3:30. Awnings were torn and reports of damage increased.

"The highest span of the roller coaster at Acushnet Park collapsed. Tree branches were broken over a wide area and there were reports of a large yacht on the rocks beside Padanaram Bridge. A young woman who refused to give her name was blown off her feet in front of the Free Public Library and stunned."

It was I who provided the sentence about the young woman; that was my first contribution to the newspaper. When I saw her — she was wearing something red — I had just emerged from City Hall and did not realize what was happening to the weather. I thought she was simply running. As she came closer, I realized that she was struggling to keep from being blown flat, that her face was contorted with fright and exhaustion, and that she was weeping.

I started toward her, but there was no running against the wind. I hung onto a telephone pole and reached out to grab her as she passed me, but a yard beyond my reach, she lost a shoe, stumbled and fell, tearing her stockings. She sat there, doubled up on the sidewalk, both knees bleeding, sobbing and weaving her head and shoulders back and forth, and crying, "No! No!" The contents of her handbag were strewn over the sidewalk. The lighter articles blew away; I grabbed for one, a white scarf, but it was gone. I helped her to her feet, picked up her things and put them in her bag. I asked her if she wanted a doctor and she brushed me away, shouting, "No! No!" more as if she could not believe, rather than as if she were answering me. Once standing, she blew on down the street, weeping.

That was the way it began, for me, with a prelude of unbelievable wildness, something gone incredibly and abruptly wrong, and of all places that it had to happen — between those pillars of predictability, the City Hall and the library. In such a location, what was occurring to the weather, to the city, and to people was ungraspable. That was the way it started, with the sound of things smashing, with the wind crying as if it blew across a taut string, with the pelting rain that fell from a sky of frantic motion, a sky the color of a jaundiced eye.

I ran up the three flights of iron stairs to the newspaper's city room to find out what the hell was happening. "It's the hurricane," said George L. Geiger, the city editor. He handed out flashlights to us. "We don't know much about what it's done anywhere else, but it's bad. We expect to lose power and lights. If it does here what it seems to have done elsewhere, there will be heavy damage and loss of life. You probably won't be able to phone us, but the night side will be here. Day people ought to be back here by six tomorrow morning at least, to start writing. If we lose our power, we'll try to arrange to print somewhere else. Take care of yourselves."

I walked out of the building feeling personally afraid — the last radio broadcast I heard urged everyone to stay under cover — and professionally incompetent. I did not own a hat or raincoat, and I was damp already. I ran from the lee side of one building to the next, headed for the waterfront. The uptown streets were largely empty by now; the storm was upon the city.

What I remember of the next several hours is fragmented, some things sharply etched, some no more than impressions, and they tumble upon each other in confusion, which is the way they happened. Over all was the aura of unreality. Everywhere — on the docks, in the street, at the beach — normality was harshly transposed: the boat was aground, the house was afloat, the living were dead, the landmark had disappeared. Incessantly in the background, there were shouts barely heard from people never seen and the sounds of foaming black water, thundering beneath the wharves.

I stood in the shelter of an old brick building and put no more than half my face and one eye around the corner to stare into the storm, southerly down the harbor and across the bay. Rain struck my face like pebbles and poured down my shirt; mixed with spray, it was salt to the taste. You could not look long, but I saw what appeared to be a wall of water coming toward the harbor; it was like a purple brush stroke. The harbor itself was full of craft in contortion. A naked man who straddled a broken piece of white masthead, was blown past me, up the Acushnet River. He clutched the spar with arms and legs, leaning low over it; his mouth was open and I do not know whether he was yelling or just trying to breathe. In a moment, he was out of sight in the spume. I never found out who he was or what happened to him.

The 60-foot dragger *Winifred M.* parted her lines at Pier 3, a short distance to the south. She was driven north to the Nye Oil Company wharf — an old stone-faced pier of the whaling era — whacked by a half-dozen heavy seas that laid her open like a split mackerel, and she sank. The whole business took about fifteen minutes.

Frank Murphy and Horace Neagus were manning the drawbridge at the head of the harbor. "We knew there was one thing we had to do," Murphy said, "and that was to turn off the hydraulic pressure under the bridge. The pressure operates the big wedges and the four 100-ton jacks that turn the draw; it's 2,800 pounds per square inch and if it let go in the storm, it would be like dynamite."

Leaving the operators' shanty on the end of the bridge pier, they ran over the planks to the platform steps. They had hardly left the little building when the sea reduced it to splinters lifting the catwalk they had just run across, and carrying it overboard at the same time. A minute later, as they reached the hydraulic base and were turning off the pressure, the platform steps were washed away. But the job was done.

"After that, Neagus and I hung onto the bridge rail all night to keep from being swept into the water, patrolling back and forth and picking up what few poor devils we could from the decks," Murphy said. "But some of the boats went into pieces so fast that God only knows what became of the sailors. Some of the biggest boats cracked against the bridge so hard that it would almost shake your grip loose. We thought the draw might go but we knew that if the bridge was letting go, the vibrations would warn us. And there was gasoline in the water, so much that every time a wave hit you in the face, it would burn your eyes."

Just east of the draw was the Pope's Island station of the New Bedford Yacht Club, a two-story building that was part of the city's waterfront heritage, familiar to countless shore people and thousands of sailors. I saw its end, and as with the America's Cup defenders in Bristol, its passing was more than a matter of wood and fastenings; when it went, all of the echoes and shadows went, too, including those of what very likely was its finest hour. That hour concerned a party, regarded as fabulous even in that splendid nineteenth-century Age of Certainty of which fabulous parties were a hallmark. My friend and dean of yachting writers, the late William U. Swan, was a guest; he once told me, gin in hand, that when it was over, the champagne corks filled three bushel baskets.

An article dated August 5, 1881, offers the bare bones of what that gathering was like. "The festivities given in New Bedford Harbor last evening by the New York Yacht Club were the gayest

Wreckage near the Pope's Island station of the New Bedford (Massachusetts) Yacht Club

of anything ever seen here in the nautical line," the story ran. "The barge on which the ball was given was towed out to her position and lashed alongside Commodore Waller's *Dauntless* about 7 o'clock and at 8, the guests began to arrive, tug *Young America* and an immense number of small boats being engaged in setting them on board. By the brilliant light of numerous lanterns, the barge and its decorations looked splendidly.

"The entertainment opened with a literary and dramatic olla, the guests being seated to witness it. The programme included banjo solos and duets, imitation of actors by Mr. Harry Hatch, and a scene from *School for Scandal*, by Miss Otis and Mr. Bird. This

[317]

was all very fine and Mr. Hatch's representation of Sothern was encored.

"The merry dance followed and the witching strains of the orchestra were foot-moving in the extreme. The ladies' toilets were exquisite and the gentlemen's varied between common full dress, yachtsmen's and naval uniforms.

"At 11 o'clock, the orchestra marched the gay assemblage to supper on the steamer *Martha's Vineyard* which, after the finishing touches had been given to the tables by Mr. Brownell of the Parker House and his effective corps of attendants, steamed out into the stream and was lashed along the port side of the barge. The banquet was one of the most elegant New Bedford ever saw. . . .

"Schooner yacht *Caroline* of the Eastern squadron, Norton and Taylor owners, made a very fine display, as did the *Skylark*, *Imperia*, *Dreadnaught*, and sloop *Minnie*, of this port. Yacht *Aroostook* was also illuminated with Japanese paper lanterns and there was a fine concert on board by a violin, flute and cabinet organ, which played Strauss music effectively. Fireworks in profusion were burned on many of the yachts from dusk until one o'clock. The grand illumination and reception of the visitors at the New Bedford clubhouse takes place this evening. . . ."

Now, as I watch that same clubhouse, the wind builds the sea. The harbor, open to the south, is vulnerable to both. The yacht club, at the harbor's head, is precisely in the target area. Before long, there is a pattern to the waves, as there is in the deeper water offshore; they come crooked, black and curling, their tops crumpling, but not breaking. One or two pleasure craft still in the anchorage are hawsing in frantic fashion, leaping as the sea rolls under them, falling into the troughs, and rolling their dark bottoms out as they attempt to recover.

The water raises the float stages, already abnormally high, and they surge and yank at their chains. The sea is rough even close to the beach; it slams against the stonework, throwing spray; it inches higher on the docks and their decks are already soaked and slippery. As every sea hisses past the spiles on its way to smash on the beach, its top thunders and splatters up through the cracks between the wharf planks, flooding in yellow foam across the deck.

The wind begins to sound like mad music. It is impossible to look into it, the eyes run streaming; it rips at the clothes. Such few clouds as there are blow in harried strings. The air is horizontal. Things are beginning to let go; plate glass buckles and smashes. All of the boats are dragging; two have parted their gear and wallow broadside like wounded birds, bound for disaster to leeward. The white water of the harbor is full of vessels adrift, their mastheads rolling in quick arcs, and when they drop into the troughs, the masts are all that show.

Docks and stages have been torn adrift; the best-driven oak pilings were not meant for this. Water has risen around the yacht club; it is up to the wheels of the automobiles in the parking lot and rising fast. Some vessels are aground; there is a big sloop in the surf in front of the club; she is hove down and being pounded and when the sea strikes her, the spray flies a hundred feet.

And now the Pope's Island station of the New Bedford Yacht Club is inundated. The sea has flooded the island, has overrun the bridge, and is hammering at the building that artist-architect Nat C. Smith took such pains with only eight years ago: "Rebuilt and Renovated Throughout — Greatly Improved Facilities Obtained Without Loss of Accustomed Atmosphere," said the headline. No building could stand the punishment being inflicted by the tons of gale-driven water pounding against the front of the clubhouse. Every time the sea hits, something smashes; every time it falls back for another blow, something drops — in pieces.

That clubhouse — which had been substantial enough to have withstood all the waterfront weather since 1877 — disintegrated as I watched it. The sea hammered in the front, the roof fell, and the building collapsed, abruptly reduced from a snug monument to a half-acre of junk, strewn, as one member observed, "from hell to breakfast." And beside it, equally symbolic, the wreckage of the little schooner yacht *Lizzie* lay against the stonework that had destroyed her, the bottom driven out of her and her masts leaning against the iron railing of the bridge.

In midharbor at New Bedford is Palmer's Island. It is about 1,000 feet long and 460 feet wide and its highest point is between 30 and 40 feet above sea level. In 1938, Captain Arthur A. Small had been keeper of the lighthouse on the north end of Palmer's Island for nineteen years; he and his wife, Mabel, lived in a white story-and-a-half house on the island.

Small was an exceptional man. He began his sea career at fourteen, fished with both the Maine and Gloucester fleets, had served aboard merchant ships, coasting vessels, sealers, freighters, and packets, had rounded the Horn and been through the Straits of Magellan several times.

A likable and attractive man, a smoker of corncob pipes, he said once, "A trip around Cape Horn seems to have a sort of romantic appeal for landsmen. I'll tell you, there's very little romance about Cape Horn, or anywhere below fifty-two south latitude, for that matter. It's cold and ugly down there. . . ."

He joined the Navy in 1906 and sailed around the world in the Great White Fleet, commanded by Admiral Robley D. Evans. He served in Coast Guard vessels and in the Coast and Geodetic Survey, as well as in the Lighthouse Service, including assignments at the Narrows in Boston Harbor and at Boston Light. He was also a painter, principally of ships and the sea, and authenticity was his hallmark.

While painting an eight-by-five-foot canvas of the clipper *A. C. Roper*, he commented, "When the picture is finished, the ship will be shown in the harbor of Hongkong. I have two charts of the harbor there on the wall, so I'll be sure to get the coastline right and I've looked at those high blue mountains enough times to remember how they should appear as a background." He did a number of murals, including a depiction of Columbus's discovery

[320]

of America for the Spanish Historical Society of St. Augustine, Florida, and once, commissioned to paint a panel for a yacht — the owner wanted Sir Walter Raleigh's fleet engaging the Spanish Armada — Small read volumes in preparation, especially so that he would get the ships' rigging exactly.

Late one afternoon in the 1930's when Captain Small made his way up the spiral staircase in the Palmer's Island light tower and reached behind the barrel-shaped lens to light the oil vaporizer, which had to be warmed up before the lamp could be lighted, he remarked with amusement, "Whenever they say anything about a lighthouse keeper, they always act as if he were some kind of hero. We're not heroes. Here I am on this island, perfectly safe, working and painting pictures, while you wander around in New Bedford, crossing streets with automobiles and trolley cars whizzing by, just missing you by a few feet. Why, you people take more chances in a week than I do in ten years."

Small and his wife were alone on the island on September 21. Having been through a number of hurricanes, being weatherwise in the manner of all deep-water sailors, he knew what the heavy atmosphere and the color of the sky meant. Shortly before dark, he prevailed upon Mrs. Small to go to the oil house, the highest point on the little island, where the water was already 3 feet deep. Palmer's Island was beginning to flood; the wind was stiff, and the sea was rolling across it, burdened with all manner of lumber and driftwood.

Leaving her in the upper part of the oil house, he forced his way through the water toward the lighthouse; it was time to light the lamp. The seas knocked him off his feet; he was hurt, and was being swept overboard. He swam, but with difficulty, because of his injury.

Mrs. Small, seeing that he was in trouble, left her place of safety and ran to the boathouse. She was an excellent oarsman and was going to row to him; he was already in deeper water than she could wade in. Small, by swimming underwater to dodge the wreck-

[321]

age, got his footing again, and was struggling to regain the station. He could see his wife going to launch a boat and then watched in horror as a heavy sea slammed into the boathouse. It collapsed upon her. The next wave swept the building away.

"I was hurt and she knew it," Small said later. "Seeing the wave hit the boathouse was about the last thing I remember. I must have been hit by a piece of timber and knocked unconscious. I came to some hours later, but all I remember was that I was in the middle of some wreckage. Then I must have lost my senses again, for I remember nothing more."

Nevertheless, even though suffering from both shock and injury, he somehow retained strength and consciousness to haul himself back to the lighthouse, and he kept the light and the fog signal operating throughout the hurricane and Wednesday night.

At 7:45 in the morning on September 22, observing that the keeper's house and other buildings on Palmer's Island had been swept away, Captain William D. Raymond and Captain Fred W. Phillips — both close friends of Small — rowed out to the island with food. Raymond contacted the Lighthouse Service for permission to have Small relieved from duty, for the rule of the service stated: "No keeper may leave his post until relieved, if he is able to walk." Raymond and Phillips arranged for a police escort over the New Bedford–Fairhaven Bridge — closed to regular traffic because of grounded boats and debris — and they took Small to St. Luke's Hospital.

On September 23, the following letter was sent from the hospital to the Superintendent of Lighthouses in Washington:

> In reporting the destruction of and loss of building and equipment at Palmer Island Light Station, New Bedford, Mass. on September 21st, 1938, the keeper made preparations all during that day, securing everything so far as possible, carrying extra oil and lamp equipment to the tower. This station felt the full force of the gale, the seas reaching clear across the island. . . .
>
> Keeper swept overboard, but by swimming underwater, made the

[322]

station again. Mrs. Small, the keeper's wife, was seen by the keeper while he was overboard. She left the oil house where he had told her to stay and evidently she tried to launch a boat to save the keeper, but she was swept away and drowned. . . . There is no shelter to be had at the station, except in the top of the tower.

Keeper remained on duty until properly relieved. The light and fog signal were in good order. Keeper removed to St. Luke's Hospital suffering from exhaustion and exposure.

(Signed) Arthur A. Small, keeper. Dictated by Arthur Small, keeper, recorded by Wesley V. Small, keeper's son.

Three days later, in Washington, Commissioner Harold D. King of the Bureau of Lighthouses described Captain Small's performance during the hurricane as "one of the most outstanding cases of loyalty and devotion that has come to the attention of this office."

E. H. Tripp of Fairhaven wrote a tribute to Mrs. Small and, implicitly, to her husband, which unquestionably reflected the feelings of many:

"A happy and courageous companion through thirty years of married life in the Lighthouse Service, in Wednesday's storm, she abandoned her refuge in an attempt to help her valiant husband, struggling for his life, to reach his post of duty and thereby lost her own.

"The manner of Mrs. Small's death shocked the community and her loss is deeply felt and mourned by her family and very wide circle of friends. A great number of people in all walks of life have visited Captain and Mrs. Small, the noted, as well as the obscure, and have met with a sincerely cordial and generous hospitality. Mrs. Small and her husband shared their enjoyment of people and books and art with their friends. And those who have been welcomed to the home circle and who enjoyed their company will grieve that, with the gracious mistress gone, the home is no more.

"All express their deepest sympathy for Captain Small and his two stalwart sons, Wesley and Allan. Wesley is skipper of the two-masted schooner *Adventure*, lying at Gloucester, and Allan spent the summer as one of the crew of the three-masted schooner *Sachem* of Essex, Connecticut.

"Mrs. Small's forty-eighth birthday came two days after the catastrophe. Mrs. Small was a member of the Fairhaven Mother's Club, for which she and Captain Small had given talks. Living by and on the sea and knowing full well the might of God's awful elements as well as sunshine on a sandy, rock-strewn isle, the brave wife of a brave man, casting aside all thought of self, nor by wind or tide dismayed, she tried to bring succor to her mate, who struggled in the raging flood.

"We, her friends who weep, may pause and say, 'There is no greater love than this — her dear memory to us a treasure will be always.'"

On September 30, there was a classified advertisement in the *Standard-Times* of New Bedford, which read: "LOST — IN HURRI-CANE FROM PALMER ISLAND, large sum of currency in canvas pouch about 6 x 8 inches. Substantial reward for return in whole or part. Wesley V. Small." In the files of the newspaper, attached to that clipping, there is a handwritten notation that reads: "Re-ported $7,000–$8,000 on Mrs. Arthur Small at time of hurricane drowning."

Captain Small visited Palmer's Island on either October 15 or 16, 1938, the first time he went there after the hurricane and perhaps the last time. He informed the Fairhaven police that he had been granted a long furlough by his superiors in order to regain his health and that he would be living in Dorchester.

About two weeks later, he wrote the following letter from Dor-chester to the Superintendent of Lighthouses, Second District:

Referring to the superintendent's letter of October 4, 1938, re-questing that this office be furnished with a report listing personal effects lost as a result of the hurricane:

The list enclosed herewith is a report covering only the outstand-ing items lost at this time.

All buildings except light tower and oil house [where he had placed

Mrs. Small for safety] were destroyed and carried away in the heavy sea that swept the entire reservation and all personal property was lost. None of the personal effects belonging to Mrs. Small, my wife, who lost her life as a result of this hurricane, are included in the list herewith.

Respectfully,

Arthur Small

Essentially, what Captain Small listed was "Personal library of several hundred volumes, many out of print, and the result of about thirty years of careful selection, $75;

"The value of the following cannot be estimated, as my personal records and data of sailing ships were sketches and notes, the result of thirty years' work and used for reference in painting the history of sailing ships, a spare-time hobby, $100."

Two things are noteworthy. In characteristically modest fashion, Captain Small asked for no compensation for a number of his paintings that were lost in the Palmer's Island house, although, as a matter of record, his work had marketable value. Further, records in the National Archives reveal that someone, not identified, recommended he be given $100, rather than the $175 he had asked for.

By March 20, 1939, the *Standard-Times* reported, "That Captain Arthur A. Small, for many years keeper of the light at Palmer's Island, never will return to New Bedford in his official capacity, is the information just received by Frank Ponte, temporary keeper of Palmer's Island light, in a letter written to him by Captain Small from the Canal Zone.

"Reading between the lines of Captain Small's letter, Mr. Ponte is of the opinion that the U.S. Treasury Department has granted Captain Small a leave of absence with pay for the next two years, at the end of which Captain Small will be retired from the Lighthouse Service on pension.

"Captain Small, following the death of his wife by drowning, the loss of $7,500, which she had with her when she attempted to save his life in the tidal flood and hurricane last September, and the injuries he sustained, was sent to the Marine Hospital at Chelsea for treatment.

"When convalescent, Captain Small was granted an indefinite leave of absence on full pay and upon his discharge from the hospital, went to Panama, where his son is employed on a millionaire's yacht."

In August of 1939, a visitor to Palmer's Island observed, "The present light keeper has a small rocky terrain, with only hurricane wreckage for company; crumbled bricks which were once the foundation of a house . . . are mute evidence of New Bedford's lighthouse tragedy."

Slightly more than forty-eight hours before, I had come to New Bedford on the steamer *Martha's Vineyard*, in search of my fortune. It was a pleasant, uneventful trip, such as thousands of tourists have known, aboard that same vessel. But at 4:30 on the afternoon of the twenty-first, the *Martha's Vineyard* and those aboard were on the threshold of trouble.

She came rolling up to Pier 9 minutes ahead of the rush of water into the harbor. Her fifteen passengers, once off the vessel, discovered that they were not going any farther; behind them, the river was rising and out beyond the dock shed, the driving rain and wind had shut everything down. They went into the company office at the head of the dock; when the first floor was flooded, they went to the second and were trapped there, watching the water still coming up. Crew members of the steamer, including porters, manned two skiffs, battled their way across the slip, and took the passengers out of the inundated building through a second-story window, rowing them across deeply flooded streets to higher ground.

As the water poured into the harbor, it picked up the *Martha's Vineyard* and suspended the steamer by its guardrail from the roof of the pier buiding. The guardrail, 7 feet above waterline, held the big vessel to the roof; all during the period of high water, the ship pounded the shed and threatened its own destruction as well. When the water receded, as rapidly as it had risen — throughout all the waterfront streets of the city, you could hear it going with an awful sucking noise like a giant drain — the steamer dropped off the roof, but her guardrail caught on the tops of four wharf spiles. There she hung, listing at a frightening angle and with her steel hull under terrible strain.

That is how I came upon her, paddling through the muck, the broken fish boxes, the hundreds of cans of motor oil floated off somebody's dock, dodging the open manholes whose covers had been blown off by the high water; I, coming with flashlight in the dripping dark to see who and what was left.

There was the good round-faced Dutchman, Albert F. Haas, the steamboat company superintendent, standing stalwart and chunky in the yellow blob of the battery-powered emergency lighting hooked up to the caplog, watching his steamer, wondering if she would break in half before they could help her.

In the weak light, the arc of her steel guardrail overhead hung like a scimitar and that is what it was for the steamer's crew who set to work with saws and axes to cut off the spiles on which she was hung. Working underneath those tons of vessel, with each stroke weakening the wood that held her suspended, they kept one hand for the blade and one for themselves, alert with each stroke for that last cracking of spile which would signal that the steamer was coming down. There was no way of knowing what she would do at the moment when her hull was freed.

It was ringing bite of the ax, steady risp-rasp of the saw, the bent backs, rising and falling with effort, the figures half in light, half in dark, chips and sawdust gathering on the dock, one man spelling another, so through the hour. Then the crack of timber came, somebody yelled a warning, they all jumped, and down came the *Martha's Vineyard*, transformed in an instant from incongruous cripple to her customary grace. Sweaty-faced, they cheered.

Two men stranded in a flooded restaurant boarded this runaway boat and gained the shore safely at Fairhaven, Massachusetts.

Haas said softly, "They saved the vessel and the pier as well. As far as I am concerned, that was heroic. They did not know what might happen."

East of the yacht club and across the highway, there was a diner. I waded toward it, past an automobile agency with its plate glass windows shattered and the new showroom models wheel-deep in salt water. From somewhere in the darkness, two men came splashing; one wore a bathing suit and shoes, the other khaki trousers and a life jacket. I assumed they were off some boat — perhaps the schooner yacht *Gallant*, which lay hove down in the nearby park — but they were looking for a couple of fellows who had been in the diner.

"What do you think happened to them?" I asked.

One of them looked toward where the sidewalk in front of the diner ought to be. Water still poured over it and a big chunk of the steel bridge rail was gone. "I suppose they're overboard somewhere," he said, and sloshed off. "I suppose they're dead," he yelled back.

They were overboard, but not the way he thought.

Halfway down the harbor, Enos E. Days, Jr., had a 38-foot cabin cruiser, *Prudence*, berthed on the north side of Union Wharf, Fairhaven. On the south side of the wharf were lying several laid-up holdovers from the port's rumrunner fleet of Prohibition days; they were heavy boats, 50 to 60 feet long. When the water rose, the rum boats floated over the wharf and parted all of *Prudence*'s lines, setting her adrift.

Meanwhile, to the north, the owner of the bridge diner, Antone J. Viau, and an employee, Edward Riendeau, were having a hard time. Water flowed through the restaurant so rapidly that by the time they got to the front door, it was too high and running too hard for them to risk getting into. As they stood there, in increasing danger every minute, *Prudence*, unmanned, and broadside to the flood and wind, was hastening to the rescue.

The cruiser was blown up the Acushnet River, over flooded Marine Park, where deeper vessels grounded, and across Route 6; she fetched up momentarily broadside to the brick front steps of the diner where Viau and Riendeau were stranded. They jumped aboard and broke a cabin door to get to the wheel, hoping to be able to steer the cruiser if the sea washed her free of the restaurant. For a moment, it looked bad; *Prudence* pounded against the steps and punched a hole a foot-and-a-half in diameter in her port side. Fortunately, most of it was above the waterline and it did not cause her to leak much.

The next series of waves carried *Prudence* clear of the diner, but the two aboard discovered immediately that there was no steering her because her rudder had been smashed. So they rode her helplessly, northeast across the upper harbor to the Fairhaven shore. There, she sheared the piazza off one house and came to rest on the lawn of another, at least a hundred feet from the water in ordinary times. Neither Viau nor Riendeau was injured. I reported both "probably drowned," and was pleased to be found in error.

Steam yacht Neelia *and schooner* Gallant, *high
and dry at New Bedford, Massachusetts*

Inevitably, the night provided a little humor. Aboard Thomas
Kearns's big steam yacht *Neelia*, aground at Marine Park, there
were lights, because she had her own power plant. In a dark and
damaged world, the glow through the cabin windows was both
incongruous and cheering. I made my way there carefully, each
step oozing, to see what was going on.

There was a ladder leaned against the side of the vessel. I arrived at the foot of it, at which moment, the glare of a bull's-eye
lantern flashed upon me and a voice said, "Freeze or I'll shoot!"
I froze. A police officer walked out of the darkness, revolver in
hand.

I said, rather lamely, "I'm a reporter for the *Standard-Times*."

"Got any credentials?"

"This is my first day. All I have is a Social Security card."

"Goddam." Then he said, without putting away his gun, "We have orders from Boston to shoot looters. This area is out of bounds, as of a half-hour ago. I had no idea who you were or what you were doing. I would have been justified in taking extreme action." He put his gun away. "And you get a goddam press pass and you come down to the station house and show it to me to-morrow morning. D'you hear?"

Then he left and let me go aboard the *Neelia*. I remember to this day how he said "extreme action." After he had gone, I was some-what unraveled.

That was not what was funny.

Once aboard the yacht, aware of my muddy feet and damp clothes, I discovered that Mr. Kearns — totally undisturbed by the fact that his vessel was high and dry on the storm-littered grass of the park — was host at a small supper. He and his guests agreed they were "quite comfortable." That was funny.

On the east side of the Acushnet, the fleet took a savage batter-ing. At Fairhaven's Union Wharf, little Joe Pinto, master of the freight boat *Eben A. Thacher* of Vineyard Haven, saved her, and very possibly the lives of her crew, when he decided it was less dangerous to try to cross the swollen river full of junk than it was to stay at the exposed dock. "When the water took her above the level of the wharf, I knew the spiles were likely to go," Joe said. "I started my engine, sent a man forward and one aft with axes, and when I threw in the clutch, I yelled at them to cut the lines.

"I didn't know whether she would steam to under it or not, and I couldn't tell whether we could dodge the wreckage and the vessels that were being swept up the river, but I had to take a chance. My keel scraped the caplog on the wharf and my propeller chopped a big piece of concrete off the top of the dock, but we got out of there. We got across the river and I saw lee, on the north side of Pier 3. Just as we were easing in, the Cuttyhunk boat *Alert* washed right over the wharf and into the slip where we were heading. A minute more and she would have dropped on top of us. We hauled out of there and found another place. . . ."

Captain Phillips, a gentleman mariner of the old school, was newly master of the *Lochinvar*, the large, twin-screwed vessel recently purchased by Amory Houghton of Corning Glass; she was undergoing repairs at the Peirce and Kilburn yard, the most southerly in the harbor and the most exposed. "We were all lying on the south side of the dock. We were on the outside, in the *Lochinvar*. Between us and the wharf lay the schooner *Quita*, and the Swedish sloop *Gladje*, with Captain Edward Coffin of Nantucket aboard her," Phillips said to me.

"The sloop parted her lines first and came down onto us under the bowsprit of the *Quita*. The *Quita* parted next and sawed our bow line right off. It was blowing hard then and all three of us were about ready to go adrift in a bunch.

"The *Lochinvar* still had a spring line and a stern line fast, and we carried the stern line forward, threw out two anchors, and let her hang off the end of the dock. Coffin had been jumping back and forth between us and his vessel and if he'd known we were going to cast off, I know he would have stayed aboard his own craft. He wanted to get back aboard her and was going to try it when she was carried down by us, but he couldn't make it.

"It's lucky he didn't, because she went right across the harbor, hit the Hathaway dock and sank after two seas had smashed her to pieces. If Coffin had stayed aboard his vessel, he never would have come out alive.

"It was one hair-raising night. Everything went by us. I saw a paint shop driving down on us, rolling end over end, but it sank before it got to us. There must have been a hundred cradles and all kinds of gear from the railways that went by us. But the worst scrape occurred when Andrew G. Pierce's 110-foot schooner *Palestine* came down on us. She poked her bowsprit right through the

[332]

stateroom window, took out two panes and their frames, and went on by. That was close."

Palestine was lost, and when the storm had passed, only the masts of Warren Burbridge's schooner *Caroline* and the cabin top and stack of Joseph Cudahy's steam yacht *Innisfail* were above water. The 100-foot dragger *Leretha*, which had been hauled out on the ways for repairs, was hurled across the tracks, stove on her port side, and dumped on her beam ends.

There is one final vignette from the New Bedford fishing waterfront. In those days, the men who made their living offshore, who remembered "Boom Tackle" Oliver, who knew the shoals called Cultivator and L'Homme Dieu the way you know your backyard, had a harder and rougher life. They were islands of men, carried their bankrolls in their back pockets, and many had no families. One of the barrooms some of them frequented between trips, a typical, steamy pub with the windows painted so you couldn't see who was inside, was only a block up from the river. On the bar, which had been polished black over the years by wiping up perpetually spilled beer, there were two big glass jars, one full of pigs' feet in brine, the other containing pickled hard-boiled eggs.

Back of the bar there was a sign; in the center of it was a picture of a bundle of ten-dollar bills, bound with a rubber band. Underneath, it said, "If I can't take it with me, I'm not going." An unsmiling, bald fellow named Charlie tended the bar; he always said, "You give me four boat crews coming here regular and I'll retire early."

The hurricane went right through the place; windows blown in and water up to the tops of the bar stools. When I went by there that night, it was black and empty; my flashlight, shining ahead, picked up the feet of a woman, standing in the mud of the pavement. I don't know what her face would look like by day, but with no more than the light that I had, and the silent city all about us,

[333]

she seemed pretty, even with a prominent gold tooth. Her eyes were dark and deep; she had interesting cheekbones. She was probably forty and looked at least fifty; when she spoke, her voice was flat and raspy.

"Ain't it a mess?" she said, staring into the dripping barroom. "To think that last night, I was sittin' right there." She pointed. "I come here every night. It's friendly. It's like — "

"Home?" I volunteered, without great enthusiasm. I was wet, cold, and tired, and she had been drinking. I had no intention of staying there, listening to her ramblings.

"Home, hell," she said. "Ten times better. They like me here. They laugh when I say funny things. And now lookit. All busted to hell. And I got nowhere to go but home. I was brought up in the Church but I be damned sometimes if I don't wonder what God is thinking of. This place didn't bother nobody." She lit a cigarette, her hand shaking, and I left her there in the dark, coughing. "You think it'll be open tomorrow?" she hollered. "Maybe tomorrow night?"

Chapter 18

THERE ARE A FEW OTHER THINGS that ought to be said.

When Harrison McDonald of Lafayette, Indiana, finally arrived in Boston on September 23, he observed, "You don't know how queer it seems to be in a normal city with lights, heat, and telephones running."

The suggestion that Boston had escaped the hurricane was born of relativity; compared to New London and Providence, from which Mr. McDonald had just come, the city was fortunate. Yet there was the matter of the city's North End to be considered; this was the home of those Italian fishermen who made up the crews of the so-called "mosquito fleet," the little boats. Ordinarily, six boats, with a total of thirty men, would have docked early Wednesday evening. When the hurricane had thundered its way past Boston, when darkness had fallen, the six boats had not come home.

It was a bad night in the North End, and no time for sleeping. These people were close: many were related; the families were large, and the fate of the six vessels affected a lot of them. Through the night, the women, children, and old men stood and talked quietly in little knots in the streets; in Fleet Street, North Street, and Moon Street, they waited, tautly and quietly, their parish

[335]

The Dorchester yacht fleet being pounded at Boston, Massachusetts

priests with them. The small stores — neighborhood gathering places crammed in fragrant disorder with fat lumps of mozzarella, strings of garlic, golden crusted loaves, and black oil-cured olives — were crowded all through the dark hours. They had telephones; there might be some news come by them. A group of youngsters remained on duty at the Eastern Packet Pier, where the Italian fleet berthed, ready to rush home with the glad tidings if any of the missing boats came up the harbor.

A report came — the *4C554*, a 45-foot vessel, had gone down off Finn's Ledge in Boston Harbor. The women, fingering their prayer beads, passed the word. They knew that number; they knew the names of the four men aboard; they knew them by their first names. The hours wore on.

Coast Guard headquarters relayed a radio message received from the British freighter *Baron Dechmont*. Outward bound from Boston, she had observed a small fishing vessel capsize off Finn's Ledge. Only one survivor had been sighted and rescued. When last seen, the capsized vessel was drifting toward Nahant.

Only one man rescued? Was it Frank Marino? Or Joe Sciafano? Or Frank's brother, Tony, the father of six, or Tony Ciulla, the father of eleven? Waiting in the streets, they looked at each other, holding back grief until they knew whose it was.

At daybreak, the Eastern Packet Pier was crowded with the anxious. The sun rose; the entire fleet that had made it home safely put to sea to search the waters of the bay for survivors of the *4C554*. As the morning passed, some better news came. Some of the little boats, scattered in the gale, had made it. The *St. Joseph*, with a crew of six, and the *Maria*, with five, both safe at Portsmouth, New Hampshire. The *Josephine F.*, with six, arrived at Gloucester, with all hands. The *Maria Giuseppe*, five aboard, wrecked off Nahant, all safe. And at 10 in the morning, the stalwart *Anna Madre*, her port bulwarks carried away, her crew of four worn out from the battle, chugged up the harbor and the hundreds on the pier greeted her with a rousing cheer as she nosed into her berth.

Then Frank Marino came home. He was suffering from shock, his face was lacerated, several of his teeth had been knocked loose, and he staggered so, still weak from immersion and his ordeal, that he could hardly get to his house on Prince Street. He had only a hazy idea of what happened when the hurricane overtook the *4C554* as she was running for the shelter of Boston Harbor.

He said he was barely conscious after a sea struck him and washed him overboard from the deck of the vessel. He struggled to stay afloat and thought he was in the water about fifteen min-

The Strandway in Boston, Massachusetts; at the hurricane's height

utes before someone aboard the *Baron Dechmont* threw him a line. He lost consciousness after he was hauled aboard the freighter; he came to his senses early Thursday morning as he was being transferred from the British vessel, off the harbor entrance, to an inbound trawler. Landed at the Fish Pier, he walked home, praying all the way that the other three aboard the 4C554 had somehow made port safely. None had; none ever did.

Surveying Boston's $6-million loss, the Boston *Globe*'s "Uncle Dudley" editorialized, "After lives and houses, our worst loss from the hurricane is trees . . . there they always were, some for a century and a half, and the assumption was that there they always would be. Then, in two hours, thousands of them are laid low.

"Did you see the fight they put up? It was game. They roared like goaded animals and mostly, they fell slowly, fighting to the end. One old fellow, an elm, at least 150 years old, if not 200, on the exposed ridge of a seaward headland was delivering a splendid battle. He met the buffets of the hurricane with contempt. 'Pfugh,' said he. 'To hell with you.' And he won; only a minor limb of him went down. But his neighbors, younger and not so strong, were less lucky. . . .

"A creature that has established and maintained itself on a spot of land from ten to one hundred years is a citizen. What is more, any orchardist or forester will tell you that a tree manages its affairs far more sensibly than do most people. It does less harm to its neighbors and gets into fewer scrapes of its own. This realization that trees are people and have rights, when it first comes home to one, is startling. In 'Specimen Days,' Walt Whitman speaks of walking out on Boston Common and sitting out underneath the great trees along the Beacon Street Mall, until he has made himself acquainted with 'their personalities.'

"Mourning will not bring back the dead. . . ."

Worcester counted seven dead, and the toll might have been higher had it not been for the quick action of a school janitor and

[339]

a teacher. Classical High School, built in 1892, was one of the city's oldest; on the afternoon of the storm, twenty-five pupils were in the school auditorium. A double window blew out, and janitor Charles W. Carrick and Miss Margaret M. Walsh, an instructor, had the pupils leave the room immediately and, because of the heavy rain, go to the basement for shelter.

Mr. Carrick went to his office and telephoned his wife. Just as he was about to hang up the receiver, the upper part of the building began to collapse; a heavy board came through the ceiling of his office and he had just time to jump under a beam for safety. Teacher and janitor quickly evacuated all the pupils, housing them in a nearby store.

They had hardly arrived there when, about 5 P.M., with a roar that rocked houses for blocks around, the massive slate roof of the school collapsed, crashed through the third floor into the assembly hall on the floor below, and ripped away much of the rear of the brick structure. As the upper part of the building disintegrated, sheathing was flung into windows of nearby houses, an immense section of wreckage crushed the porch of an adjacent dwelling, bricks were scattered the length of the street, heavy timbers were thrown about, and falling brick crushed and buried three automobiles.

The New York Times of September 22 reported from Northfield, Massachusetts: "Two students at Northfield Seminary, Miss Norma Stockberger and Miss Audrey Lucas, were killed instantly and two others were seriously injured — Miss Mary Kidder and Miss Lucille Carle — when a tall brick chimney crashed during the height of the hurricane. The chimney crashed through the roof of the school dining hall at 6:15 o'clock, while the students were eating dinner. There were 140 girls in the hall at the time and it is considered miraculous that many more were not killed or seriously injured."

Harold B. Ingalls was chaplain of the school at that time and he recalled: "Suddenly [in the afternoon of the twenty-first], the storm became ferociously worse and threatening; some trees and hundreds of branches fell. My wife and I lived in a house owned by the school, but just across the street from the campus. We went from window to window on all four sides of the house and marveled that, at that point, we could not see that any building had been damaged. Of course, visibility was poor and most of the campus buildings were not within sight of our windows. Electric power in the town had failed by that time.

"Suddenly two girls from Gould Hall appeared at our door. Elizabeth Colvin and Margery Smith, roommates, had somehow managed to get across the campus to report the tragedy in Gould. I immediately got raincoat, etc., and called to our neighbor, Russell Roberts, a school employee who lived in the apartment above us, to do the same and come with me, telling him there had been a bad accident at Gould Hall.

"We were there quickly — either the first, or among the first four or five men to arrive. I am not sure whether the school power plant was still operating or we were dependent upon our flashlights, but we could see at once the extent of the devastation and managed to get to the most seriously injured persons. I do recall there was no electricity later as we continued to work. Some other men arrived and cars took the injured to the school infirmary.

"The wind at its height hit the large chimney full force and snapped it off at or very near the roof level. It must have been almost horizontal when it crashed through the ceiling of the dining room, leaving (I think I am accurate) a clear pattern of its shape overhead. Most, if not all of those killed or seriously injured were at one table for ten, I believe.

"Quick work by an intelligent, dedicated group of faculty members present (all women at the moment) was responsible for saving at least one life, possibly more. Miss Elizabeth Homet, biology teacher, quickly saw that one girl was lying on her back with blood gurgling out of her mouth, turned her over and administered first aid. There were others who helped in similar ways, while some went for professional medical help.

"Miss Annie Mildred Herring, dietitian, was aware that there was a possibility a second chimney — not as tall or wide as the first, but quite large — might topple, and she rounded up all who could walk and sent them to the basement, where there was a large, safe area.

"I recall having stopped at the school infirmary to see if any help was needed. The school physician and two or three nurses, aided by faculty and community people who had had some nursing or first-aid experience, had things well under control, though they were overworked. I cannot recall how many patients there were there or how many injured and placed in a dorm until the next day. I remember, of course, the four mentioned in the *New York Times* story. Lucille Carle, 'Bushy' — loved by all — did not make it. Eleanor Shedd was very seriously injured, hospitalized for months, but finally made a good recovery.

"There was no possible way to get to any hospital that night, nor could any help get in from any direction. Nor was communication elsewhere possible. Later that night, I was asked to try to get to Greenfield by truck, with a crew of men who went ahead and hand-sawed or chopped enough space between fallen trees and branches so that we could get through. It was my sad responsibility to call and notify parents of the dead girls and those most seriously injured of what had happened. (I think I managed to get *The New York Times* also, but I am not sure.) It took some roundabout routing, but we managed to reach nearly all of the parents, although it took the rest of the night.

"I wish I had kept a daily record of events immediately following September 21 and for months thereafter. The problems resulting from the storm were many. Most related to structures, etc., were quickly solved, temporarily at least. But the emotional and intellectual (especially theological) problems required longer periods

Fire as well as flood, struck Peterborough, New Hampshire.

and a vast amount of counseling and guidance. I suspect that not all of them were solved and that there are still scars. . . ."

Miss Betty Goff was a student at Northfield; she escaped injury, and in a letter to her parents, Mr. and Mrs. W. W. Goff of Westerly, Rhode Island, shortly after the storm, she said that forty girls were hurt when the chimney fell. Miss Goff wrote: "Wednesday, two chimneys fell over and through the roof at Gould Hall. As it was, they fell through the dining room and all the girls were just eating. Two girls were killed and fifteen taken to a hospital out of town and twenty-five here in the hospital. A lot more were cut and bruised.

"They took the girls out of the cellar (where they finally landed) and wrapped them up in blankets and sent them in bunches all over the campus to different buildings. I was drying dishes when they came in here. It was awful to see them, all cut and crying and fainting. We went into the living room and they were lying all over the room, wrapped in soaking wet blankets. Most of them finally went to the hotel to sleep but a lot slept here.

"It's just like being on an island here. All the wires are down and nobody can get across the river or send any mail except by air. Last night, we were given stamps and told to write home a very short letter saying we were all right and the mail went out in five minutes.

"None of the girls from Gould Hall have been back to their hall, so we lent them clothes to wear. I think tonight they are to go back, but not eat there. I just can't explain any more about it here, but everyone is in a daze and has been in a daze since Wednesday."

At some point, any thoughtful record of the hurricane must necessarily address itself to the matter of suicide. I have mentioned one instance in which a storm victim considered surrendering to the elements, but decided against it. In other episodes, persons familiar with the subjects and circumstances suggested that already depressed people, given the opportunity of the hurricane, consciously decided they did not choose to survive.

Although the hurricane was on Wednesday, September 21, and Aurelio Giorni, forty-three, well-known New York pianist and composer, did not die until Friday night — when he leaped from a Pittsfield, Massachusetts, bridge and drowned in the fast-flowing flood waters of the Housatonic River — it is not unreasonable to cite his death as an example of this phenomenon. Many hurricane-related deaths did not occur for days, weeks, or even months after the fact and in the particular instance — even with the heavy rains preceding the storm — the Housatonic would not have been as high and raging as it was, had it not been for the downpour of the

Undermined and weakened by flood waters, this bridge was swept away at Springfield, Massachusetts.

hurricane. And one who knew Mr. Giorni well suggested it was, in fact, the condition of the river as a result of the bad weather which prompted him to end his life *at that moment in that place*.

Friends knew that Giorni was greatly disappointed when he was notified only a few days before the hurricane that his services at Smith College would not be required in the coming term. He had hoped to have classes there, even though the professor whose place he had been taking had returned. He was also genuinely disappointed when none of his compositions were given place on the South Mountain program and he was not among the performers at the Berkshire Chamber Music Festival, which he attended on that Friday night. Another factor contributing to his mental state was the discouraging notices by music critics given his Symphony in D Minor, played for the first time at Carnegie Hall, New York, the preceding April.

Of the symphony, H. Howard Taubman of *The New York Times* wrote on April 26, 1938: "A new symphony by Aurelio Giorni, who was a member of the Elshuco Trio, had its first performance last night. It did not leave one with an eagerness to hear it soon once more. . . . There was a lack of definition and accent in the work. It was as if the composer had been weighted down by the huge apparatus of the full symphony orchestra. . . ."

Dr. Modestino Criscitiello knew Giorni well; they had been friends since they had first met at Princeton years before, and Mr. and Mrs. Giorni were visiting the Criscitiellos in Pittsfield at the time when Giorni ended his life. I asked Dr. Criscitiello if he would comment on the relationship, if he believed any existed, between the act and the storm.

"Aurelio Giorni was a very sensitive individual with a high moral sense of honesty and integrity," Dr. Criscitiello told me. "Though he was recognized as an unusually well-qualified pianist, especially in the field of chamber music, his main interest was in composition. He apparently had talent for this and was trained by several well-known worldwide composers.

[*346*]

"Because of financial circumstances, he was forced to teach and perform. This left him little time for composition. I am in no position to judge his creative efforts, but I can attest to the fact that he did not write music for the masses and thus sell easily. Rather, he strove to express his highly sensitive and noble nature through his own music. He instinctively tried to emulate the master composers of the past. Johannes Brahms was one of his fervent idols. He had hoped to be appointed to the faculty of Smith College, where he would teach and to some extent perform. This would also give him more time and the setting for composition. Unfortunately, the opening on the staff which he had hoped to fill did not materialize.

"Several months before the fatal event in Pittsfield, he deliberately stepped in front of a moving vehicle. Due to the alertness of the driver of the car, a tragedy at that time was averted. On the day of the fatal event in Pittsfield, he had been at one of the Coolidge Festival concerts, at which he was neither a performer nor was he represented as a composer. He apparently was very depressed. The weather was clear and calm. Our streams were high and swift, caused by the deluge from previous days.

"On the way from the concert hall to our home, he came to a bridge over the Housatonic River. The water was high and swift. I do not believe that the elements had anything to do with his act. I do not believe that the condition of the water was the *cause* of his suicidal mood. The stage had already been set for his act. The high and on-rushing water under the bridge was merely *the catalytic agent* for his act. It precipitated his fatal performance just as the onrushing vehicle had in the previous unsuccessful attempt several months before.

"A very sad story. Aurelio Giorni was a casualty of our materialistic society."

On September 24, the Boston *Transcript*'s Washington bureau reported, "Although granting that New Englanders had scant warning to prepare themselves against the tropical hurricane, Dr. Charles C. Clark, acting chief of the U.S. Weather Bureau, said today that the bureau forecasters, on the basis of the data on hand, could hardly have given any greater advance warning, for the tropic storm — the worst in the history of the Northeast — was a freak; it did not follow the usual pattern. . . .

"Up to the time it reached Hatteras, there was no indication that it would be particularly dangerous, and it seemed quite likely that it would go out to sea well off the Atlantic Seaboard. However, from Cape Hatteras, the storm center headed north with enormously increased momentum, covering on Wednesday six hundred miles in twelve hours, an average of fifty miles an hour. This is believed to be the fastest movement ever recorded by a major tropical disaster."

Owing to the unusually rapid rate of progress of the storm across New England, the winds on the right or east side of the path were very destructive, while strong winds did not extend far to the westward. At the Harvard Meteorological Observatory at the top of Blue Hill, Milton, Massachusetts, gusts of approximately 173 and 186 miles per hour were recorded during the storm's height. Wind velocity of 111 miles an hour was recorded on the summit in three five-minute periods at 6:05, 6:20, and 7:12 P.M. The gusts of 173 and 186 miles an hour occurred during the passage of 7 miles of wind in 2½ minutes at 6:59 P.M. and the passage of 4 miles of wind in a little over a minute at 6:15 P.M.

The most sensitive recorder on the hilltop, a French windmill anemometer, started to disintegrate when registering a five-minute velocity of 80 miles. It broke under a gust of 100-mile-an-hour velocity.

Damage to property along the coast was largely due to the storm wave. At the Battery, New York City, it was 6.44 feet above mean sea level. Along the coast of Connecticut, Rhode Island, and on the shores of Narragansett and Buzzards Bay, the highest tide ranged from 12 to 25 feet above mean low water, being highest on the southern shores of Massachusetts, where the maximum stage occurred about 5 or 6 P.M. At Point Judith Coast Guard station, the water rose 18 feet above mean low water; at Fairhaven, it was estimated at 25 feet.

Even to this day, statistics concerning the hurricane, especially concerning lives lost, vary considerably. It is generally accepted, however, that there were 680 lives lost and property damaged to a total of $400,000,000. Comparable figures for the San Francisco earthquake and fire of 1906 were 450 lives and $350,000,000 property damage, and for the Chicago fire of 1871, 200 lives and a $200,000,000 loss.

Seven hundred and eight suffered injuries; 4,500 homes, summer cottages, and farm buildings were destroyed; 15,139 homes, summer cottages, and farm buildings were damaged; 2,605 boats were lost and 3,369 were damaged. A total of 19,608 families applied for emergency help or assistance in rehabilitating themselves.

Twenty-six thousand automobiles were smashed; 275,000,000 trees were broken off or uprooted, amounting to 2.6 billion board feet of timber downed, and nearly 20,000 miles of electric power and telephone lines were blown or knocked down. A total of 1,675 head of livestock and between 500,000 and 750,000 chickens were killed. Railroad service between New York and Boston was interrupted for seven to fourteen days while 10,000 men filled 1,000 washouts, replaced nearly 100 bridges, and removed thousands of obstructions from the tracks, including a number of houses and 30 boats. More than a half-million telephones were silenced, isolating 240 communities. In order to repair these, Bell System crews rolled into New England from as far south as Virginia, from as far west as Arkansas and Nevada; more than 2,300 trained men with 615 motor vehicles were loaned by 14 telephone companies.

[349]

The Bell System listed materials needed to effect hurricane repairs as: 400 miles of cable, 31,000 poles, 72 million feet of wire, and 50 carloads of telephone hardware.

The storm destroyed $2,610,000 worth of fishing boats, equipment, docks, and shore plants. Orchardists also suffered greatly. During the first part of September, it was anticipated that the total apple crop would be 2.8 million bushels from Massachusetts, 1.8 million from the orchards of Connecticut, almost one million from Maine, and lesser amounts from New Hampshire, Vermont, and Rhode Island, in that order. Agriculturists estimated that at least half of the total apple crop was still on the trees when the hurricane struck and that growers received from $1 million to $2 million less than they had expected earlier in the month.

Chapter 19

AFTER IT WAS OVER, there were comments of several sorts.

Bernard DeVoto said, "The face of New England had been changed forever. . . . But one had seen, had listened in darkness, had realized the community rallying."

As for John Q. Stewart, associate professor of astronomical physics at Princeton University, he concluded that "newspapers, especially outside New England, gave the stupendous hurricane of September 21 very inadequate treatment. For two or three days immediately following the disaster, bits of it were front-page items, but the whole account was not available until the neurotic interests of editors had jumped to fresher happenings. . . .

"A seaboard as wealthy as any in the world and its hinterland . . . felt the shock. There had been no warning worth the mentioning. . . . A sophisticated population died by hundreds, with little or no knowledge of what raw shape of death this was which struck from the sky and the tide. In the long and laudable annals of the government's weather forecasters, that day's record makes what must be the sorriest page."

Then there was the question of God's involvement. The Reverend Dr. Arthur Lee Kinsolving of Boston's Trinity Church said,

"There is no valid evidence that Christianity ever assumed the world would provide maximum security and comfort. The guest at a hotel may make such demands, but we are in no such position to expect this sort of attention from God." In Springfield, Massachusetts, the Reverend Dr. Earl Vinie, speaking at East Church, rejected the notion that the storm was an act of God. He said, "These so-called 'acts of God' you find referred to in your old insurance policies are a direct carryover of certain outgrown religious teachings found scattered throughout the pages of the Old Testament. Those who taught those things were mistaken."

As for me, I walked the docks and beaches during the following days, attempting not so much to discover the truth of why it had happened as to accept the reality of what had happened. If the dark wildness of Wednesday remained unbelievable (Thursday dawned benign, quiet, its water characteristically gentle), the miles and acres of destruction over which I crawled and stumbled were equally incredible even when one walked them in the unforgiving light of day.

It takes some time to sort out an experience like this. If you have seen the sea sun-sparkled and glassy, clear and clean, swirling about the bare feet of a child and have watched it in the same place, only hours later, dirty, ugly, and as high as a two-story house, crushing things and people, it stretches the mind to accept the contradictions.

And there are so many other things — the row of boathouses, shops, and shanties, silvered by generations of weather, that had been a fundamental of childhood; it might not have been so bad if something had been left that was recognizable, but as it was, the buildings were gone, the land on which they stood was gone, and the land remaining was so alien in form as to repudiate and confound the memory.

The smell of bodies! In places, you could taste it in the food and it came through closed windows into your bedroom at night.

[352]

I remember watching a pair of horses, hooves planted in wet sand and heavy haunches straining, dragging the side of a house off a pile of storm junk ten feet high. I was counting empty foundations, trying to put together a news story on how many dwellings there had once been on the empty beach, and I said to nobody, watching the horses, "There is a corpse under there. I can smell it." And there was. I knew exactly what it would look like, because by then, I had seen enough of them.

It was a savage leveler, that storm. Living on the beach was expensive in summer but it was cheap in winter, so both the rich and the poor were there. The year-around poor knew about the water; mostly, they got out, but the domestics of the wealthy died because they had never done any boating, or swimming either, and once overboard, they panicked. Assuredly, the wealthy died, too, because they had known the sea and the beach for a long time and they trusted both to be essentially as they had always been, since Grandfather's time and beyond. Grandfather was a shrewd man; he would not have built a house in a place that wasn't safe, would he?

Nothing was ever the same again after the hurricane. The new buildings were different. The social leveling it started persisted, and the steam yacht became one with the dinosaur. The war that threatened became fact. It was established that landmarks did not *have* to endure.

But with the war, the Depression was over. I put my curled-up, salt-rimed shoes on a heatless radiator in my room and bought another pair, on credit. For my part in covering the story of the hurricane, I received a raise in pay from $20 to $25. The raise enabled me to think about marriage, which I did, and if it seems to you that I have made something rather personal out of a national catastrophe, so be it.

It was, in fact, one of the most thoroughly personal things I have ever experienced, and in one of the most thoroughly terrible ways.

[353]

In twenty-four hours, I established a career and a direction in life. The price I had to pay for it was to watch the only world I had ever known well writhe in torment for the few moments required to destroy it.

Acknowledgments

CHAPTER ONE

Contents of news broadcast from issues of New Bedford (Mass.) *Standard-Times*, July-August, 1938. Statistics of July, 1938, weather, same source.

CHAPTER TWO

Greater New Bedford news items from *Standard-Times*, August to September, 1938.

CHAPTER THREE

The New York Times, New York *Herald Tribune*, September 21–26, 1938; Carnegie Hero Fund Commission case minute on William P. McGrath; correspondence with Frank McLoughlin, deputy commissioner, public information, New York City Police Department, on unknown Queens hitchhiker; Times Square–Southold, Long Island, drive, by Russell Owen, *The New York Times*, September 23; Brooklyn *Eagle*, September 23; Northport *Observer*, September 22; *Suffolk County News*, September 23; Huntington *Long Islander*, September 22; Smithtown *Long Island Messenger*, September 23; Southold *Long Island Traveler*, September 29; New York *Sun*, September 23–24; Sag Harbor *Express*, September 22; Ernest S. Clowes, *Hurricane of 1938 on Eastern Long Island* (Bridgehampton, New York: Hampton Press, 1939).

CHAPTER FOUR

William T. Helmuth III, *The Hurricane of 1938 in Retrospect* (Garden City, New York: J. C. Nichols, 1954).

Bay Shore story, by Gustave Zismer, New York *Sun*, September 22; also by Lloyd G. Record, *Suffolk County News*, September 23; Bay Shore *Sentinel*, September 22; Amityville *Record*, September 23; Countess Charles de Ferry de Fontnouvelle story by Associated Press, September 22; Southampton *Press*, September 23; Hampton *Chronicle*, September 30; Southampton *Times*, January 13, 1939, address on the hurricane delivered by Wallace H. Halsey before the American Shore and Beach Preservation Association; George E. Burghard story, special commemorative issue, Hampton *Chronicle*, September 26, 1968, and copy of manuscript, East Hampton Library; New York *World Telegram*, September 24; Associated Press file, September 23; Pat McGrady story, Patchogue *Advance*, September 23.

CHAPTER FIVE

I am especially indebted to the late Jeannette E. Rattray, former publisher of the East Hampton *Star*, and her son, Everett T. Rattray, editor of that publication, not only for making available to me the very helpful files of their newspaper but for leading me to the invaluable collection, for which Mrs. Rattray was responsible, in the East Hampton Library, of Long Island newspapers dealing with the 1938 hurricane. Graeme Elliott's account was published in the East Hampton *Star*.

CHAPTER SIX

Elmer Davis account, *The New York Times*, September 24; H. I. Phillips eulogy, New York *Sun*, October 21, in his column, The Sun Dial; New Haven *Register*, September 22, 23; Hartford *Courant*, September 22 to October 2, including T. H. Parker account, the "Battle of Colt's Dike," and the Claude Adams story.

CHAPTER SEVEN

New London *Day*, September 21 to October 7; U.S. Bureau of Lighthouses correspondence, National Archives.

CHAPTER EIGHT

I am very grateful to Joseph C. Richards of West Haven and John P. Cooke of North Haven for the extensive interview in which they told the story of the Bostonian.

Westerly *Sun*, September 25; Boston *Globe*, September 24; Providence *Journal*, September 23; Boston *Herald*, September 25; Harry Easton's account, New Haven *Register*, September 24; *The New York Times*, September 24, New Haven Railroad statement.

CHAPTER NINE

For the story of the Geoffrey Moore family and other information concerning Watch Hill, I am indebted to the late Charles F. Hammond, publisher of *Seaside Topics*, and to his daughter, Marcelle Hammond Ham. These accounts were republished in a special pictorial issue of *Seaside Topics* (Utter Company, Westerly, R.I.).

Providence *Journal*, September 22 to October 9, including stories by Andrew Clarke, James B. Stickley; Carnegie Hero Fund Commission case minute on Henry M. Morris; William A. Cawley story, Associated Press file, September 23; Burgess-Marshall amateur radio account, Westerly *Sun*.

CHAPTER TEN

I am indebted to Alfred A. Niska for giving me details on what happened to the tug *May* and especially for enabling me to locate Captain Paul D. Higgison, for whose meticulously recorded account I am grateful.

CHAPTER ELEVEN

Van Wyck Mason and L. D. Lacy accounts, *The New York Times*, September 23; Charles Toomey account, New York *Journal American*, September 22. Ralph Rivers account by Robert L. Wheeler, Providence *Journal*, October 2; Manuel Azevedo story, Federal Writers Project files, National Archives.

CHAPTER TWELVE

Newport *News*, September 22–October 6. Of the many who assisted me in this task, none contributed more or more generously than my friend Catharine Morris Wright, who made it possible for me to interview residents of Jamestown on Conanicut Island, including Joseph Matoes, and I am grateful to her.

The Sarkis Kayarian account is from the Federal Writers Project files in the National Archives.

CHAPTER THIRTEEN

New Bedford *Standard-Times*, September 23 to October 9; Fall River *Herald News*, September 23 to October 1. I am grateful to James Gill for writing to me of his hurricane experience, to my friend Joseph Slight, for his recollections of the storm and its aftermath, and to Captain Ernest Woodcock for the account of what happened to *Tar Baby*.

[357]

CHAPTER FOURTEEN

Vineyard Gazette, September to October. I thank Mr. and Mrs. Donald LeMar Poole for their helpful comments on Menemsha. The excerpt from Benedict Thielen's *House by the Sea* was published in *The Yale Review* (Spring, 1939).

CHAPTER FIFTEEN

Falmouth *Enterprise*, *Cape Cod Standard-Times*, September to October; Wareham *Courier;* Carnegie Hero Fund Commission case minute on Hayward Wilson; Tabor Academy *Log* files. I am indebted to Raymond A. Dennehy, Jakob M. Svendsen, Mrs. Parker Converse, Benjamin D. Dexter, former Wareham Police Chief Chester A. Churchill, and Leroy P. Ellis for interviews or letters.

CHAPTER SIXTEEN

I thank Mrs. Ruth Taylor for permitting me to read and quote from her very helpful diary. Worcester *Telegram*, September 23 to October 1. I am grateful to Edwin L. Perkins, who granted an interview, and to my friend Lena K. Arden, who wrote her recollections for me.

CHAPTER SEVENTEEN

Captain Arthur A. Small's correspondence with the Superintendent of Lighthouses is from the National Archives; Mrs. Small's eulogy is from the Fairhaven *Star*, September 29.

CHAPTER EIGHTEEN

Boston *Globe*, Boston *Herald*, Boston *Transcript*, Worcester *Telegram*, September 22 to October 15. I am indebted to Mr. and Mrs. Harold B. Ingalls for their account of the tragedy at Northfield Seminary. The letter from Betty Goff was published in the Westerly *Sun*, September 28. I am grateful to Dr. Modestino Criscitiello for his letter concerning Aurelio Giorni.

Charles F. Brooks, Blue Hill Meteorological Observatory, Harvard University, "Hurricane into New England," *Annual Report of the Board of Regents of The Smithsonian Institution, 1939* (Washington, D.C.: U.S. Government Printing Office, 1940). (Reprinted with changes from *The Geographical Review*, vol. 29, January 1939.)

I. R. Tannehill, Marine Division, Weather Bureau, Washington, "Hurricane of September 16 to 22 1938," *Monthly Weather Review*, vol. 66, no. 9 (U.S. Department of Agriculture, Weather Bureau, September 1938).

New York–New England Hurricane and Floods — 1938. Official Report of Relief Operations (Washington, D.C. The American National Red Cross, October 1939).

New England Telephone and Telegraph Company, *Annual Report* for the year 1938 (Boston, February 21, 1939).

New Haven Railroad. *The Devastation and Restoration of New England's Vital Life-Line* (New Haven, 1938).

Boston *Globe*, September 23 Federal Fisheries Bureau loss estimates from Associated Press file, October 14.

I am especially appreciative of the efforts in my behalf by the staffs of the Connecticut State Library, Hartford; Westerly Library; Providence Public Library; New Bedford Free Public Library; Millicent Library, Fairhaven; Wareham Library; Marion Library; and by the librarian of the *Berkshire Eagle*.

Index

Brooks, Eleanor, 269
Brown, Arthur M., 286
Brown, Edward, 149
Brown, Jennie, 296–297, 300–303
Brown, Richard, 279
Brown, Mrs. Victor, 279
Browne, Mrs. Chester, 78
Brownell, Clarence H., 234
Brundage, Walter, 136–137
Bryant, Marguerite, 278–279
Burgess, Wilson E., 175–176
Burghard, George E., 56–72
Burghard, Mabel (Mrs. George), 56–72
Burr Brothers' wharf (New London), 115
Burrows, Claude, 81
Bushnell, Edwin, 138
Bushnell, Ernest G., 137–178
Butler, David, 255
Butler, Fanny, 279
Butler, Norman, 184
Buzzards Bay, Mass., 248, 271, 273, 274, 281, 348

Cahoon, Charles H., 249
Cahoon, Samuel T., 270
Camp, Mrs. John McKesson, 158
Campbell, Colin, 137
Cape May, N.J., 33
Cape Cod, Mass., 265–276, 281–284
Cape Cod Canal, 281–284
Carle, Lucille, 340, 342
Carlson, Mrs. Carl, 109–110
Carr, William H., 38
Carrick, Charles W., 340
Carter, Dr. Earl, 135
Caswell, Norman, 220–223
Catskill, 125–126
Cawley, William A., 174
Chabot, Capt. Jules, 35
Chapman, Alfred H., 167
Chapman, Mary, 167
Chappaquoit (Falmouth), Mass., 267
Chappell, F. H. and A. H., Coal companies (New London), 120
Chappell Lumber Co. (New London), 114, 119
Charlestown; Charlestown Beach, R.I., 158, 180–182, 186
Charlestown Pond, R.I., 181, 187
Chellis, Carl, 222, 224
Chellis, Clayton, 220–224
Chellis, Marion, 220–224
Cheshire, Conn., 109

Chilmark (Martha's Vineyard), Mass., 258
Christie, Joe, 168
Churchill, Chief Chester A., 280
Ciulla, Tony, 337–338
Civilian Conservation Corps, 186
Clark, Dr. Charles C., 348
Clark, Josephine, 258–261
Clark dike (Hartford), 100–101, 104
Classical High School (Worcester), 340
Clowes, Ernest I., 46, 51, 90
Cluett, Wilby, 80
Coast Guard. *See* U.S. Coast Guard
Coe, Mrs. Henry E., 75
Coffin, Capt. Edward, 332
Cogswell, Harold G., 49
Coleman, Samuel, 83
Coleman, Timothy, 109
Coleman, William, 109
Collins, Lou, 168
Colt dike (Hartford), 100–104
Colt Firearms Co. (Hartford), 101, 103
Colvin, Elizabeth, 341
Conanicut Island, R.I., 220–224
Congdon, William E., 133
Connecticut, 93–153, 159, 177, 350. *See also* individual place names
Connecticut River, 96–105, 111, 133
Consolidated Edison Co., 33–34
Conte di Savoia, 36–37
Conti, Gino E., 213
Converse, Mrs. Parker, 291–292
Converse Point (Marion), 291–292
Cook, Raymond R., 263
Cooke, John P., 146–148, 151
Corey, William, 295
Cornell, Howard, 248
Cornell, John, 248
Cornell, Katharine, 254–255
Cornfield, 126–127
Coxe, George Harmon, 275
Crampton, Bill, 298–299
Crescent Beach (Mattapoisett), Mass., 295–306
Criscitiello, Dr. Modestino, 346
Cromwell, Conn., 104–105, 108
Cross, Gov. Wilbur L., 142
Cross Mills, R.I., 187
Crump, Chief William R., 265, 266
Cruz, Tony, 291–292
Cupples, Norman P., 249
Cuttyhunk Island, Mass., 248–249
Cythera, 115

[362]